THE TORONTO GUIDE

D1473876

THE TORONTO GUIDE

MARGARET AND RODERICK MacKENZIE

Chronicle Books • San Francisco

Library of Congress Cataloging-in-Publication Data

MacKenzie, Margaret, 1953-
    The Toronto guide / Margaret and Roderick MacKenzie.
        p.   cm.
    Includes index.
    ISBN 0-87701-628-3
    I. Toronto (Ont.)—Description—Guide-books. I. MacKenzie.
Roderick, 1952-   .   II. Title.
F1059.5.T683M34 1989
917.13′541044—dc19
                                        88-32981
                                            CIP

Design by Barbara Hodgson
Maps by Anna Gamble, Margaret MacKenzie and Barbara Hodgson
Cover photograph by E. Otto/Miller Comstock Inc.
Typeset by The Typeworks
Printed and bound in Canada by D. W. Friesen & Sons Ltd.

10   9   8   7   6   5   4   3   2   1

Chronicle Books
275 Fifth Street
San Francisco, California
94103

For Jim, Kenn, Jon and Martha

ACKNOWLEDGEMENTS

We gratefully acknowledge the contributions of the following people: Doug Carrick for his golf course recommendations and descriptions; Graham Henderson for his assistance in the Night Life chapter; Brian Pel for his photographs; David Crighton for his drawings of Toronto landmarks; and Ruth Goodfellow, Claire Beattie and Carolyn Lofquist for their late-night typing. We would also like to thank Shaun Oakey for his excellent editorial guidance.

Last but not least, a very special thanks to Deborah Hurst and Brent Makohn for their great efforts in contributing the Restaurants chapter and assisting with the Shopping chapter.

CONTENTS

Contents

LIST OF MAPS

ABOUT TORONTO 1

A FIVE-STAR CITY

In just a few short years Toronto has burst onto the world scene and directly into the limelight as a truly cosmopolitan city. Visitors flock here from around the globe, and thousands of people settle here every month, not just from across Canada but from the world over. It's no wonder. Toronto now has a multitude of top-quality hotels and dining spots. It has exceptional attractions such as the Royal Ontario Museum, the CN Tower, the Ontario Science Centre, the Metro Zoo and the

Toronto's central waterfront with the Western Gap in the distance. (Photo by Ottmar Bierwagen)

McMichael Canadian Collection. It's home to the Blue Jays, the Maple Leafs, the National Ballet, the Toronto Symphony and the Canadian Opera Company. It's the site of the International Caravan celebration, the Festival of Festivals, Chinatown, Harbourfront, Ontario Place, Black Creek Pioneer Village and Caribana, one of the world's largest West Indian festivals. More than that, it's a liveable city. Visitors are amazed by our safe, clean, efficient subway, by how easy it is to navigate the city streets, by the vast range of cultural experiences, city services and stores to shop in, and, most of all, by the friendliness of the natives. Whether you're visiting, planning to stay or already here, you'll soon agree that this "city that works" is truly first class.

GETTING ORIENTED

Although the Municipality of Metropolitan Toronto is spread out over a huge land area, getting to know the downtown core and your way around the city is very easy. The city streets were laid out in the simple grid system used by British land surveyors. This means they run either east-west or north-south (with a few exceptions). To Torontonians, "downtown" is bordered by Bloor St. on the north, Lake Ontario to the south, Bathurst St. on the west and Jarvis St. on the east. This downtown is then bisected by the city's largest retail artery, Yonge St. (which, according to the *Guinness Book of World Records,* is the world's longest street). Most of the city's major attractions, large hotels, famous restaurants and exclusive shopping are located in the downtown core.

Torontonians tend to give directions

Looking north along University Ave.'s central boulevard. (Photo by Brian Pel)

by naming the nearest major east-west, north-south intersection—for example, they'll tell you the Royal Ontario Museum is just south of Bloor St. at Queen's Park.

Telling north from south can be tricky at first. Keep in mind that Lake Ontario (when you can see it) is to the south; so is the can't-be-missed CN Tower, the world's tallest free-standing structure and world-famous landmark. The land also gently rises to the north as it slopes away from the lake.

When you're exploring the city, remember that north-south streets start numbering at the lake, and east and west streets start numbering from Yonge St. Pay attention to the east and west designations in an address. There is a very long walk between 565 Queen W. and 565 Queen E.

Hwy. 401, a major link to both eastern and western Ontario, traverses the northern part of the City of Toronto. The Don Valley Pkwy. (called "The Parkway") follows the Don River from the 401 down into the downtown core. The Parkway connects at its south end to the Gardiner Expressway, which from there runs west across the southern limit of the city, eventually becoming the Queen Elizabeth Way ("QEW") and heading south into the Niagara Peninsula. From the QEW, the traveller can turn north onto Hwy. 427, which connects the QEW with Hwy. 401 near Lester B. Pearson International Airport in the northwest corner of Metropolitan Toronto.

A note to visitors who intend to drive in the city: though our roads and highways are well maintained and well marked, like any major city we do have morning and afternoon rush hours, when traffic can be very heavy. It is at times like those that Torontonians refer to the Don Valley Parkway as the Don Valley Parking Lot. Plan to avoid rush hours whenever possible.

When residents speak of "Toronto," they typically mean the Municipality of Metropolitan Toronto, which consists of the City of Toronto, the City of North York, the City of York, the Borough (Canada's only) of East York, the City of Scarborough and the City of Etobicoke. Toronto's municipal structure of government was the first of its kind in North America.

Toronto is on the "Golden Horseshoe" of southern Ontario, a heavily

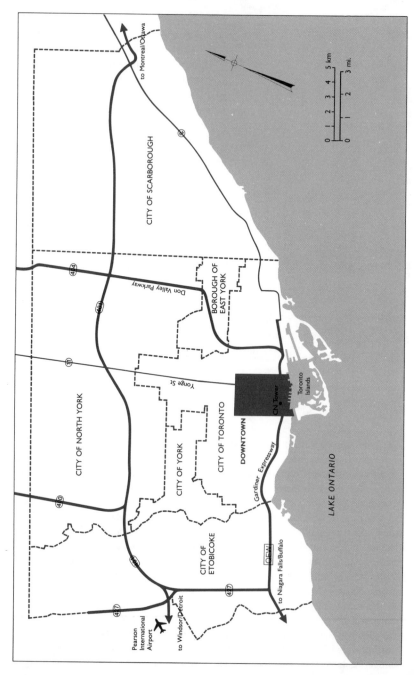

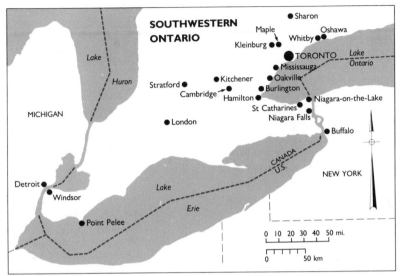

populated band starting in the Niagara–St. Catharines area of the Niagara Peninsula, running around the western end of Lake Ontario through Hamilton, Burlington and Oakville and continuing east through Toronto to Oshawa and Whitby.

HISTORY

BEGINNINGS

Toronto's location is by no means a mere historical accident. For thousands of years before Europeans explored this part of North America, the indigenous peoples had been using the mouth of the Humber River, near present-day Bloor and Jane streets, as the southern terminus of what is one of the most famous portage routes in North America. Historians call it the Toronto Carrying Place, and it started at the mouth of the Humber River and ran 45 km (28 mi.) north through Toronto to the Woodbridge–Kleinburg area and then beyond

to the Holland River and Holland Landing. There, canoes could be put into the water and paddled down the Holland River to Lake Simcoe and then Georgian Bay. This portage allowed paddlers to by-pass about 960 km (600 mi.) of dangerous travel on Lakes Erie and Huron and, above all, allowed them to avoid Niagara Falls.

Archaeological findings indicate that several prehistoric cultures lived in the Toronto region including the Laurentian Stone Age culture and the later Point Peninsula people. In the early 1600s, European explorers came upon Seneca Indians of the Iroquois nation settled in large villages at the mouths of both the Humber and Rouge rivers, part of present-day Toronto.

EXPLORATION

1615, Sept 9   A 19-year-old Frenchman and 12 Huron companions arrive at the mouth of the Humber River. The first European ever to set eyes on the site of future Toronto, Etienne Brûlé had been sent by Samuel de Champlain from Lake Simcoe to gather the support of friendly Indians for a war upon the Iroquois. Brûlé later lived with the Indians for a time but ran afoul of them and was ultimately murdered and eaten by them near Penetanguishene, Ont.

SETTLEMENT

1649   Various European traders and French explorers and priests begin visiting the Toronto Carrying Place. Among them are LaSalle, Radisson, Brébeuf, Marquette and Joliette.

1720   The French establish a trading post at Toronto near the mouth of the Humber River.

1750   The French establish a royal fort, known as Fort Rouillé, on what is now part of the CNE grounds.

1763   With the signing of the Treaty of Paris, New France, including the Toronto region, is surrendered by France to the British.

1770   Jean-Baptiste Rousseau from Montreal builds a permanent house on the east bank of the Humber River to carry on the business of fur-trading. Rousseau is considered Toronto's first citizen.

1787, Sept 23   The British complete the Toronto Purchase: three Mississauga Indian chiefs sell the Toronto region for £1,700 in cash and goods.

1791   Britain's North American possessions are divided into Lower Canada (Quebec) and Upper Canada (Ontario).

1792   British veteran of the American Revolutionary War, Col. John Graves Simcoe, is appointed governor of Upper Canada.

THE TOWN OF YORK

1793, July 30   Governor Simcoe, his family and his military party land at Toronto and establish a fort in the vicinity of today's Fort York, and a blockhouse on what is today Hanlan's Point on Toronto Island. Toronto Harbour was considered one of the best harbours in North America and of great military significance.

1793, Aug 27   Simcoe names his new capital York, after the Duke of York.

1813   During the War of 1812, American forces capture York and burn down the Parliament Buildings. A year later, British troops, in retaliation, invade and burn Washington, D.C., including the president's residence, which, when repainted, becomes known as the White House.

An early 20th-century view of Toronto from the spire of St. James' Cathedral. (Metropolitan Toronto Library, T 33051)

1824 The *Colonial Advocate* is first published by William Lyon Mackenzie and quickly attains a popular following in Upper Canada.

1829 York's population rises to 9000, due to increased Scottish, Irish and English immigration.

TORONTO AS A CITY

1834, March 6 The Town of York becomes the City of Toronto. Mackenzie's *Colonial Advocate* attacks the change of status as a Tory plot to raise taxes.

1834, March 30 Mackenzie is elected the first mayor of Toronto.

LATER LANDMARK YEARS

1837, Dec Mackenzie heads a rebellion to oust the provincial government. His rag-tag army advances south along Yonge St. to attack the city. The attack fails and the rebels retreat to Montgomery's Tavern (in the vicinity of Yonge and Eglinton), where they are completely defeated within days. Mackenzie flees to the U.S., but will return to become a member of provincial Parliament.

1842 Gas lighting is installed on Toronto streets.

1843 King's College, the predecessor of the University of Toronto, enrolls its first students.

1857 A census of Toronto indicates 42,000 citizens, of which 10,000 are British, 14,000 are Irish, 12,500 are native-born and 5500 are American.

1867 Toronto is designated the capital of Ontario.

1869 Timothy Eaton opens his first store on Yonge St. between Queen and Richmond.

1878 The Canadian National Exhibition begins. It will become the world's largest annual fair.

1899 Toronto's population exceeds 200,000.

1904 The Great Fire of Toronto. The conflagration destroys much of the downtown business district.

1914 European immigration has increased the population to 470,000.

1914 The Royal Ontario Museum opens.

1931 Maple Leaf Gardens opens. The Toronto Maple Leafs win their first Stanley Cup.

1932 The British Empire's tallest building at that time, the Bank of Commerce skyscraper, is finished.

1934 City of Toronto celebrates its centennial.

1953 The Municipality of Metropolitan Toronto, North America's first regional government, is created.

1954 The Yonge St. line, Canada's first subway, begins service.

1965 Toronto's new City Hall is completed.

1967 The Toronto–Dominion Centre opens, the first of many skyscrapers in the financial district.

1977 The CN Tower is erected.

POPULATION

The 1986 census indicated that the Municipality of Metropolitan Toronto is Canada's largest city with a population of 2.2 million. The City of Toronto proper has a population of 612,000. It is estimated that the Toronto vicinity—that is, within a radius of 80 km (50 mi.)—contains more than 4 million people.

Since the Second World War, many immigrants have come to settle in Toronto. More than 70 ethnic groups now reside here, many in distinct enclaves, and over 100 languages are spoken in Metro. In order of decreasing population, the main ethnic groups are British, Italian, Chinese, Portuguese, Jewish, East Indian, German, French, Greek, Polish, Ukrainian, Dutch, Spanish, Filipino, Korean and Japanese.

Its tremendous ethnic diversity has made Toronto one of the world's most cosmopolitan cities and offers the visitor seemingly unending cultural and dining experiences.

WEATHER

Ontario's weather is similar to that of the northeastern United States. Contrary to the old joke, "Yes, we have two seasons, winter and July," Toronto has four distinct seasons. Although Lake Ontario tends to moderate the climate, making the winters less harsh than farther inland, Toronto does suffer from occasional extremes and can be uncomfortably hot in the summer and icy cold in the winter. Visitors are well advised to pack appropriate clothing.

Snow is a given in the winter, although in recent years it has tended not to remain long. When it does snow in Toronto, the city is well prepared with a busy fleet of snow-removal vehicles and plows. Nonetheless, winter storms can produce some memorable traffic jams.

For Torontonians, spring is March, April and May, though winter can maintain its grip until mid-April. Springs are mild, with rain to be expected. Appropriate clothing means a sweater and a light jacket, with a change of warm-weather clothing just in case.

Summer usually opens in June and runs through July and Aug. Toronto is known for generally hot summers, and every summer one or two heat waves occur. At those times, it is blistering hot (sometimes over 90°F/32°C) and humid. Light, loose clothing, hat and sunglasses are a necessity. But please note that some summer days and evenings can be

WEATHER CHART	Mean Low Temperature		Mean High Temperature		Average Number Days of Precipitation	Average Monthly Precipitation		Average Number Hours of Sunshine
	°C	°F	°C	°F		cm	in.	
Jan	−8	17	−1	30	14	6.1	2.4	92
Feb	−7	19	0	32	12	5.2	2.0	112
Mar	−3	27	4	39	12	7.0	2.7	145
April	3	38	12	53	11	7.3	2.9	182
May	9	48	18	65	11	6.6	2.6	233
June	14	58	24	75	10	6.4	2.5	253
July	17	63	27	80	9	7.3	2.9	281
Aug	17	63	26	78	10	7.3	2.9	252
Sept	13	55	21	70	9	6.6	2.6	192
Oct	7	45	15	59	10	6.1	2.4	149
Nov	2	36	8	46	12	7.0	2.7	81
Dec	−5	24	1	35	14	7.3	2.9	75

Soaring skyscrapers at the heart of the financial district near King and Bay. (Photo by Brian Pel)

cooler, so you'll also need some warmer clothing, such as a cotton sweater.

Fall means Sept, Oct and Nov. Cool weather prevails. Pack sweaters and jackets. True "Indian summers" can occur in late Sept and Oct, so you should include lighter clothing. Fall in Ontario is famous for its colours, with "Muskoka colour weekends" a delight to both natives and visitors.

The unpleasant winter months are Dec, Jan and Feb. The dampness from Lake Ontario chills you to your bones at temperatures that Northern Ontario residents consider downright balmy. Dress warmly, prepared for the cold and the wet. Waterproof boots, gloves, scarves, hats and heavy coats are required. Experience teaches that a layered clothing approach is best. That way, you can regulate your temperature by adding or removing clothing as needed. Salt protectant for boots is advisable.

COMMERCE AND INDUSTRY

A port and commercial centre since its beginnings, Toronto boasts a wide array of business and industry. Toronto is Canada's business financial centre, as the King and Bay towers attest. The headquarters of about 200 of the country's top industrial companies and most of Canada's major banks, investment dealers and law firms are located here. The Toronto Stock Exchange trading volume places it among the world's top 10 exchanges. Many of Canada's corporate elite call Toronto home, and a trip through the affluent districts of Rosedale, Forest Hill and the Bridle Path gives you an idea of just how well business is doing. The sprawling industrial parks of North York, Mississauga and Scarborough house thousands of the region's small, medium and large businesses.

In the late 19th century, Canada's prime minister, Sir Wilfrid Laurier, predicted, "The 20th century belongs to Canada." While there was a time when many thought Sir Wilfrid had missed the mark, recent years have proved the "beaver" to be very bullish. From 1983 to 1988, Canada's economy grew faster than that of any other of the big seven industrial countries. Most of that growth centred in Ontario and, for that matter, Toronto. "The 20th century belongs to Toronto" may be a prediction that is right on the money.

ESSENTIAL INFORMATION 2

EMERGENCY PHONE NUMBERS

Some emergency numbers listed here apply only to the City of Toronto proper. For other metropolitan areas, check the inside front cover and page 2 of the Metropolitan Toronto White Pages telephone directory.

Police, Fire, Ambulance
In Metro Toronto dial 911. Anywhere else dial "0" for operator and say "This is an emergency."

Doctor
For a referral, call the Ontario Medical Association Physician Inquiry Service at 963-9383, Tues to Thurs 9 A.M. to 3:30 P.M. Other days and after hours, call out-patient service at the nearest hospital.

Dentist
For a referral, call the Academy of Dentistry. Mon to Fri 8:30 A.M. to 4:30 P.M., call 967-5649. Mon to Fri 4:30 P.M. to 1 A.M. and weekends and holidays 9 A.M. to 1 A.M., call 924-8041.
   Dental Emergency Service is provided at 1650 Yonge St. (near St. Clair), Sun to Thurs 9 A.M. to 1 A.M.; Fri to Sat 10 A.M. to 2 A.M. Call 485-7121.

Legal Assistance
The Law Society of Upper Canada operates a referral service at 947-3330, Mon to Fri 9 A.M. to 5 P.M.

Poison Information Centre
Call the Hospital for Sick Children at 598-5900 or Toronto East General Hospital at 469-6245.

Optician
Call Public Optical, 69 Queen St. E., 364-0740. Glasses in one hour. They have a large inventory of soft contact lenses as well. Hard contact lenses can be ordered (3-to-4-day turnaround). Open Mon to Wed 9 A.M. to 6 P.M., Thurs 9 A.M. to 8 P.M., Fri 9 A.M. to 6 P.M. and Sat 9 A.M. to 5 P.M.

Veterinarian
Willowdale Animal Clinic is always open. Call 222-5409.

Rape Crisis
Call 597-8808 (24 hours).

Distress and Suicide
Call 598-1121 or 486-1456.

AIDS Information
Call AIDS Info Line at 924-5200 or City of Toronto AIDS Hotline at 392-AIDS.

Community Services, Emergencies
Call 863-0505. Staff keeps a list of 120 emergency numbers covering such situations as shelter for battered women, counselling for crisis intervention and services for seniors.

Alcoholics Anonymous
Call 487-5591.

Alcohol/Drug Crisis
Call Addiction Research Foundation at 595-6128.

Visitor Health Insurance and Health Information
Hospital Medical Care, call 597-0666, Mon to Fri 9 A.M. to 9 P.M., Sat 9 A.M. to 5 P.M.

Ontario Blue Cross, call 429-2661, Mon to Fri 8 A.M. to 4 P.M.

Check whether your health insurance plan extends coverage outside your province or country. Prescriptions must be written by an Ontario physician to be filled in Ontario, so bring an adequate supply of your prescribed medicines.

Lost or Stolen Credit Cards
American Express 474-9280 (24 hours)
MasterCard   232-8020 (24 hours)
Diners Club   974-4515 (24 hours)
VISA (Royal Bank) 974-5460 (24 hours)

Royal Bank personnel will refer you to other bank VISA offices.

Marine and Aircraft Emergencies
Call Toronto Metro Marine at 967-3008 or Air and Marine Search and Rescue (Trenton) at 1-800-267-7270.

MAJOR HOSPITALS

All hospitals listed here have emergency rooms.

Doctors Hospital
45 Brunswick St. at College
923-5411
This hospital has two full-time interpreters on staff and can provide services in about thirty languages.

Mount Sinai Hospital
600 University Ave. at College
596-4200

Hospital for Sick Children
555 University Ave. at College
597-1500

Toronto General Hospital
200 Elizabeth St. at College
595-3111

Wellesley Hospital
160 Wellesley St. E.
at Sherbourne
966-6600

Womens College Hospital
76 Grenville St. at Bay
966-7111

St. Michael's Hospital
30 Bond St. at Queen E.
360-4000

Toronto Western Hospital
399 Bathurst St. at Dundas W.
368-2581

Sunnybrook Medical Centre
2075 Bayview Ave. between
Lawrence and Eglinton E.
486-3000

Etobicoke General Hospital
101 Humber College Blvd.
at Hwy. 27
747-3400
Closest hospital to Pearson International Airport.

AUTOMOBILES

Ontario's Rules of the Road
Seatbelts are mandatory. Infants must be secured into infant car seats.

If you are involved in an accident that results in a personal injury or property damage over $700, you must notify the police and remain at the scene of the accident.

Right turns on red lights, unless otherwise indicated, are permitted after you have come to a full stop.

A flashing green arrow or light allows you to turn left while a red light holds oncoming cars at bay.

Speed limits and distances are posted in metric. (To convert kilometres to miles, multiply by 6 then divide by 10.)

Pedestrians have the right of way at crosswalks. Crosswalk signs show a large black X on an orange background.

When approaching a stopped or stopping streetcar from the rear, you must come to a complete stop no closer than 2 m (6½ ft.) behind its rear door to allow passengers to enter and disembark.

Studded tires are banned.

Having a radar warning device in your car is illegal, even if it is not hooked up.

It is illegal to have excessively tinted windshields or side-front windows that obscure a clear view of the front-seat occupants.

For further information on local traffic laws, call CAA Toronto Traffic Laws Advisory Section at 964-3170.

Emergency Road Service

The CAA provides 24-hour emergency road service to its members and members of other auto clubs. Call 966-3000. The Ministry of Transportation patrols major highways for disabled vehicles and can be counted on for assistance.

Towing

Street parking in downtown Toronto is scarce and expensive. It's even more expensive if you get towed from a no-parking zone during rush hour (7 A.M. to 9 A.M. and 3:30 P.M. to 6 P.M.). If towed, call the police at 324-2222, and their computer will locate your car. Towing charges range from $55 to $85; impoundment charges can add $10 a day. Payment can be made in cash or with VISA, MasterCard or American Express—no cheques.

Road Conditions

Call the Ministry of Transportation Highway Information Centre at 235-1110.

CAA and AAA Service

Members of both associations are entitled to all services provided by any CAA club in Ontario. Listed under "Canadian Automobile Association" in the White Pages.

Ontario Provincial Police

Major expressways such as Hwy. 401 are within the jurisdiction of the OPP. They can be reached through the White Pages, or dial "0" and ask the operator for Zenith 50000.

Documents and Insurance

Drivers in Ontario must maintain a minimum public liability insurance of $200,000. A valid foreign driver's licence is good for three months in Canada.

VISITOR INFORMATION

THE METROPOLITAN TORONTO CONVENTION AND VISITORS ASSOCIATION

Personnel answer all visitor enquiries and offer complete information about Toronto. Head office is at 207 Queen's Quay W. at Harbourfront, Suite 509. Open Mon to Fri 8:30 A.M. to 5 P.M. Their information booth at the southwest corner of Yonge St. and Dundas, just outside the Eaton Centre, is open daily 9 A.M. to 7 P.M. (summer), 9:30 A.M. to 5:30 P.M. (winter). Their Information Line is 368-9821. From southern Ontario, N.Y., Ohio, Mich. and Pa., call toll free 1-800-387-2999. Mailing address is 207 Queen's Quay W., Suite 509, Box 126, Toronto, ON M5J 1A7.

ONTARIO TRAVEL INFORMATION CENTRES

Toronto Eaton Centre (level 1)
Open all year. Mon to Fri 10 A.M. to 9 P.M.; Sat 9:30 A.M. to 6 P.M.

Other locations on highway approaches to Metro (all are open from 8 A.M. to 8 P.M. mid-May to Labour Day; reduced hours the rest of the year):

Niagara Falls
West on Hwy. 420 off the Rainbow Bridge at 5355 Stanley Ave. (currency exchange available).

St. Catharines
Garden City Skyway on QEW (currency exchange available).

Barrie
Northbound lane of Hwy. 400, at Barrie.

Windsor
110 Park St. E. at Windsor–Detroit Tunnel (currency exchange available), or 1235 Huron Church Rd., east of the Ambassador Bridge (currency exchange available).

VISITOR INFORMATION— ONTARIO

Travel information is available from the Ontario Ministry of Tourism and Recreation's Travel Centre (965-4008), at the Eaton Centre, on the basement level near Eaton's. Open Mon to Fri 10 A.M. to 9 P.M.; Sat 9:30 A.M. to 6 P.M. You can also write Ontario Travel,

Queen's Park, Toronto, ON M7A 2R9, or phone toll free 1-800-268-3735.

VISITOR INFORMATION— CANADA

Call the Canadian Government Office of Tourism in Ottawa at (613) 954-3854, Mon to Fri 8:30 A.M. to 5 P.M.

WEATHER

Call Environment Canada (676-3066) for a recorded report 24 hours a day. On TV, WeatherNow channel (Rogers cable 20) broadcasts continuous weather reports.

PUBLIC HOLIDAYS

New Year's Day, 1 Jan *
Good Friday, date varies *
Easter Monday, Mon after Good Friday *
Victoria Day, fourth Mon in May *
Canada Day, 1 July *
Civic Holiday, first Mon in Aug **
Labour Day, first Mon in Sept *
Thanksgiving Day, second Mon in Oct *
Remembrance Day, 11 Nov **
Christmas, 25 Dec *
Boxing Day, 26 Dec *

* statutory holiday—government offices, banks and most businesses closed
** civic holiday—government offices and banks closed, some businesses closed

LOST AND FOUND

For items lost on buses, subways and streetcars:
Toronto Transit Commission
393-4100
Mon to Fri 9 A.M. to 5 P.M.

For items lost on GO buses and trains:
GO Transit
965-8844
Mon to Fri 11 A.M. to 7 P.M.

Police Lost and Found
324-2222

FOREIGN VISITORS

Toronto is home to approximately 50 consulates. Consult the Yellow Pages.

INTERPRETER SERVICES

The bilingual staff of the Metropolitan Toronto Convention and Visitors Association at the Eaton Centre can provide some French translation assistance.

Several private businesses are listed in the Yellow Pages under "Translators and Interpreters."

The College of Family Physicians of Canada will provide referrals to doctors who speak a second language. Call 493-7513, Mon to Fri 8 A.M. to 4 P.M.

If you need health care in your own language, the Doctors Hospital at 45 Brunswick St. (923-5411) employs two full-time interpreters and has a multilingual staff.

CUSTOMS REGULATIONS

Every 30 days, U.S. citizens going home after 48 hours or more can take with them $400 (U.S.) worth of duty-free merchandise. If you are 21 or over, this may include 200 cigarettes, 100 cigars (not Cuban), one pound of smoking tobacco and 32 oz. of alcohol. After a visit of less than 48 hours, only $25 (U.S.) worth of merchandise may be taken back duty free. U.S.-manufactured goods purchased in Canada may be brought back duty free and are not included in the basic exemption.

BANKING

Over 50 foreign banks have branches in Toronto. Check the Yellow Pages under "Banks." Banking hours are no longer uniform, so phone ahead. Extended hours are usually offered on Thurs and Fri, and Sat banking is available (see next column). Many banks and trust companies maintain 24-hour automated tellers throughout the city, and many of these feature inter-bank services such as Interac. The Toronto Dominion Bank has Green Machines throughout the city. Two convenient downtown locations are the Eaton Centre and underground at the Toronto-Dominion Centre. The Canadian Imperial Bank of Commerce has Instant Teller machines at 16 subway stations.

CURRENCY EXCHANGES

Foreign visitors may exchange currency at all major banks and at foreign exchange dealers. Downtown, currency can be exchanged at:

Bank of America Canada
Several downtown locations, including 4 King St. W., 16th floor (360-8022), open Mon to Fri, and the Royal York Hotel lobby (863-7324), open daily. Also at both terminals of Pearson International Airport.

Deak International
Seven locations, including 10 King St. E. (863-1611); Manulife Centre, 55 Bloor St. W. (961-9822), 60 Bloor St. W.

(923-6549) and the Sheraton Centre, 123 Queen St. W. (363-4867). All locations except King St. are open Sat.

Guardian Trust
123 Yonge St. near Richmond
863-1100

Union Currency Exchange
Union Station, Ticket Hall
61 Front St.
367-0808
Open daily 7:30 A.M. to 5:30 P.M.

SATURDAY BANKING

Among others, the following are open for business:

Bank of Nova Scotia
292 Spadina Ave. at Dundas
866-6633
10 A.M. to 1 P.M.

Canada Trust
50 Bloor St. W. at Yonge
962-4711
9 A.M. to 5 P.M.

Bank of Montreal
291 Spadina Ave. at Dundas
867-4759
10 A.M. to 3 P.M.

The Toronto-Dominion Bank
501 Dundas St. W. at Spadina
982-2111
8 A.M. to 4 P.M.
65 Wellesley St. E. at Church
961-8602
9 A.M. to 3 P.M.

Canadian Imperial Bank of
Commerce
Eaton Centre (lower level)
Yonge St. at Dundas
980-4770
10 A.M. to 3 P.M.

Royal Trust
60 Bloor St. W. at Bay
922-5078
9 A.M. to 3 P.M. Most branches are open Sat.

National Trust
50 Bloor St. W. at Yonge
925-1173
8 A.M. to 3 P.M.

POST OFFICE

Most post offices throughout the city are open Mon to Sat 10 A.M. to 6 P.M. Drugstores and other small stores that have post office facilities are designated by a red, white and blue Canada Post sign in the front window.

Two downtown post offices are:

Atrium on Bay
595 Bay St. at Dundas
Mon, Tues, Wed, Sat 10 A.M. to 6 P.M.; Thurs and Fri 10 A.M. to 9 P.M.

First Canadian Place
New Directions Outlet
100 King St. W. at Bay
Mon to Fri 10 A.M. to 6 P.M.; Sat 10 A.M. to 5 P.M.
This post office also sells postal souvenirs and has an extensive philatelic section.

Toronto's first post office, at 260 Adelaide St. E., opened in 1833. This national historic site is now open to the public (see Sightseeing).

TELEPOST

This fast message delivery service is available through the CN/CP Public Message Centre (368-6041). Messages sent before 6 P.M. will be delivered the next day.

LATE NIGHT SERVICES

PHARMACIES (24 Hour)

**Owl Drug
68 Wellesley St. E. at Church
266-8724**

**Shoppers Drug Mart
700 Bay St. at Gerrard
979-2424**

GROCERIES

**Bloor Super Save
384 Bloor St. W. at Spadina**
Open 24 hours.

**A&P Grocery Store
3142 Yonge St. near Lawrence**
Open Mon 9 A.M. through Sat 9 P.M.

7-Eleven stores
Open 24 hours throughout Toronto. Downtown stores are 200 Jarvis St. at Dundas and 796 Bloor St. W. at Crawford.

RESTAURANTS

If you are hunting for a restaurant in the wee hours of the morning, the following are open 24 hours a day:

**Fran's
24 College St. at Yonge
923-9867
21 St. Clair Ave. W. at Yonge
925-6336
2275 Yonge St. at Eglinton
481-1112**
Fran's is a Toronto institution. Not gourmet, but good, consistent food.

**Howard Johnson's
801 Dixon Rd. at Hwy. 27
(near Pearson International Airport)
675-6100**

**People's Foods
76 Dupont St. at St. George
961-3171**
One of Toronto's landmark greasy spoons.

**Just Desserts
306 Davenport Rd. at Bedford
922-6824**
Open 24 hours on Fri and Sat only. Rest of week open until 3 A.M. Incredible desserts. The late night line-ups are worth it.

**Golden Griddle Pancake House
11 Jarvis St. at Front
865-1263
45 Carlton St. near Yonge
977-5044**

In a city the size of Toronto, a considerable number of eating establishments offer late night meals. We recommend the following:

Bloor Street Diner
50 Bloor St. W. near Yonge
2nd floor
928-3105
Open until 3 A.M.

Bemelmans
83 Bloor St. W. near Bay
960-0306
Open Mon to Sat until 3 A.M., Sun until midnight.

Sai Woo
130 Dundas St. W. at Bay
977-4988
Open Mon to Sat until 2:30 A.M., Sun until 1:30 A.M.

Dessert Dessert
2352 Yonge St. at Eglinton
485-1725
Open Tues to Sat until 3 A.M., Sun until 1 A.M., closed Mon.

Free Times Café
320 College St. near Spadina
967-1078
Open Mon to Thurs until 1 A.M., Fri and Sat until 3 A.M., closed Sun.

Toby's Goodeats
93 Bloor St. W. near Bay
925-2171
725 Yonge St. at Bloor
925-9908
Open Mon to Sat until 3 A.M., Sun until 1 A.M.
Toby's has several other downtown locations with similar hours.

See also Restaurants (Late Night).

BABY SITTERS

Many major hotels can arrange baby sitters for you if notified in advance. The Yellow Pages lists many baby-sitting services under "Baby Sitters."

LIQUOR/WINE/BEER

In Ontario the statutory drinking age is 19, and proof of age may be required. Licensed premises such as hotels, lounges and restaurants are permitted to serve alcohol from 11 A.M. to 1 A.M. Mon to Sat, and from noon to 11 P.M. Sun. The consumption of alcohol in a place other than a residence or a licensed premise is a criminal offence.

Ontario's drinking and driving laws carry stiff penalties. Police run spot checks year-round. It is a criminal offence to refuse to take a breathalyzer test or to produce a breathalyzer reading in excess of 0.08%.

Liquor, imported wines and beers and limited brands of domestic wines and beers are available at government-owned Liquor Control Board of Ontario (LCBO) stores. Domestic wines are also available through independent stores operated by the respective wineries. The LCBO has several rare-wine shops in Toronto, called Vintages, with knowledgeable, helpful staff. Domestic beer and ale is sold primarily through the retail outlets of the Brewers' Retail Association, known as The Beer Stores. LCBO and Brewers' Retail outlets are listed in the White Pages. Independent wine stores are listed in the Yellow Pages under "Wineries."

2   Liquor, Wine, Beer/Dry Cleaning/Shoe Repairs

Centrally located liquor stores are:

Cumberland Terrace
2 Bloor St. E. at Yonge
Open Mon to Fri 9:30 A.M. to 9:30
P.M., Sat 9:30 A.M. to 6 P.M.

87 Front St. E. at Jarvis
Mon to Thurs and Sat 9:30 A.M. to
6 P.M., Fri 9:30 A.M. to 9 P.M.

Union Station
Mon to Fri 9:30 A.M. to 10 P.M., Sat
9:30 A.M. to 6 P.M.

1121 Yonge St.
near Summerhill subway
Mon to Sat 9:30 A.M. to 10 P.M.

Eaton Centre
(lower level at north end)
Yonge St. at Dundas
Mon to Fri 9:30 A.M. to 9:30 P.M., Sat
9:30 A.M. to 9 P.M.

Centrally located Beer Stores are:

614 Queen St. W. at Bathurst
Open Mon to Sat 10 A.M. to 9 P.M.

345 Bloor St. E. near Sherbourne
Mon to Fri 10 A.M. to 9 P.M., Sat 9:30
A.M. to 9 P.M.

1123 Yonge St.
near Summerhill subway
Mon to Wed 10 A.M. to 10 P.M., Thurs
and Fri 10 A.M. to 11 P.M., Sat 9:30
A.M. to 10 P.M.

St. Lawrence Market
15 Market St.
Mon to Fri 10 A.M. to 9 P.M., Sat 7 A.M.
to 9 P.M.

The most popular Vintages store is at:

2 Cooper St. at Queen's Quay E.
Open Mon to Thurs and Sat 9:30 A.M.
to 6 P.M., Fri 9:30 A.M. to 9 P.M.
This store carries more than 700 brands
of wine.

DRY CLEANING/SHOE REPAIRS

Knob Hill Cleaners and Laundry
463 Bloor St. W. at Brunswick
923-6541
One-hour dry cleaning.

Cadet Cleaners
Atrium on Bay
595 Bay St. at Dundas
598-1929
Same-day service.

Sketchley Cleaners
Toronto-Dominion Bank Tower
(lower level)
55 King St. W. near Bay
365-9807
Same-day service if dropped off by 10
A.M.

Most hotels offer one-day dry cleaning.

Two stores that do leather and suede
cleaning are:

Peter Pan
2531 Yonge St. near Eglinton
481-3341
Free pick-up and delivery.

Premier Cleaners
33 Yonge St. at Front
362-0861

30

These stores will take care of minor emergency shoe repairs while you wait:

Novelty Shoe Rebuilders
119 Yonge St. near Adelaide
In business for over 50 years, Novelty has repaired all styles of footwear. Also a wonderful place to people-watch.

Express While You Wait Shoe
Repair
Eaton Centre (2nd level)
Yonge St. at Dundas

Market Square Shoe Service
80 Front St. E. near Jarvis

RADIO/TELEVISION

AM RADIO STATIONS

590 CKEY, classic hits
680 CFTR, top 40
740 CBL, CBC English, informational, current and public affairs
790 CIAO, multilingual, mostly Italian
860 CJBC, CBC French
900 CHML, light rock
1010 CFRB, easy listening, news
1050 CHUM, hits of yesterday and today
1220 CHSC, adult contemporary
1320 CFGM, country
1350 CKAR, soft rock
1430 CJCL, nostalgia music, Blue Jay baseball, Maple Leaf hockey
1480 CKAN, classic hits
1540 CHIN, multilingual

FM RADIO STATIONS

88.1 CKLN, specialty programming, classical, jazz

89.5 CIUT, talk shows, community programming
91.1 CJRT, educational, classical, jazz
94.1 CBL-FM, classical, arts
94.9 CKQT, easy listening, some ethnic programming
95.3 CKDS, easy listening
96.3 CFMX, classical
97.3 CJEZ, easy listening
98.1 CHFI, adult contemporary
99.1 CKO, all-news
99.9 CKFM, light rock
100.7 CHIN, multilingual
102.1 CFNY, progressive rock
104.5 CHUM, album rock
105.7 CHRE, adult contemporary
107.1 Q107, progressive rock

NETWORK AND CABLE TV

Five cablevision companies service Metro Toronto. Listed below are the cable channels of Rogers Cable, which services the downtown area.

2 WGRZ NBC Buffalo (cable 15)
3 CKVR CBC Barrie (cable 33)
4 WIVB CBS Buffalo (cable 5/16)
5 CBLT CBC Toronto (cable 6)
6 GLOBAL Toronto
7 WKBW ABC Buffalo (cable 9/17)
8 WROC NBC Rochester
9 CFTO CTV Toronto (cable 8)
10 WHEC CBS Rochester
11 CHCH Hamilton (cable 11)
12 CHEX CBC Peterborough (cable 35)
13 CKCO CTV Kitchener (cable 34)
TVO FRENCH Toronto (cable 13)
17 WNED PBS Buffalo (cable 18)
19 CICA TVOntario Toronto (cable 2)
23 WNEQ PBS Buffalo
25 CBLFT CBC Toronto, French (cable 12)

29 WUTV Buffalo (cable 19)
41 GLOBAL Toronto (cable 3)
47 CFMT Toronto (cable 4)
57 CITY Toronto (cable 7)

PAY TV

Arts and Entertainment (cable 29)
CNN News (cable 25)
Family Channel (cable 30)
First Choice (cable 24)
MuchMusic (cable 22)
Nashville Network (cable 27)
The Sports Network (cable 26)

NEWSPAPERS/MAGAZINES

Three daily newspapers make Toronto North America's most competitive newspaper city.

The Globe and Mail
Canada's only national newspaper. The Metro edition is published mornings Mon through Sat. Certainly Toronto's best foreign news and business coverage.

The Toronto Star
The newspaper with the biggest readership in Canada. Great entertainment section, and many Torontonians feel their weekend incomplete without the Saturday *Star*. The Friday edition includes the informative "What's On" section. Published seven days a week, with morning and evening editions Mon through Fri.

The Toronto Sun
Toronto's answer to London tabloids. Excellent sports coverage. Provides the right-wing viewpoint. Published every morning.

Other interesting publications with a Toronto focus include:

NOW
A weekly tabloid containing entertainment, news and reviews. Free.

Metropolis
Another weekly tabloid containing entertainment, news and reviews. Features a useful "Eight Days a Week" chart. Free.

Xtra!
A bi-weekly gay guide to Toronto. Free.

FOREIGN NEWSPAPERS

Reflecting a thriving multicultural population, many foreign newspapers and magazines are available in Toronto. One excellent source is Lichtman's News and Books, at 144 Yonge St. near Richmond (368-7390), 1430 Yonge St. near St. Clair (922-7271) and 842 Yonge St. near Bloor (924-4186).

TIPPING/PROVINCIAL SALES TAX

A 10 to 15% tip is customary in restaurants and taxis.

A retail sales tax of 8% is levied by the Province of Ontario on almost all goods and services. Visitors who accumulate $100 worth of receipts for certain types of merchandise to be used outside of Ontario may apply for a retail sales tax refund. For more information call the Retail Sales Tax District Office at 487-1361.

WHERE TO STAY   3

WHERE TO STAY

In a city as large and as popular as Toronto, there is ample accommodation to fit every taste and budget. If price is no object, you can certainly pay for and receive first-class treatment in the city's finer hotels. If you're travelling on a budget, alternative accommodations and bed and breakfast houses can make for an affordable visit.

We have described only recommended accommodations. Hotels are listed by price, based on double occupancy in early 1989 (not including sales tax). The Metropolitan Toronto Convention and Visitors Association recommends that you contact the accommodation of your choice to confirm the rate before your visit.

Tourism Ontario inspects and grades hotels, motels and other accommodation on a one-to-five star system. Its official Ontario/Canada accommodations directory is available from the Ontario Ministry of Tourism and Recreation by calling toll free 1-800-268-3735. As well, the following accommodation services can help you find suitable lodgings.

Accommodation Toronto
596-7117
Free hotel reservation service provided by the Hotel Association of Metropolitan Toronto. Call daily 9 A.M. to 9 P.M.

Econo-Lodging Services
494-0541
Free reservation service for groups, individuals and families. Covers all Toronto hotels plus furnished apartments and tourist homes. Call Mon to Fri 9 A.M. to 5 P.M.

DOWNTOWN ACCOMMODATION

1 Venture Inn
2 Four Seasons Hotel
3 Park Plaza Hotel
4 Windsor Arms Hotel
5 Hotel Plaza II
6 Brownstone Hotel
7 Town Inn
8 Cromwell Apartments
9 Sutton Place Hotel
10 Prestige Executive Accommodation
11 Westbury Hotel
12 Carlton Inn
13 Hampton Court Hotel
14 Primrose Hotel
15 Quality Inn—Essex Park
16 Delta Chelsea Inn
17 Neill-Wycik Co-op College
18 Holiday Inn Downtown
19 Bond Place Hotel
20 Toronto International Hostel
21 Sheraton Centre
22 Hilton International Toronto
23 Journey's Court
24 Executive Motor Hotel
25 King Edward Hotel
26 Hotel Victoria
27 Strathcona Hotel
28 Royal York Hotel
29 L'Hotel
30 Novotel Toronto Centre
31 Hotel Admiral
32 Toronto Harbour Castle Westin
● CN Tower
■ SkyDome
→ Traffic direction
   Not all one-way streets are shown

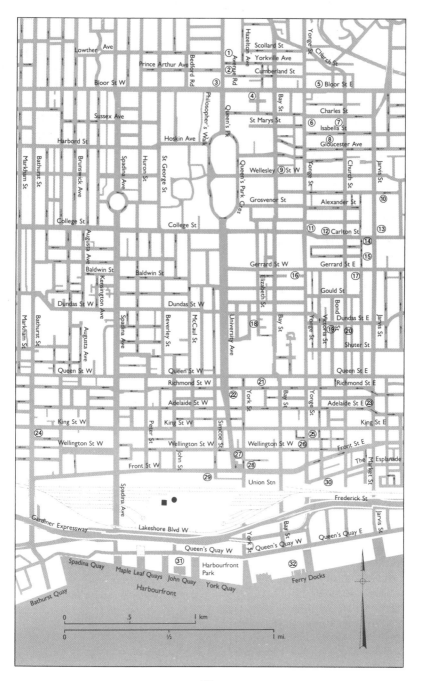

HOTELS

DOWNTOWN

Four Seasons Hotel
21 Avenue Rd. near Bloor
964-0411
1-800-268-6282 toll free (Canada)
1-800-332-3442 toll free (U.S.)
Double $240–$260
In 1985 the prestigious Institutional Investor poll of top-level international financiers and executives rated 6 Four Seasons hotels in the top 50 in the world including No. 1 in both Canada and the U.S.A. This superb hotel is the chain's flagship.

The Four Seasons chain aims to recreate the style of the grand hotels that adapted to the needs of each guest. Sumptuous furnishings include original art and antiques. Award-winning service includes 24-hour room and valet services, multilingual concierge, twice-daily maid service, non-smoking floor, first-class dining rooms, well-equipped health club and pool, and courtesy limousine service to the financial district.

Located in fashionable Yorkville amidst some of Toronto's most exclusive shops, this is one of the favourite hotels of visiting movie stars. Elizabeth Taylor, Jane Fonda and Peter Ustinov have all stayed here.

The King Edward Hotel
37 King St. E. near Yonge
863-9700
1-800-225-5843 toll free
Double $210–$260
More than any other hotel in the city, the King Eddy treats you to first-class service in a setting of Edwardian opulence. Designed by E. J. Lennox, Canada's most famous architect at the

King Edward Hotel

time (he also designed Old City Hall), the hotel opened its doors in 1903. Even if you don't stay here, the palatial lobby with its 24-m (80-ft.) high ceiling, the marble staircase to the mezzanine level, the fabulous baroque plaster-work ceiling in the Café Victoria, and the Edwardian ballroom are more than worth the visit.

For many years the King Eddy was "the" fashionable hotel in Toronto and one of the most fashionable in the British Empire. But as the business heart of the city moved west of Yonge St., the King Eddy slipped into a gradual decline, until in 1979 a $25-million renovation made it once again one of Toronto's most prestigious hotels. It offers 315 rooms, valet parking, 24-hour room service, a health club/spa and a most attentive concierge staff.

If you do stay at the King Eddy, you will be in good company. Over the years Rudyard Kipling, Lloyd George, the Archbishop of Canterbury, Margaret Thatcher, Queen Sophia of Spain, and a scandal-stirring Liz Taylor and Richard Burton have been guests here.

The Sutton Place Hotel
955 Bay St. at Wellesley
924-9221
1-800-268-3790 toll free
Double $200–$290
With the financial district on one side and the city's most fashionable shops on the other, the Sutton offers premiere service and luxury with a European ambience. The hotel contains 208 guest rooms and 72 luxurious suites. Amenities include 24-hour room service, concierge service, fitness centre and a courtesy limousine to the financial district in the morning. The Sanssouci Restaurant has a deservedly excellent reputation.

The Sutton Place is another Toronto hotel preferred by visiting movie stars, and its proximity to the provincial legislature at Queen's Park makes it a favourite haunt of politicians and their hangers-on.

L'Hotel
225 Front St. W. near University
597-1400
1-800-268-9420 toll free (Ont. and Que.)
1-800-268-9411 toll free (all other provinces)
1-800-828-7447 toll free (U.S.)
Double $180–$215
Many of the 600 rooms in Toronto's newest luxury hotel have panoramic views of downtown or Lake Ontario. L'Hotel is only a short walk from the financial district and is attached to Canada's largest convention centre.

This CP hotel is virtually connected to the CN tower, so guests have the option of rising to the Top of Toronto revolving restaurant for dinner. The impressive Skylight Lounge, a three-storey atrium complete with an overhead

Enjoying drinks amidst the greenery of the Skylight Lounge at L'Hotel.

canopy of fig trees, is an elegant spot for lunch or drinks. The hotel offers a fitness club, concierge, non-smoking floors and laundry/valet service. Approximately half the rooms come with fully stocked computerized bars.

Hilton International Toronto
145 Richmond St. W.
near University
869-3456
1-800-268-9275 toll free
Double $165–$195
The 600-plus-room Hilton is close to City Hall, the Eaton Centre and the financial district, and along with the Sheraton and the Royal York it is con-

nected to a huge shopping mall beneath the streets of downtown. The service here is more personalized than you'd expect from a hotel of this size. Trader Vic's Polynesian Restaurant is popular. Services include health facilities, 24-hour room service, concierge and business services (typing, FAX, etc.).

The Sheraton Centre
123 Queen St. W. near Bay
361-1000
1-800-325-3535 toll free
Double $165–$195

Close to City Hall, the Eaton Centre and the financial district, the Sheraton is one of three hotels connected to an extensive underground shopping mall

(about 60 shops are housed in the mall level of the Sheraton itself). Though it has more than 1400 rooms, service is still very high quality. The expansive landscaped gardens, including a 9-m (30-ft.) waterfall, distinguish this hotel from many others in the city. Features non-smoking floors and six restaurants and lounges. The Long Bar, containing the longest stand-up bar in the city, is a great place to enjoy a quiet drink while you overlook Nathan Phillips Square. The hotel's extensive sports/health complex includes an outdoor roof-top jogging track and Canada's largest hotel indoor swimming pool.

The Hotel Admiral
249 Queen's Quay W.
near Spadina
364-5444
1-800-387-1626 toll free
Double $140–$170

Beautifully located in the heart of Harbourfront, this 157-room hotel offers great views, 24-hour room service, concierge service and as well as its own fine restaurants and lounges, proximity to those at Harbourfront's Pier 4. The Admiral's Promenade Deck is certainly one of the more refined places to sunbathe in the city.

One of the attractions of the Sheraton Centre Hotel—its beautifully landscaped gardens and waterfall.

Park Plaza Hotel
4 Avenue Rd. at Bloor
924-5471
1-800-268-4927 toll free
Double $165
Right on the edge of Yorkville, the 200-room Park Plaza has long been a popular spot with tourists and residents alike. It's convenient to the University of Toronto, the Royal Ontario Museum and Queen's Park. The renovated Café Terrace, the hotel's roof-top lounge, which over the years has been a favourite haunt of journalists (including Ernest Hemingway) will reopen in late 1989.

Toronto Harbour Castle Westin
1 Harbour Square at Bay
869-1600
1-800-228-3000 toll free
Double $135–$200
Popular with conventioneers, the 976-room Harbour Castle sits right next to Lake Ontario—in fact, the Toronto Islands ferries arrive and depart directly behind the hotel. All the amenities you would expect from a large hotel, includ-

ing non-smoking floors, four full-service restaurants and a sports club. Most rooms have a beautiful view of the lake.

Hotel Plaza II
90 Bloor St. E. at Yonge
961-8000
1-800-223-0888 toll free
Double $127–$149
You can't get more central. This 256-room hotel, on top of the Hudson's Bay department store at the busy Yonge/Bloor intersection, is convenient to subways and plenty of shopping.

The Royal York Hotel
100 Front St. W. at York
863-6333
1-800-268-9411 toll free (Canada)
1-800-828-7447 toll free (U.S.)
Double $125–$170
An institution in Toronto, the Royal York Hotel opened its doors the year of the great stock market crash of 1929. To this day it remains the largest hotel in the British Commonwealth. Its coppertop roofs are to many Torontonians an integral part of their city's skyline. Directly across from Union Station and in the heart of the financial district, the hotel is always busy, but with 1600 rooms it is seldom booked solid and is a good bet if you're having trouble getting into another hotel. Watching the bustle in the hotel lobby is a form of entertainment in itself.

There is plenty of choice within the hotel for eating and drinking, with seven bars and lounges and six dining rooms including the well-known Benihana of Tokyo.

The Royal York is aptly named—Queen Elizabeth, Prince Philip and thirteen other members of the royal family

The largest hotel in the British Commonwealth, Toronto's regal Royal York.

have stayed here, as well as such non-royals as Winston Churchill, Charles de Gaulle, Raquel Welch and Frank Sinatra. Pets allowed.

Novotel Toronto Centre
45 The Esplanade near Yonge
367-8900
1-800-221-4542 toll free
Double $119–$150
Great location close to the theatre district, St. Lawrence Market and downtown shopping. A cozy 266-room hotel with an arcade façade designed to complement the historic streetscape.

Delta Chelsea Inn
33 Gerrard St. W. near Yonge
595-1975
1-800-268-1133 toll free
Double $119–$143
They must do something right. This hotel reputedly has the highest occupancy rate in the city. Just north of the Eaton Centre, the Chelsea offers 997 rooms, valet service, 24-hour room service, non-smoking floors, recreation facilities and a children's creative centre. They will also provide you with maps of jogging routes near the hotel. "Quiet" house pets allowed with a security deposit.

The Windsor Arms Hotel

The Holiday Inn Downtown
89 Chestnut St. near Dundas
977-0707
1-800-HOLIDAY toll free
Double $119–$139
What can we tell you about a hotel whose slogan is "the best surprise is no surprise"? Next to Nathan Phillips Square and the new City Hall. Pets allowed.

The Brownstone Hotel
15 Charles St. E. at Yonge
924-7381
1-800-263-8967 toll free
Double $110
This older hotel with 109 rooms is near bustling Bloor and Yonge streets and close to some of Toronto's best shopping.

The Windsor Arms Hotel
22 St. Thomas St. near Bloor
979-2341
1-800-668-8106 toll free
Double $105–$180
Toronto's only hotel in the true European tradition, the Windsor Arms is small (81 rooms), extremely elegant and possesses an international reputation. It is tucked away on a quiet back street near the heart of Toronto's most luxurious shopping district. The Windsor Arms is one of only 10 Canadian hostelries associated with the exclusive French Relais and Chateau, whose members must adhere to the 5 C's: Character, Calm, Comfort, Cuisine and Courtesy. Each hostelry must be small (less than 100 rooms), individually furnished with antiques, and must maintain an atmosphere of casual elegance.

In addition to first-class personalized service, the Windsor Arms is home to four exceptional restaurants and two lounges, and it keeps one of the most extensive wine cellars in Canada. The European-style Courtyard Café features an enormous glass-covered garden and cuisine naturelle.

The hotel's rigid policy of ensuring the privacy of its residents has ensured a steady stream of celebrity guests.

The Hampton Court Hotel
415 Jarvis St. at Carlton
924-6631
1-800-387-5510 toll free
(Ont. and Que.)
1-800-387-2701 toll free (U.S.)
Double $110
Near Maple Leaf Gardens and the Eaton Centre. The Hampton Court's 163 rooms wrap around an outdoor court-yard and heated pool, an innovative design in its day. (This is the hotel where the hoteliers who own and operate the world-renowned Four Seasons chain got their start.)

The Westbury Hotel
475 Yonge St. near Carlton
924-0611
1-800-387-0647 toll free
Double $104–$140
Almost next door to Maple Leaf Gardens, the 545-room Westbury is only a short walk south to the Eaton Centre or north to Yorkville. Creighton's, their highly praised dining room, serves meals prepared by an award-winning chef.

The Town Inn
620 Church St. near Bloor
964-3311
Double $95–$135
Just south of Bloor and just east of Yonge, this hotel has 200 suites, an indoor pool, saunas and outdoor tennis courts.

The Quality Inn—Essex Park
300 Jarvis St. near Carlton
977-4823
1-800-228-5151 toll free
Double $95
This hotel, overlooking Toronto's famous Allan Gardens, was built in 1930. The Toronto Historical Board is considering having it designated a historic site. It has 109 rooms and most of the amenities you would expect for this price.

The Venture Inn
89 Avenue Rd. near Bloor
964-1220
1-800-387-3933 toll free
Double $95
There are several Venture Inns in Toronto. This one (71 rooms) is conveniently close to Yorkville and the Royal Ontario Museum.

Hotel Victoria
56 Yonge St. near King
363-1666
Double $90–$110
Recently refurbished, this small hotel is close to the O'Keefe Centre, Union Station and the financial district.

The Primrose Hotel
111 Carlton St. at Jarvis
977-8000
1-800-268-8082 toll free
Double $89–$119
Not far from Maple Leaf Gardens, this 338-room hotel is also convenient to the Eaton Centre and fashionable Bloor St.

The Carlton Inn
33 Carlton St. near Yonge
977-6655
1-800-268-9076 toll free
Double $89–$110
Maple Leaf Gardens is next door, and the subway is a few steps away. Though this 536-room hotel offers economy accommodation, it contains an indoor pool, restaurant and lounge and is close to the Yonge St. strip.

The Strathcona Hotel
60 York St. at Wellington
363-3321
Double $75–$90
This small (196 rooms) hotel is close to the financial district, Union Station and the subway.

The Bond Place Hotel
65 Dundas St. E. near Yonge
362-6061
1-800-268-9390 toll free (Ont.,
Que., eastern Canada, U.S.)
1-800-387-1557 toll free (western
Canada, Nfld.)
Double $75
This 300-room hotel is almost next door to the Eaton Centre. You don't have the facilities or the amenities of the more expensive hotels, but the rooms are more than adequate, and price and location are ideal.

Journey's Court
111 Lombard St. at Jarvis
367-5555
1-800-668-4200 toll free
Double $70
Strictly rooms (196); no food, bar or fitness facilities, but a bargain price for a downtown hotel.

The Executive Motor Hotel
621 King St. W. near Bathurst
362-7441
Double $56–$63
The Executive offers budget accommodation in a motel-style setting. One advantage is being able to park your car close to your room. House pets allowed.

METROPOLITAN AREA

Because the Metropolitan area is so large, some of these hotels may be a considerable distance from the downtown core.

The Prince Hotel
900 York Mills Rd.
Don Mills
444-2511
1-800-268-7677 toll free (Canada)
1-800-542-8686 toll free (U.S.)
Double $140–$150
South of Hwy. 401 between Leslie St. and Don Mills Rd. The Prince offers excellent accommodation and services in a wooded ravine setting. The Katsura Japanese Restaurant's elegant design and the beautiful surroundings have made it a favourite with Asian businesspeople.

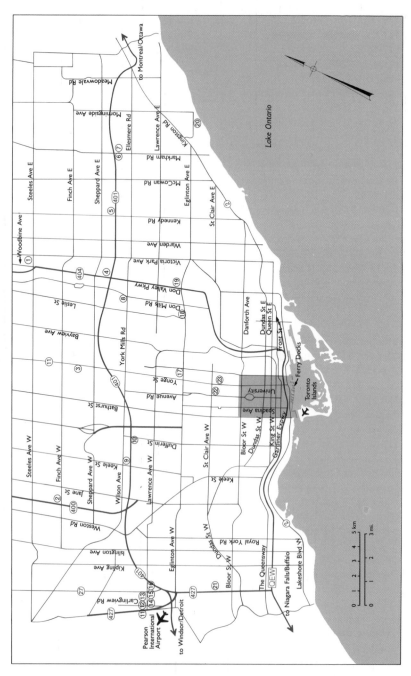

METROPOLITAN AND AIRPORT ACCOMMODATION

1 Chimo Hotel
2 Journey's End
3 Novotel North York
4 Ramada Hotel Don Valley
5 Wharton Renaissance Hotel
6 Venture Inn
7 Howard Johnson Hotel
8 Prince Hotel
9 Skyline Triumph Hotel
10 Holiday Inn Yorkdale
11 Airport Hilton
12 Bristol Place Hotel
13 Constellation Hotel
14 Marriott Hotel
15 Howard Johnson's Toronto Airport Hotel
16 Skyline Hotel
17 Roehampton Place Hotel
18 Inn on the Park
19 Radisson Hotel Don Valley
20 Guild Inn
21 Valhalla Inn
22 Bradgate Arms
23 YWCA Woodlawn Residence
 Downtown
-⑩- Highway

The Bradgate Arms
54 Foxbar Rd. at Avenue Rd. and St. Clair W.
968-1331
1-800-268-7171 toll free
Double $135–$155
This 109-room hotel evolved out of two older apartment buildings refurbished and connected by an elegant atrium with a marble floor and trees. Its often recommended dining room and a cozy library complete with fireplace add to the ambience.

Wharton Renaissance Hotel
2035 Kennedy Rd.
Scarborough
299-1500
1-800-387-5353 toll free
Double $135
North of Hwy. 401. Toronto's first postmodern hotel. The 388-room Renaissance is close to the Metro Toronto Zoo and the Ontario Science Centre. Elegant dining room and beautiful Japanese restaurant overlooking the city. Health club, 24-hour room service, non-smoking floors, a mini putting green and most of the amenities you'd expect from a large hotel. Pets allowed.

The Radisson Hotel Don Valley
1250 Eglinton Ave. E.
Don Mills
449-4111
1-800-228-9822 toll free
Double $120–$160
With 354 rooms, two restaurants and well-equipped fitness facilities including indoor and outdoor pools. Pets allowed.

Dining in the Terrace Café overlooking the Nordic Garden at the Valhalla Inn.

Inn on the Park
1100 Eglinton Ave. E.
Don Mills
444-2561
1-800-268-6282 toll free (Canada)
1-800-332-3442 toll free (U.S.)
Double $118–$143
Overlooking the beautiful Don Valley ravine, this hotel is beside 240 ha (600 acres) of parkland, providing ample opportunity for jogging, cycling or hiking. An elegant Four Seasons chain hotel, it offers 24-hour room service, valet service, complimentary morning limousine service, multilingual concierge and a

complete health club. Fifteen minutes from downtown via the Don Valley Pkwy.

The Holiday Inn Yorkdale
3450 Dufferin St.
Downsview
789-5161
1-800-HOLIDAY toll free
Double $115
Just south of Hwy. 401. A 373-room hotel next door to the Yorkdale Shopping Centre, a huge and diversified indoor mall and a Toronto attraction in its own right. Pets allowed.

The Valhalla Inn
1 Valhalla Inn Rd.
Etobicoke
239-2391
1-800-268-2500 toll free
Double $115
Just east of Hwy. 427 and convenient to Pearson International Airport. The 250-room Valhalla is built around a beautiful garden courtyard complete with pool. Facilities include supper club, health spa and a dining room with a menu that includes traditional Scandinavian entrees. Pets allowed.

Novotel Mississauga
3670 Hurontario St.
Mississauga
896-1000
1-800-387-7811 toll free
Double $115
Offers 325 reasonably priced rooms and is convenient to the airport. A real French bakery take-out on the premises. Small pets allowed.

The Chimo Hotel
7095 Woodbine Ave.
Markham
474-0444
1-800-387-9779 toll free
Double $110
North of Hwy. 401 and just east of Hwy. 404, the Chimo Hotel is close to the Metro Toronto Zoo and not far from the Ontario Science Centre. The hotel offers dining room, lounge and fitness facilities including daily memberships at a nearby tennis/squash/racquetball centre.

The Skyline Triumph Hotel
2737 Keele St.
North York
633-2000
1-800-648-7200 toll free
Double $109
North of Hwy. 401. The Skyline has 204 rooms and is convenient to the airport and Canada's Wonderland amusement park.

Novotel North York
3 Park Home Ave. at Yonge
North York
733-2929
Double $105–$120
Near the business centre of North York—the fastest growing city in Canada. It has 262 rooms and is noted for its in-house bakery.

The Guild Inn
201 Guildwood Pkwy.
Scarborough
261-3331
1-800-268-1133 toll free (Canada)
1-800-877-1333 toll free (U.S.)
Double $99
Definitely not your usual hotel accommodation. Set in 35 ha (90 acres) of beautiful woodlands at the top of the scenic Scarborough Bluffs, it's a great spot from which to explore the bluffs or the nearby Rouge River parkland. Lots of wood panelling and antiques. The Sunday brunch is one of the best values in the city. The Guild Inn is a short distance from the Metro Zoo and is the home of the Spencer Clark Collection of Historic Architecture (see Sightseeing/Great Buildings). Pets allowed with a security deposit.

Ramada Hotel Don Valley
185 Yorkland Blvd.
Willowdale
493-9000
Double $94–$106
Just north of Hwy. 401 and east of the Don Valley Pkwy., this hotel offers 285 rooms and is 12 minutes from downtown. Also close to the Metro Zoo and the Ontario Science Centre.

Sheraton Parkway Hotel
Hwy. 7 at Hwy. 404
Richmond Hill
881-2121
1-800-325-3535 toll free
Double $89–$109
North of Hwy. 401 and west of the Don Valley Pkwy. The Sheraton has 217 rooms, suites with whirlpool baths, and a fitness club. It is near the Metro Zoo and the Ontario Science Centre.

The Howard Johnson Hotel
40 Progress Court
(Hwy. 401 and Markham Rd.)
Scarborough
439-6200
1-800-654-2000 toll free
Double $88–$120
Halfway between the Metro Zoo and
the Ontario Science Centre, in the east
end of the city. With 192 rooms, indoor
pool and 24-hour restaurant. Pets allowed.

Roehampton Place Hotel
808 Mt. Pleasant Rd.
near Eglinton
487-5101
1-800-387-8899 toll free
Double $80–$100
Of the 112 rooms, 20 have kitchenettes.
A less expensive hotel because of its
location slightly outside the downtown
core.

The Venture Inn
50 Estate Dr.
Scarborough
439-9666
1-800-387-3933 toll free
Double $68
Near Markham Rd. and Hwy. 401. This
hotel is minutes from the Metro Zoo
and offers budget accommodation. Pets
allowed.

The Journey's End
66 Norfinch Dr.
Downsview
736-4700
1-800-268-0405 toll free
Double $55
Just east of Hwy. 400 and north of Hwy.
401. This economy hotel is convenient
to the airport and is the closest in the
city to Canada's Wonderland amusement park. Pets allowed.

NEAR THE AIRPORT

As in most cities, the airport strip hotels
are large and for the most part well run.
They cater to travellers on the run.

The Bristol Place Hotel
950 Dixon Rd. near Carlingview
675-9444
1-800-828-7491 toll free
Double $150
Recent renovation and upgrading have
placed this hotel at the top of its cate-
gory. There are 267 rooms, non-
smoking floors, 24-hour room service,
concierge, valet parking and health club.
One of its several restaurants, The Peel
County Feed Company, maintains a particularly convivial ambience. Pets allowed.

Delta Meadowvale Inn
6750 Mississauga Rd.
821-1981
1-800-268-1133 toll free
Double $150
In the Meadowvale Business Park, 20
minutes west of the airport. The usual
hotel amenities plus tennis, squash and
nearby golf. Pets allowed with security
deposit.

The Marriott Hotel
901 Dixon Rd. at Carlingview
674-9400
1-800-228-9290 toll free
Double $145
Contains 423 rooms and a health club, indoor pool, non-smoking floor, concierge, 24-hour room service and Japanese steak house. Pets allowed.

The Airport Hilton Toronto
5875 Airport Rd.
677-9900
1-800-268-9275 toll free (Canada)
1-800-445-8667 toll free (U.S.)
Double $139
This is the closest hotel to the airport and offers 256 deluxe guest rooms and 154 mini-suites. The usual Hilton amenities. Pets allowed in first-floor rooms only.

The Skyline Hotel
655 Dixon Rd. at Hwy. 27
244-1711
1-800-648-7200 toll free
Double $115–$135
One of the largest airport hotels, offering 715 rooms and suites, 24-hour room service, indoor pool, health club and valet services. Canadian, Italian, Creole and continental cuisine, and adjacent movie theatres.

The Constellation Hotel
900 Dixon Rd. at Carlingview
675-1500
1-800-268-4838 toll free
Double $95–$130
The Constellation offers 835 rooms, seven restaurants, 24-hour room service, concierge, non-smoking floors, indoor/outdoor pool, full health club including massage, and many shops. Small pets allowed.

Howard Johnson's Toronto
Airport Hotel
801 Dixon Rd.
675-6100
1-800-654-2000 toll free
Double $65–$94
Offers 242 rooms, non-smoking floor, indoor pool and sauna, dining room and 24-hour coffee shop. Free stop-over parking for up to three weeks if you stay at the hotel the night before you fly out. Bus shuttle service to the airport at a nominal fee. Pets allowed.

The Celebrity Inn
6355 Airport Rd.
677-7331
Double $59–$69
Offers 100 rooms, sports lounge featuring two 12-foot screens, coffee shop and dining room. Pets allowed in first-floor rooms only.

ALTERNATIVE ACCOMMODATION

Toronto International Hostel
223 Church St. near Dundas
368-0207
Separate men's and women's dormitory accommodations with 96 beds; no meals, but kitchen facilities are available. Rooms are closed between 10 A.M. and 4:30 P.M., and the front door gets locked at midnight. The maximum stay in the busy period is three nights for a member and one night for a non-member. You may need a reservation for summer weekends. If you are a member of the Canadian Hostelling Association (membership is $18 a year), the charge is $10 a night, nonmembers $14.

3

**Neill-Wycik Co-operative College
96 Gerrard St. E. near Church
977-2320**
Singles $30–$32, Doubles $35–$40
Ryerson Polytechnical Institute's student residence becomes rental accommodation from mid-May to the end of Aug. Single and twin bedrooms, daily maid service, linen changed twice a week, shared kitchen facilities and a café serving natural foods. There is even a roof deck for sunbathing. They tout themselves as the "Club Med of the Don."

**The YWCA Woodlawn Residence
80 Woodlawn Ave. E. near Yonge
923-8454**
Women only. Single room, private bath and breakfast, $36. Double room, private bath and breakfast, $50.

The University of Toronto, its associated colleges and York University provide rental accommodation during the summer (generally mid-May to mid-Aug) in their student residences. These rooms are usually available for a fraction of what you pay at a hotel.
　The U of T colleges are downtown. Services vary between residences, and many colleges limit the length of your stay. Phone ahead for details and reservations.

**Glendon College
487-6773**

**Knox College
978-4508**

**New College
978-2468**

**Trinity College
978-2523**
Separate men's and women's accommodation.

**University College
978-2532 or 978-2520**

**University of St. Michael's College
926-7117**

**Victoria College
585-4523**

**Wycliffe College
978-2870**

**York University
736-5020**

APARTMENT HOTELS

**Cromwell Apartments
55 Isabella St. E. near Yonge
962-5604**
Furnished apartments downtown, near the subway. Weekly maid service, free underground parking, laundry facilities and fully equipped kitchens. Daily rates: studio $50, 1-bedroom $70, 2-bedroom $90. Also monthly rates.

EXECUTIVE APARTMENTS

Prestige Executive Accommodation
77 Maitland Place near Jarvis
922-6292
Fully furnished condominium and luxury apartments. Has 24-hour security with card access, indoor pool, gym, convenience store and dry-cleaning facilities. Daily rates: 1-bedroom $99, 2-bedroom $110, penthouse $120. Also weekly and monthly rates.

BED AND BREAKFAST

The Downtown Toronto Association of Bed and Breakfast Guest Houses
977-6841
(9:30 A.M. to 1 P.M. daily)
Doubles $50–$65
This association will make suggestions and bookings for you at member bed and breakfast guest houses. All guest houses are older homes, are non-smoking, offer a full breakfast and are on a 24-hour transit line.

The Metropolitan Bed and Breakfast Registry of Toronto
964-2566 or 928-2833
(Mon to Fri 9:30 A.M. to 7 P.M.)
Doubles $40–$70
Suggestions and bookings. All member guest houses are convenient to the TTC.

The Metropolitan Toronto Convention and Visitors Association
979-3141
Mon to Sat 9 A.M. to 5 P.M.,
Sun 9:30 A.M. to 5 P.M.
They will provide bed and breakfast information.

TRAILER PARKS/ CAMPGROUNDS

If you prefer to stay at a campground farther out from Toronto, during the summer you can phone 963-2992 for a 24-hour recorded report on vacancies in the government park campgrounds. Campground prices listed here are based on 1988 season rates.

Glen Rouge Campground
392-2541
Serviced sites $15 a night, unserviced sites $11.50. Open May to Oct. On Hwy. 2 just east of Sheppard Ave., or take Port Union exit off Hwy. 401. On 10 ha (25 acres) of wooded land close to the Metro Zoo; 117 sites, 87 with electricity and water. Washrooms, showers and trailer pump-out station. Maximum stay is nine days.

Cedar Beach Park
Musselman's Lake
R.R. #2, Stouffville
640-1700
Rates run from $14 to $16 a night. Open mid-May to mid-Oct. All 540 sites have showers, flush toilets, hydro, water, cable TV and telephone connections. A variety of recreation pursuits are available as well. Pets allowed.

KOA Toronto West
Campbellville
854-2495

Rates are $14 a night plus $3.50 for service hook-ups. Open 1 May to mid-Oct. Take the Campbellville exit 312 off westbound Hwy. 401. Go north on the Guelph line and follow KOA signs. Near Mohawk Raceway, if you're a harness racing fan. Of the 130 sites, 100 have electricity and water. Swimming and other recreation available. Pets allowed.

Toronto North KOA
R.R. #1, Bradford
775-5494

Rates are $16 a night plus hook-ups. Open May to 1 Oct. Located on the northwest corner of the intersection of Hwys. 400 and 88. A total of 175 sites of which 161 are serviced with water and electricity. Laundromat and games room. Pets allowed.

The Milton Heights Campground
R.R. #3, Milton
878-6781

Rates are $14 a night plus hook-ups. Open year-round. Off Hwy. 401 at Hwy. 25 (exit 320). Drive north to Campbellville Rd., west to the Townline, then south to the campground entrances. Of 450 sites, 100 have electricity, sewers and water, 100 have electricity and water only. Pets allowed.

RESTAURANTS 4

When it comes to restaurants, Toronto is truly international. People have settled here from all over the globe, and the full spectrum of ethnic tastes and textures they brought with them is yours for the ordering. Torontonians eat out more than any other Canadians—three times a week, on average—and that's reflected in the quality food and service of the more than 4000 restaurants that thrive here.

The ones we've recommended, located mainly in the downtown core, represent the wide variety of cuisines (and prices) available in our city.

Toronto restaurants with more than 30 seats must provide a no-smoking section. You'll usually be asked which you prefer.

The price scale we've used is based on the average cost of dinner for two without drinks and before tax:
$ = under $30; $$ = $30–$50;
$$$ = $50–$70; $$$$ = over $70.
B = breakfast, L = lunch,
D = dinner.

BRITISH

Hop and Grape　　　$–$$
14 College St. near Yonge
923-2818
Authentic English pub on the ground floor serves many imported beers. Upstairs dining rooms feature fine traditional fare such as roast lamb and beef tenderloin with Stilton and port butter, and a large selection of wines by the glass. L, D daily. Major cards.

Pimblett's　　　$
263 Gerrard St. E.
at Berkeley
929-9525
Jolly good English fare in rooms festooned with Victorian bric-a-brac. Prix fixe menu. D daily. Major cards.

Sherlock's Prime Rib　　　$$
Restaurant
12 Sheppard St.
near Richmond W.
366-8661
Roast beef and Yorkshire pud in olde England. Holmes would feel at home here savouring Dr. Watson's rice and raisin pudding. Closed Sun. L Mon to Fri, D Mon to Sat. Major cards.

Porker's Stern　　　$
244 Adelaide St. W. at Duncan
597-2183
Reputedly the best pub grub in town. Closed Sun. L, D Mon to Sat. Major cards.

Many traditional British pubs serve respectable pub grub along with a selection of domestic and imported beers. Slip away from the hustle and bustle and enjoy a pint of ale and some bangers, beans and mash. See Nightlife (Pubs and Bars).

CAJUN

Southern Accent　　　$$
595 Markham St. near Bloor W.
536-3211
Two intimate dining rooms serving Louisiana classics in the heart of Markham Village. Great summer patio. D daily. Late night tapas. Major cards.

Zaidy's $$
225 Queen St. W. near University
977-7222
Try their blackened and spiced delicacies from the Deep South. Closed Sun. L Mon to Fri, D Mon to Sat. Major cards.

CARIBBEAN

Bahamian Kitchen $$
14 Baldwin St. near McCaul
595-0994
Seafood's the specialty—try the Acklins Steamed Conch (spiced with thyme, lemon and hot peppers) at this low-key tropical spot. Closed Sun. L, D Mon to Sat. Major cards.

Essex Park Bistro $$
Essex Park Hotel
300 Jarvis St. near Gerrard E.
977-4823
Interesting continental dishes with a Cajun touch. Pleasant dining room with pianist providing background music. Chicken Bonkers, Blackened Catfish and Shrimp-Cargo delight. Indulge in the tempting dessert trolley. B, L, D daily. Major cards.

The Real Jerk $
1362 Queen St. E. at Greenwood
463-6906
Jamaican spice in an island-family restaurant. Enjoy the Jerk, a traditional Jamaican dish, served up to a constant reggae beat. The T-shirts are collector's items. L Tues to Sat, D daily. Some cards.

Tiger's Coconut Grove $
12 Kensington Ave.
near Dundas W.
593-8872
A refreshing café in Kensington Market run by Tiger himself. Serves Jamaican specialties and the freshest fruit juices. Closed Sun. L, D Mon to Sat. No cards.

Also
The Bamboo, see Nightlife/Rock Clubs

CHINESE

Chinese Junk $$
245 Queen's Quay W. (Pier 4)
360-5865
Enjoy Cantonese seafood specialties in this large, picturesque dining room overlooking Toronto's harbour. Summer: L, D daily. Winter: D Tues to Sun, closed Mon. Major cards.

The Fireplace $
340 Jarvis St. near Carlton
968-0071
Tasty Szechuan and Cantonese cuisine with a difference—no MSG! Ginger pineapple chicken and eggdrop soup are our favourites here. L, D Mon to Fri, D Sat, Sun. Major cards.

The Great Wall $
444 Spadina Ave. at College
961-5554
Szechuan, Hunan and Peking cuisines are all served with equal zest in this busy, popular restaurant. Specialties include tea-smoked duck and crabs in black bean sauce. Cool the palate with a Tsing Tao beer, imported from China. Closed Mon. L, D daily. Major cards.

Hsin Kuang Restaurant $
346–348 Spadina Ave.
at Dundas W.
977-1886
Hong Kong dining palace, beautifully
decorated in red and gold, offers a large
menu (over 140 items) with something
for all tastes. The sweet and sour
chicken with lichee nuts is excellent.
B, L, D daily. Major cards.

Hunan Palace $
412 Spadina Ave. near College
593-9831
Nicely decorated (linen tablecloths) restaurant features Hunan, Cantonese,
Mandarin, Szechuan and Mongolian
dishes. The hot and sour soup is a must.
Take-out menu too. Unlicensed. L, D
daily. Major cards.

Lee Gardens $
358 Spadina Ave. near Dundas W.
593-9524
Perhaps the most popular Cantonese-
style restaurant. Seems to be full all the
time with both tourists and local
Chinese residents. The specialty is
Haka-style dishes. Enjoy hot and spicy
sliced beef and chili pepper brought to
the table on a sizzling hot plate. Take-
out too. Only beer from the bar.
D daily. VISA only.

Lichee Garden $
Atrium on Bay
595 Bay St. at Dundas W.
977-3481
This has been one of Toronto's favourite Cantonese restaurants since 1948.
Beautiful surroundings sometimes include a pianist tickling the ivories. The
Moy-Tun Stove—an appetizer for two
served at your table on a broiler—is

sensational. Take-out available. L, D
daily. Major cards.

Sai Woo $
130 Dundas St. W. near Bay
977-4988
Named for China's most beautiful lake,
this Toronto institution has been serving splendid Cantonese dishes since
1954. The Sai Woo Ribs are always a
honey-garlic delight. Twelve-page
menu. Take-out available too. L, D daily.
Major cards.

CONTINENTAL

Abundance $$
81 Church St. at Adelaide E.
368-2867
Good food in an enjoyably casual
atmosphere. The wide-ranging menu in-
cludes salads, pastas, burgers and spe-
cialty entrees such as salmon in parch-
ment and fried farm-raised Louisiana
catfish fillets (with hush-puppies, of
course!). Closed Sun. L, D Mon to Sat.
Major cards.

Beaujolais $$$
165 John St. near Queen W.
598-4656
Imaginative dishes with delicately ex-
ecuted sauces, to be savoured in the airy
Monet-clad room. Try the Grand Beginning and the Grand Dessert— samplings
of many delights. L Mon to Fri, D Mon
to Sat. Major cards.

Duncan Street Grill $$
20 Duncan St. near King W.
977-8997
Upscale grilled meats, seasonal salads, pleasant pastas and substantial sandwiches in this neon and marble art deco room. L, D daily. Major cards.

Emilio's $$
127 Queen St. E. at Jarvis
366-3354
Enjoyable pastas, salads and other tasty dishes in a fashionably funky atmosphere. Give the Chicken Taipei a try—chicken breast in a wonderful gingery-peanut sauce. Bananas au Rhum is a dessert specialty. Closed Sun. L Mon to Sat, D Tues to Sat. Some cards.

Fenton's $$$–$$$$
2 Gloucester St. at Yonge
961-8485
A Toronto classic. Whether you eat upstairs (pricier) or down, the food is exemplary and the wine list extensive. A gourmet food shop is attached. L Sun to Fri, D daily (except downstairs on Sun). Major cards.

Karin $$–$$$
80 Scollard St. at Bay
964-0197
The hardworking kitchen changes its menu twice daily to take advantage of fresh market selections. Modern decor, relaxed surroundings. Closed Sun. L Mon to Fri, D Mon to Sat. Major cards.

Bellair Café $$
100 Cumberland St. at Bellair
964-2222
Very popular, very fashionable, and the food is reliably good. With its patios and terraces, it's a perfect perch for people-watching. L, D daily. Major cards.

Bistro 990 $$$
990 Bay St. near Wellesley
921-9990
Enjoy a selection of wines by the glass in an elegant Mediterranean atmosphere. Favourites at this popular spot include steak with a choice of Bordelaise or anchovy pepper sauce followed by Tarte Tatin for dessert. Pleasant copper-trimmed bar upstairs. L Mon to Fri, D daily. Major cards.

Summer patios, like this popular one in the business district, are everywhere. (Photo by Brian Pel)

Brownes Bistro $$–$$$
2 Woodlawn Ave. E. at Yonge
924-8132
Busy chefs in an open kitchen prepare
pastas with a nouvelle touch and many
grills such as lamb sausage, ribs, chicken
and a lovely beefsteak frites. Sparsely
furnished, quietly elegant room serves a
well-heeled clientele. Closed Sun.
D Mon to Sat. Major cards.

Bumpkin's $
21 Gloucester Ave. near Yonge
922-8655
There's something to please everyone
on this wide-ranging menu. A choice of
more than 25 main dishes includes
roasts of beef and lamb, chicken, fish and
shellfish at very reasonable prices.
Closed Sun. L Mon to Fri, D Mon to Sat.
Major cards.

Lotus $$$$
96 Tecumseth St. near King W.
368-7620
Toronto's hottest chef, Susur Lee, cre-
ates spectacular "Eurochinese" cuisine
with products captured on his daily
forays into Kensington and Chinatown
markets. A celebration of tastes, and no
heavy sauces. Closed Sun. D Mon to Sat.
Major cards.

Palmerston $$$$
488 College St. near Bathurst
922-9277
Jamie Kennedy, one of Toronto's most
popular chefs, prepares imaginative
dishes in an open kitchen. Haute vogue
spot. Flavourful grills on the patio in
summer. D daily. Major cards.

The Parrot $$
325 Queen St. W. at Beverley
593-0899
This small storefront dining room has
grown from humble vegetarian begin-
nings to embrace French and Italian
cuisine. The menu changes weekly and
always pleases. L Tues to Fri, D daily.
Major cards.

Peter Pan $$
373 Queen St. W. near Spadina
593-0917
One of Queen St.'s premier dining spots
for the young at heart, who pack themselves into this refurbished 1930s diner.
Modern variations on classical themes.
L, D daily. Major cards.

Stelle $$$
807 Queen St. W. near Bathurst
868-0054
Small, trendy place featuring dishes in-
fluenced by eclectic combinations of in-
ternational cuisines—all known for
being spicy-hot-hot-hot. You won't be
let down by chef Greg Couillard's
Jamaican Jump Up soup! D daily.
Major cards.

Tall Poppies $$
326 Dundas St. W.
near University
595-5588
Across the street from the Art Gallery
of Ontario, enjoy classical dishes served
with innovative twists. The Chef's
Whim usually pleases. Masterpiece desserts include a crème brûlée with fresh
fruit. Private treed patio for fine-
weather dining. Closed Sun. L Mon to
Sat, D Tues to Sat. Major cards.

Inside Tall Poppies restaurant across from the Art Gallery of Ontario on Dundas St. W. (Photo by Brian Thompson)

Telfer's Restaurant   **$$$$**
212 King St. W. at Simcoe
977-4447
This large, high-ceilinged favourite is known for splendid modern and classical cuisine. Weekend dancing to live music. Close to Roy Thomson Hall and the Royal Alexandra Theatre. Closed Sun. L Mon to Fri, D Mon to Sat. Major cards.

EAST INDIAN

Bombay Palace   **$$**
71 Jarvis St. near Adelaide E.
368-8048
Over 100 curry selections on the menu, ranging from mild to very spicy. Buffet at lunchtime. L, D daily. Major cards.

Indian Rice Factory   **$**
414 Dupont St. near Spadina
961-3472
Cozy family-run restaurant serving top-notch food. L, D daily. Major cards.

Shala-Mar   **$**
427 Donlands Ave.
near O'Connor
425-3663
Excellent Indian cuisine. Cool the spicy fire with a Kingfisher beer imported from India. Closed Mon. L, D Tues to Sun. Major cards.

**The Moghul Indian Curry $$
House**
33 Elm St. near Yonge
597-0522
563 Bloor St. W. at Bathurst
535-3315
Mild curries tickle the palate in this elegant, subdued dining room. Our favourite is Murgh Makhni—chicken tandoori in butter sauce with cashews and pistachio nuts. L Mon to Fri, D daily. Major cards.

Woodlands $
177 College St. near McCaul
593-7700
Savour authentic Punjabi-style dishes in this tiny place much frequented by the surrounding U of T community. Closed Sun. L Mon to Fri, D Mon to Sat. Major cards.

FRENCH

Auberge Gavroche $$$
90 Avenue Rd. near Bloor W.
920-0956
Affordable prix fixe and à la carte menus provide consistently good cuisine, in a comfortable country inn atmosphere. Has a patio too. Closed Sun. L Mon to Fri, D Mon to Sat. Major cards.

Gaston's $$
35 Baldwin St. near Beverley
596-0278
Prix fixe and excellent French food (our favourite is the pepper steak) prepared in the classical manner by one of the city's better known chefs (Gaston Schwalb once ran for mayor). All-year patio. L Mon to Fri, D daily. Major cards.

La Bastille $$
51 St. Nicholas St. near Bloor W.
961-1774
Three cozy dining rooms in a historic row house. Traditional French cuisine, with two prix fixe menus. L Mon to Fri, D daily. Major cards.

Le Bistingo $$$–$$$$
349 Queen St. W. near Spadina
598-3490
Unarguably the best French restaurant in Toronto. An evening here is an event to remember—how can you forget a dessert called the Torment of Love? Closed Sun and all holidays. L Mon to Fri, D Mon to Sat. Major cards.

Le Pigalle $$
315 King St. W. near University
593-0698
Enjoyable French dishes in an elegant room hung with the portraits of 19th-century Parisian women. Summertime patio. L Mon to Fri, D daily. Major cards.

Le Trou Normand $$–$$$
90 Yorkville Ave. near Bellair
967-5956
Fine Northern French food in one of Toronto's oldest French restaurants. Outside dining in the summer. L Mon to Sat, D daily. Major cards.

GREEK

Anesty's $
16 Church St. near Front E.
368-1881
Belly dancers entertain you Thurs
through Sat evenings. Light, airy atmosphere, well-prepared Greek food, and
usually busy. Closed Sun. L Mon to Fri,
D Mon to Sat. Major cards.

Penelope $$
33 Yonge St. at Front
947-1159
Any of the Olympic gods or goddesses
would be well fed here. Perfectly
prepared lamb dishes and salads. Closed
Sun. L Mon to Fri, D Mon to Sat. Major
cards.

Danforth Ave.
The Greeks who immigrated to Canada
in the 1950s and 60s settled mostly in
the Danforth area, in Toronto's east
end. Today, over 70 Greek restaurants
line Danforth between Broadview and
Jones avenues. Dining out in the Greek
community is a wonderfully flavourful
experience. Souvlaki, moussaka,
baklava—all tempting, all terrific. Here
are three places that will please. All are
$; L, D daily; major cards.

Astoria Shish Kebob House
390 Danforth Ave. near Logan
463-2838

Mr. Greek
568 Danforth Ave. at Carlisle
461-5470

Omonia Shishkabob Restaurant
426 Danforth Ave. near Chester
465-2129

HUNGARIAN

Continental $$
521 Bloor St. W. near Bathurst
531-5872
Bloor St.'s bustling stretch from Spadina
to Bathurst is home to many Hungarian
restaurants. This one's one of the best,
dishing up standard favourites like
goulash and schnitzels. Unlicensed. L, D
daily. No cards.

Country Style $
450 Bloor St. W. near Bathurst
537-1745
Wholesome foods in portions that
won't leave you hungry. You can't beat
the hospitality—or the prices. Unlicensed. L, D daily. No cards.

ITALIAN

Centro Grill and Wine Bar $$–$$$
2472 Yonge St. near Eglinton
483-2211
A beautifully appointed restaurant, with
superlative Italian cuisine care of one of
Toronto's most respected restau-
rateurs. Extensive wine list (more than
200 selections) features Italian and Cali-
fornian wines by the bottle or glass. Enjoy a drink in the lower level piano/pasta
bar. Closed Sun. D Mon to Sat. Major
cards.

Cibo $$
1055 Yonge St. near Roxborough
921-2166
Choose from blackboard specials—
delicious fresh pastas, salads, fish and
veal dishes—prepared in an open
kitchen. Selections change daily. Summer patio. L, D daily. Major cards.

La Bruschetta $$–$$$
1325 St. Clair Ave W.
near Lansdowne
656-8622
Bruschetta Too
423 Queen St. W. near Spadina
586-0318
Homemade Italian cuisine: the freshest pastas and delectable daily specials. Both closed Sun. L, D Mon to Sat (except no Sat lunch at Bruschetta Too). Major cards.

La Fenice $$$
319 King St. W. near John
585-2377
Begin with a choice from the tempting antipasto trolley and go on to enjoy one of the many grills. A real treat, made even better by the terrific service. Closed Sun. L Mon to Fri, D Mon to Sat. Major cards.

La Pergola $$
154 Cumberland St.
near Avenue Rd.
922-3543
Reliable Italian specialties in a cozy Mediterranean atmosphere right down to grapes on the vine at the entrance. L Mon to Fri, D daily. Major cards.

Noodles $$$
1221 Bay St. near Bloor W.
921-3171
Innovative, up-to-date Italian fare in a high-tech dining room. Closed Sun. L, D Mon to Sat. Major cards.

Old Angelo's $$
45 Elm St. at Bay
597-0155
A relaxed Italian trattoria with a nice mix of modern and traditional on the menu. Try the Tortellini ai du Funghi (veal-stuffed pasta in a creamy mushroom sauce) in a cozy booth for two. Closed Sun. L Mon to Fri, D Mon to Sat. Major cards.

Roberto's $$
2622 Yonge St.
near Eglinton
489-2153
The homemade garlic bread—served hot—is alone worth the trip. Absolutely sensational. The blackboard menu has never let us down, with specialties such as veal limone, fried calamari and a silky smooth tortellini alla crema—all cooked in the southern Italian style. Small and cozy. Closed Mon. D Tues to Sun. Major cards.

San Lorenzo $$$
125 King St. E. near Church
366-2556
Delicious appetizers, homemade pastas, and well-sauced meats and fish in elegant art deco rooms. Closed Sun. L Mon to Fri, D Mon to Sat. Major cards.

Trattoria Giancarlo $$–$$$
41 Clinton St. at College
533-9619
Good variety of pasta, freshly grilled entrees, and fresh fruits and cheeses at this popular restaurant in the heart of Toronto's Little Italy. Busy patio in nice weather. Summer: L Thurs and Fri. All year: D Tues to Sat. Major cards.

JAPANESE

Benihana $$–$$$
Royal York Hotel
100 Front St. W. at York
368-2511
This Japanese steak house specializes in
the entertaining art of teppanyaki-
hibachi cuisine. One of the master chefs
prepares the meal right at your table.
Closed Sun. L Mon to Fri (except holidays), D Mon to Sat. Major cards.

Masa Dining Lounge $$–$$$
195 Richmond St. W.
near University
977-9519
Enjoy delicate Japanese specialties such
as salmon teriyaki, sushi and sashimi.
Tatami rooms are available for
"authentic" Japanese dining. L Mon to
Fri, D daily. Major cards.

Nami $$$
55 Adelaide St. E. near Church
362-7373
Elegant, dimly lit Japanese restaurant.
Specialty dishes include miso (soybean)
soup, shrimp and vegetable Tempura
Moriawase, and sushi. We always enjoy
Nakemono—meals for two cooked at
the table. Closed Sun. L Mon to Fri,
D Mon to Sat. Major cards.

Tanaka of Tokyo $$
1180 Bay St. at Bloor W.
964-3868
Steak and seafood prepared by master
teppanyaki chefs. Tatami rooms are
available for more intimate dining.
L Mon to Fri, D daily. Major cards.

*At Benihana's in the Royal York Hotel, dinner is
prepared by master chefs right at your table.*

KOSHER

Greenfields $
355 Wilson Ave. near Bathurst
636-0163
Fine Kosher dining with many fresh fish
and pasta selections. Sample the delicious ice cream made in their kitchen.
Monogrammed chocolates with your
coffee. Closed Fri and Sat. D Sun to
Thurs. Major cards.

KOREAN

Korea House $
666 Bloor St. W. near Christie
536-8666
Korean specialties such as spicy beef
Beemipap served in an airy, casual atmosphere. The menu also includes Japanese
dishes, and a sushi bar lines one wall.
L, D daily. Some cards.

Korean Village Restaurant $
and Tavern
628 Bloor St. W. near Christie
536-0290
Pleasant dining room decorated with
Oriental screens. Koon Man Doo
(Korean dumplings) are tender and delicious. L, D daily. VISA only.

MALAYSIAN

Ole Malacca $$
886 St. Clair Ave. W.
near Dufferin
654-2111
Hot and sweet combine exotically in the
Ole Malacca's Malaysian dishes. Try
cooking your own satay on a table-top
grill. Closed Sun. L Mon to Fri, D Mon
to Sat. Major cards.

Rasa Ria $–$$
615 Bloor St. W. near Bathurst
532-1632
Authentic Malaysian dishes often
brought to your table by the chef himself. This cozy restaurant is popular with
the movie crowd before or after a re-
run film at the nearby Bloor Cinema.
L Mon to Sat, D daily. Major cards.

MEXICAN

Chi-Chi's Mexican Restaurante $$
80 Front St. E. near Church
364-5755
(other suburban locations)
Chi-Chi's features Mexican-garbed ser-
vers and a wide-ranging menu of Mexi-
can favourites. Special menu for the
small-fry gringos. L Mon to Sat, D daily.
Major cards.

The Peasant's Larder $$
221 Carlton St. near Parliament
967-9141
Serves authentic Mexican dishes such as
enchiladas, burritos and tortillas. They
also carry a number of Jamaican "jerk"
specialties. L Mon to Sat, D daily. Major
cards.

Viva Zapata $–$$
2468 Yonge St. near Eglinton
489-8482
Their tacos and burritos are freshly
made, not too spicy, and always enjoyable. L Mon to Sat, D daily. Major cards.

MIDDLE EASTERN

Kensington Kitchen $
124 Harbord St. near Spadina
961-3404
Excellent Middle Eastern dishes, and the
best falafel in town. Try it with the tab-
bouleh salad and hummus. Informal
dining, pleasant rooms. Patio in good
weather. L, D daily. Some cards.

MOROCCAN

The Sultan's Tent $$
1280 Bay St. near Bloor
961-0601
Wonderfully romantic atmosphere—
low banquettes, Moroccan music and
belly dancing to accompany the pleasant
Moroccan dishes, eaten with fingers or
forks. Features a five-course prix fixe.
Closed Sun. L, D Mon to Sat. Major
cards.

NORTH AMERICAN
(American and Canadian)

Ed's Warehouse　　　$$
270 King St. W. at Duncan
593-6676
For its opulence alone, this roast beef emporium is worth a visit. The flagship of Ed Mirvish's restaurant row next to his Royal Alexandra Theatre. Other Ed's, next door and with the same hours, include Ed's Chinese (593-7344), Ed's Italian (593-5392) and Ed's Seafood (977-3938). L Mon to Fri, D daily. Major cards.

Hart's Restaurant　　　$
225 Church St. at Dundas E.
368-5350
Good salads, burgers, chicken and casual bonhomie. Closed Sun. L Mon to Fri, D Mon to Sat. Some cards.

Hughie's Burgers, Fries and Pies $
22 Front St. W. near Yonge
364-2242
Great burgers and sinful desserts. American Indian decor. L Mon to Sat, D daily. Major cards.

The Liberty　　　$$
105 Church St.
at Richmond
363-7071
Touted as an "American Brasserie." You'll find most meat and fish entrees grilled. An inventive selection of salads and pasta dishes as well. Known for their steak-frites and fabulous Tarte Tatin. Closed Sun. L Mon to Fri, D Mon to Sat. Major cards.

Metropolis　　　$$
838 Yonge St. near Bloor
924-4100
An excellent restaurant that incorporates fresh local produce in sensational all-Canadian dishes. Closed Sun. L, D Mon to Sat. Major cards.

Pentimento　　　$$$
881 Yonge St. near Davenport
927-1979
Small "New North American" style restaurant serves well prepared pastas, fish and burgers. The hot herb-buttered cornbread is a dream. Whimsical Memphis-design dining room. Closed Sun. L Mon to Fri, D Mon to Sat. Major cards.

Senator Restaurant　　　$$$
249 Victoria St. near Dundas
364-7517
A plush diner, and a Toronto landmark, specializing in Californian cuisine and wines. The fries can't be beat. Closed Sun. B (from 8 A.M.), L Mon to Sat, D Tues to Sat. Some cards.

Studebaker's　　　$
150 Pearl St. near University
691-7960
Decorated à la 50s and frequented by visiting big league sports teams, as well as by the Bay St. and sports crowds. Closed Sun. L Mon to Fri, D Mon to Sat. Major cards.

PERUVIAN

The Boulevard Café   **$$**
161 Harbord St. near Spadina
961-7676
Peruvian home-style specialties such as
Camarones Ajillo (a spicy shrimp dish)
or Coderoa la Parilla (broiled lamb
chops) in a cozy Latin venue. One of
Toronto's best summer patios. L, D
daily. Some cards.

POLISH

Sir Nicholas Restaurant   **$$**
91 Roncesvalles Ave.
near Queen W.
535-4540
Right in the heart of the Polish community, the lively Sir Nicholas dishes up
such delightful traditional Polish fare as
perogies and cabbage rolls. Live entertainment and dancing every night.
Closed Mon. L, D Tues to Sun. Major
cards.

PORTUGUESE

O Barco   **$**
277½ Augusta Ave. near College
597-8700
Forceful seafoods prepared in the
Portuguese manner. A guitarist enter-
tains nightly. Closed Wed. L, D Thurs to
Tues. Major cards.

The Boat Restaurant   **$**
158 Augusta Ave. near Dundas W.
593-9218
Excellent seafoods from the Azores,
amid lively dancing every night. Closed
Mon. L, D Tues to Sun. Major cards.

SCANDINAVIAN

Danish Food Centre   **$**
101 Bloor St. W. near Bay
920-5505
For a terrific quick lunch, pop into this
popular spot for an open-faced sandwich
with traditional Danish toppings.
Cafeteria-style dining. Closed Sun.
B (from 7:30 A.M. Mon to Fri, 9 A.M.
Sat), L, D Mon to Sat. Major cards.

Copenhagen Room   **$$**
101 Bloor St. W. near Bay
920-3287
Enjoy hearty Danish entrees such as
Scallops Anjorgen, scallops cooked in
white wine and served on spinach with a
Danish cheese sauce. Danish buffet and
live entertainment Tues only. Closed
Sun and holidays. L, D Mon to Sat. Major
cards.

Vikings Dining Room   **$$**
5 St. Nicholas St. near Yonge
922-1071
A long-standing member of Toronto's
restaurant community, featuring enjoyable Scandinavian specialties. Closed
Sun. L Mon to Fri, D Mon to Sat. Major
cards.

SPANISH

Costa Basque   **$$**
124 Avenue Rd. near Davenport
968-0908
The kitchen prepares the cuisine of
Spain's Basque region with the freshest
ingredients, and there's a guitar player
to serenade you Tues through Sat.
Closed Sun. L Mon to Fri, D Mon to Sat.
Major cards.

Don Quijote Restaurante $–$$
300 College St. near Spadina
922-7636
Well-prepared Spanish specialties and
one of the city's best paellas. Flamenco
dancing nightly. Closed Sun. L, D Mon
to Sat. Major cards.

SWISS

Bistro Bernard $$
6 St. Joseph St. near Yonge
926-1900
A comfortable and intimate restaurant,
serving excellent à la minute cuisine
(fresh ingredients, prepared and cooked
after ordering). Try the beef tenderloin
in a meaux mustard sauce. There's also a
daily fresh fish. Closed Sun. L, D Mon to
Sat. Major cards.

Delisle Restaurant $
1560 Yonge St. near St. Clair
960-1707
Authentic Swiss fondues and raclette.
Over 35 wines by the glass. L, D daily.
Major cards.

Mövenpick $$
165 York St. near Adelaide W.
366-5234
133 Yorkville Ave.
near Avenue Rd.
926-9545
These two are the only North American locations of this Swiss megachain.
Swiss specialties include air-dried beef
and rössli. The desserts—especially the
ice cream—are heavenly. Each location
has several restaurants. At York St., the
main dining rooms are La Belle Terrasse
and, slightly more expensive, The Rössli.
The Grape and Cheese Bar serves fondues and raclettes, and The Verandah is

primarily a take-out, with a few tables.
At the Yorkville location, The Bistretto
is the main dining room. The slightly
pricier La Pêcherie serves seafood.
B (from 7:30 A.M.), L, D daily. Major
cards.

THAI

Bangkok Garden $$–$$$
18 Elm St. near Yonge
977-6748
This elegant restaurant in the Elmwood
Club serves splendid authentic Thai specialties. Try the Tom Yum Talay—
delicious lemony fisherman's catch
soup—and don't miss the fabulous Yum
Nua (Royal Barge)—tenderloin of beef
tossed with shallots, mint, toasted
chilies, dressed in lime and served in a
cucumber boat. Two dining rooms ex-
quisitely decorated with Thai art. Ask
for a table in the "River" section (has an
indoor pond) and be sure to take in the
mask display. Closed Sun. L Mon to Fri,
D Mon to Sat. Major cards.

Satay-Satay $
700 Bloor St. W. near Christie
532-7489
Sizzle your satay on table-top hibachis.
Many flavourful combinations and mild
or spicy sauces. D daily. Major cards.

Siam $
70 Yorkville Ave. near Bay
923-7011
A family-run restaurant serving over 50
Thai dishes, ranging from mild to hot on
the spice-dial. The summer patio upstairs is a great place to watch the street
parade on Yorkville. May to Aug: L, D
daily. Sept to April: closed Mon, L Tues
to Sat, D Tues to Sun. Major cards.

VIETNAMESE

Saigon Maxima $
414 Dundas St. W. near Beverley
598-9759
Authentic Vietnamese cuisine in a no-frills dining room. A favourite is #178—Jumbo Shrimp with rice. Another winner is the Combination Platter. Very popular place with Toronto's Vietnamese. L, D daily. Some cards.

Saigon Star $$
4 Collier St.
near Yonge and Bloor
922-5840
Vietnamese cuisine with a French touch served in a bamboo-lined room. We recommend the Imperial rolls and one of the delicately spiced brochettes. Closed Sun. L, D Mon to Sat. Major cards.

The Original Vietnam $
842 Bloor St. W. near Ossington
531-8763
Breathtaking sauces and friendly service shine in this small restaurant. Be sure to try one of the rich and flavourful soups. The chicken broth with pork-stuffed wonton is very popular, as are the seafood dishes. Closed Mon. D Tues to Sun. VISA only.

BREAKFAST

Satisfactory breakfasts can be eaten at most hotel dining rooms and coffee shops. The King Edward's Café Victoria (from 7 A.M. daily) and the Park Plaza's Prince Arthur Room (from 7 A.M. Mon to Fri; weekend brunch) are two of Toronto's favourite power brekkie spots. Here are some other spots for those who enjoy breakfast with or without a jolt of power.

Bregman's $
1560 Yonge St. near St. Clair
967-2750
Popular spot for fresh coffee and pastries. Flaky croissants too. Breads, bagels and goodies all baked on the premises. B (from 7 A.M.), L, D daily. Major cards.

The Brothers Restaurant $
698 Yonge St. near Charles
924-5084
Traditional diner serving one of the best bacon and egg breakfasts in town. Often a line-up on Sat morning. Closed Sun. B (from 7 A.M.), L, D Mon to Sat. No cards.

Golden Griddle $–$$
Pancake House
45 Carlton St. near Yonge
977-5044
11 Jarvis St. near Front E.
865-1263
Carlton St. opens at 6 A.M. daily, also L, D daily. Jarvis St. open 24 hours daily. Major cards.

Patachou Patisserie   **$**
1095 Yonge St.
near Summerhill subway
927-1105
875 Eglinton Ave. W. at Bathurst
782-1322
French bakery serves fresh pastries and
coffee for a quick breakfast. Try one of
the wonderful croissants (cheese, almond, chocolate) and café au lait in a
bowl. Opens Mon to Sat at 8:30 A.M.
Yonge St. opens at 10:30 A.M. Sun;
Eglinton closed Sun. Also L, early D Mon
to Sat. Closes at 6 P.M. Unlicensed. No
cards.

Also
Mars Restaurant, see Greasy Spoon
Fran's, see Late Night
Senator, see North American
See Delis

You can sample one of hundreds of brands of
beer at the very popular Rotterdam brew pub.
(Photo by Brian Thompson)

BREW PUBS

Amsterdam Brasserie and   **$**
Brew Pub
133 John St. near Adelaide W.
595-8201
The Brasserie dining room has delicious
prix fixe and à la carte "designer"
meals—some fish, some pasta, some
Italian, some Thai—to be washed down
with terrific beer brewed on the
premises. The bar menu includes
burgers, wings and fish and chips. Very
popular with the singles and after-work
crowd—the large room is usually
packed. L, D daily. Major cards.

Rotterdam Brewing Company $
600 King St. W. near Bathurst
868-6882
The world's biggest brew pub, with 21 copper kettles on view. The Rotterdam serves over 375 kinds of beer, including its own fresh brew. Same food as the Amsterdam. L, D daily. Major cards.

DELIS

Druxy's $
Many locations including
1 Bloor St. E. at Yonge
925-5885
Eaton Centre
Yonge St. and Dundas
979-9747
115 Yonge St. at Adelaide
360-0057
Decent salads and fresh-sliced corned beef at this fast-food chain. Eat in or take out. Unlicensed. B (from 6:30 A.M. Mon to Fri, later on weekends), L, D daily. No cards.

Gert's Deli $
St. Lawrence Market,
lower level
92 Front St. E. at Jarvis
This popular lunch spot features hearty soups and sandwiches. Stop in after shopping at the Farmer's Market on Sat. Unlicensed. Closed Sun and Mon. Open 8 A.M. to 5:30 P.M. Tues to Sat. No cards.

Meyers Deli $–$$
69 Yorkville Ave. at Bay
960-4780
185 King St. W. at University
593-4190
These fashionable delis turn out traditional items. Live jazz Tues to Sat nights at the Yorkville location; Fri and Sat nights at King St. Yorkville: L, D daily, also B Sat. King: L, D daily, also B (from 8:30 A.M.) Mon to Fri. Major cards.

Pancer's Delicatessen $
4130 Bathurst St.
near York Downs
633-1230
Unarguably the best deli in the city, and also the oldest. Mrs. Pancer has been making everything on the premises for the past 33 years. B (from 8 A.M.), L, D daily. VISA only.

Shopsy's Delicatessen $$
Restaurant
33 Yonge St. at Front
365-3333
From humble beginnings on Spadina, Shopsy's has moved into large, pleasant surroundings. Wide selection of traditional deli foods, and a take-out section too. The large patio is busy in summer. B (from 7 A.M. Mon to Fri, 8 A.M. weekends), L, D daily. Major cards.

Switzer's Delicatessen $
322 Spadina Ave. near Dundas W.
596-6900
Beehive-hairdoed waitresses tote Mandel's cream cheese and lox on bagels. An original Toronto deli. B (from 8 A.M. Mon to Sat, 9 A.M. Sun), L, D daily. Some cards.

Yitz's Delicatessen Restaurant $
346 Eglinton Ave. W.
at Avenue Rd.
487-4506
A favourite spot with the locals. Join the hubbub at Sunday morning breakfast. B (from 10 A.M.), L, D daily. Major cards.

DESSERT/ICE CREAM

Simply Delicious Desserts $
279 Queen St. W. near Duncan
971-5863
A bouncing little hot spot dishing up delightful sweets with gourmet coffees and teas till the wee hours. Unlicensed. Closing times: Mon to Thurs 3 A.M., Fri 4:30 A.M., Sat 4 A.M., Sun 1 A.M. Some cards.

Courtesy of David Crighton © 1989

Dooney's Café $
511 Bloor St. W. near Brunswick
536-3293
Choice of many sweets plus Italian ice cream and cappuccino. Busy patio in summertime. Also L, D daily. Major cards.

Just Desserts $
306 Davenport Rd.
near Avenue Rd.
922-6824
Choose from a zillion (well, 50) decadent desserts. Unlicensed. Open 24 hours on the weekend, closes at 3 A.M. Mon to Thurs. No cards.

Slice of Cake Café $
7 Balmuto Ave. near Bloor W.
923-9494
Drop in for coffee and a treat while shopping on Bloor or after a movie at the Uptown. Also L Mon to Sat, D daily. Major cards.

Greg's Ice Cream
200 Bloor St. W. near Avenue Rd.
Fresh homemade ice cream, whose flavours change daily. Choice of many different, but equally decadent, toppings. Open daily from noon. No cards.

Laura Secord
(Many locations)
Canada's favourite candy lady serves hand-scooped ice cream from most outlets. A Canadian institution for over 75 years.

Lisa's Treats and Sweets
386 Bloor St. W. near Brunswick
Lisa scoops the newest craze in ice cream—Toronto's own gelato fresco, a uniquely rich and flavourful ice cream that has a lower calorie content than you'd think. Open daily from 9 A.M. No cards.

W. D. Kones
Atrium on Bay
595 Bay St. near Dundas
Smooth and creamy ice cream scooped onto a choice of cones. Try the home-made waffle cone. Open Mon to Sat from 10 A.M., Sun from 11 A.M. No cards.

You can always get a quick meal from one of Toronto's many street vendors.

FAST FOOD/BURGERS

Fast-food carts have sprouted on corners throughout Toronto in the past few years. If you don't feel like sitting down, try a hotdog or sausage on a steamed poppyseed bun from one of the many vendors.

The following fast-food restaurants have many outlets around town and serve up top-quality quickie meals. Check the White Pages for the closest location. Different times at different locations.

Bersani & Carlevale $
Sandwiches and salads with an Italian perspective. VISA only.

Cultures $
Salads and sandwiches. No cards.

Foodworks on Bloor $$
549 Bloor St. W. at Bathurst
531-1195
Good, casual fare—steaks, burgers, dogs and chili. They grind their own meat on the premises. L, D daily. Major cards.

Harvey's $
(36 Toronto locations)
One of the best fast-food burgers in town. Those great fries are freshly cut. No cards.

Lick's $
285 Yonge St. near Dundas
362-5425
2383 Kingston Rd. near Midland
267-3249
People line up for Lick's home-made burgers. Unlicensed. L, D daily. No cards.

Toby's Goodeats $
11 Toronto locations, including
93 Bloor St. W. at Bay
925-2171
542 Church St. at Wellesley
929-0411
725 Yonge St. at Bloor
925-9908
Eaton Centre
Yonge St. at Dundas
591-6994
A dozen variations on the burger and a respectable Eggs Benedict. Open till 3 A.M. Mon to Sat at Bloor, Yonge and Eaton Centre locations, Thurs to Sat at Church. L, D daily. Some cards.

Rhodes $$
1496 Yonge St. near St. Clair
968-9315
Upbeat, fashionable restaurant and bar. Blond wood decor. Gourmet burgers and other toney foods. L, D daily. Major cards.

GREASY SPOON

Mars Restaurant $
432 College St. at Bathurst
921-6332
Always busy because of its out-of-this-world food. Try the bacon and eggs and homemade muffins. Cabbies love the place, but on the weekends the yuppies take over. Some of the staff and clientele date from opening day in 1951. B (from 5 A.M.), L, D daily. VISA only.

Courtesy of David Crighton © 1989

73

HOTEL DINING

Café Victoria   **$$$$**
King Edward Hotel
37 King St. E. near Yonge
863-9700
The baroque ceiling and splendidly appointed room provide a pleasant backdrop to continental dining. Sunday brunch is delightful. Traditional afternoon tea is served with elegance every day from 3 until 5:30 P.M. in the Lobby Lounge. B (from 7 A.M.), L, D daily. Major cards.

Creighton's   **$$–$$$**
Westbury Hotel
475 Yonge St. near Carlton
924-0611
Opulent dining in the grand hotel style. Fine cuisine from the kitchen of two-time World Culinary Olympics gold medal champion chef Gunter Gugelmeier. B (from 7 A.M.) Mon to Fri, L Sun to Fri, D daily. Major cards.

Trader Vic's   **$$–$$$**
Hilton International Toronto
145 Richmond St. W.
at University
869-3456
You can almost feel the South Sea zephyrs in this exotic Polynesian setting. Well-executed Polynesian dishes—try the Bongo Bongo soup. L Mon to Fri, D daily. Major cards.

Windsor Arms Hotel
22 St. Thomas St. at Bay
979-2341
Superb dining and service in any of this charming hotel's dining rooms. The Courtyard Café, where visiting celebrities often dine, has an innovative continental menu. Of the Three Small Rooms, the most formal, The Restaurant, serves fine French cuisine. Fondues are the specialty at The Wine Cellar. Or you can savour grilled salmon, lamb, chicken and the like at The Grill. Escape to a bygone era while enjoying afternoon tea from 3 till 6 P.M. in the Fireside Lounge.

Courtyard Café   **$$$**
B (from 7 A.M.), L, D daily.
The Restaurant   **$$$$**
Closed Sun. D Mon to Sat.
The Wine Cellar   **$$$**
Closed Sun. L Mon to Fri, D Mon to Sat.
The Grill   **$$–$$$**
D daily.
All take major cards.

LATE NIGHT

Bemelmans   **$**
83 Bloor St. W. near Bay
960-0306
A bar and restaurant with very chi-chi food and patrons. Back patio in summer. Open till 3 A.M. Mon to Sat, Sun till midnight. Major cards.

Bloor Street Diner   **$$**
50 Bloor St. W. near Yonge
2nd floor
928-3105
Neon lights and a big menu. Open till 3 A.M. daily. Major cards.

Fran's $
20 College St. near Yonge
923-9867
21 St. Clair Ave. W. at Yonge
925-6336
2275 Yonge St. at Eglinton
481-1112
Open 24 hours. Round-the-clock B, L,
D. Major cards.

Also
Toby's, see Fast Food/Burgers
Just Desserts, see Dessert/Ice Cream
Simply Delicious Desserts, see
Dessert/Ice Cream

PIZZA

Camarra's Pizzeria $
and Restaurant
2899 Dufferin St. near Lawrence
789-3222
People have driven miles to enjoy
Camarra's pizza. One of Toronto's best.
Take out or eat in. Closed Tues. L Mon
and Wed to Sat, D Wed to Mon. Major
cards.

Il Fornello $
486 Bloor St. W. near Bathurst
588-3491
1968 Queen St. E. near Woodbine
691-1466
Very popular. Pizza with tasty, imaginative toppings baked in a wood oven. Try
the herbed extra-virgin olive oil on the
table. Bloor: L Mon to Fri, D daily.
Queen: L, D daily. Major cards.

Massimo Pizza and Pasta $
504 Queen St. W. near Bathurst
867-1803
302 College St. near Spadina
967-0527
Delicious pizza, one of the best slices in
town. Eat in or take out. L, D daily (except Queen closed Sun). College location unlicensed. Some cards.

Poretta's $
97 Harbord St. near Spadina
920-2186
Good pizza with choice of regular or
whole wheat crust. Menu also offers traditional pastas, salads and meats. Pleasant dining room, with a patio in good
weather. Closed Mon. D Tues to Sun.
Major cards.

POOL HALLS

A fine espresso is never hard to find
among North America's highest concentration of billiard rooms, but meals in
these places have been limited to fast
foods. Two trendy pool halls have recently opened, both licensed and encouraging patrons to enjoy a sit-down
meal before or after picking up a cue.
Who knows—maybe gourmet bowling
is next.

Q Club $
1574 Queen St. E. near Coxwell
469-3660
L, D daily (with a lighter menu after
10 P.M.). Major cards.

Squeeze Club Billiards $
817 Queen St. W.
near Claremont
365-9020
L, D daily. VISA only.

SEAFOOD/FISH AND CHIPS

Old Fish Market $$
12 Market St. at Front E.
363-0334
Spacious restaurant with full range of
fish and shellfish on the ample menu.
L Mon to Sat, D daily. Major cards.

Coasters—A Shellfish Bar $
12 Market St. at Front E.
(upstairs)
862-7129
Dine on fresh shellfish in a very casual
atmosphere. Ask for a booth. Refresh-
ing sangria by the jug in hot weather.
L, D daily. Major cards.

Filet of Sole $$
11 Duncan St. near King W.
598-3256
Menu changes daily with a large selection of fresh fish and shellfish from
around the world. Complimentary
crudités and dip (served in a china boat,
of course). Henry's Oyster Bar features
freshly shucked oysters and clams.
L Mon to Fri, D daily. Major cards.

Joso's $$$
202 Davenport Rd.
near Avenue Rd.
925-1903
Enjoy the freshest seafood and skillfully
prepared dishes such as squid ink
risotto. Unusually but tastefully
decorated with paintings and sculptures
of nudes. Closed Sun. L Mon to Fri,
D Mon to Sat. Some cards.

Lobster Trap $$$
1962 Avenue Rd. near Wilson
787-3211
Nova Scotia lobster arrives every day.
D daily. Major cards.

Pier 4 Storehouse Restaurant $$
Harbourfront
245 Queen's Quay W.
863-1440
Large selection of seafood as well as tra-
ditional turf favourites such as rack of
lamb and meaty ribs. Lovely view of
Toronto's harbour. Summer: L, D daily.
Winter: L, D Sun to Fri, closed Sat.
Major cards.

Rodney's Oyster House $$
209 Adelaide St. E. near Jarvis
363-8105
Rodney, purveyor of the freshest
shellfish to restaurants around town,
prepares the delicacies for patrons in
this no-frills cellar bistro. Choose from
five types of oysters, hard and soft
clams, lobsters and more. Closed Sun.
L, D Mon to Sat. Major cards.

The Mermaid $$
330 Dundas St. W.
near University
597-0077
One of Toronto's oldest seafood dining
rooms. Well-executed dishes. Closed
Sun. L Mon to Fri, D Mon to Sat. Major
cards.

Whaler's Wharf $$
144 Front St. W. at University
593-5050
(other suburban locations)
The nautical motif is an apt background
to the treasures of the sea. L Mon to Fri,
D daily. Major cards.

These are some of Toronto's favourite fish and chip emporiums. All prepare freshly cut chips. As well, most of the restaurants listed under Nightlife/Pubs have fish and chips on their menus.

Alfred's $
649 Yonge St. near Bloor
929-9764
Closed Sat and Sun. L, D Mon to Fri. No cards.

The Fish and Chip Shoppe $
287 Davenport Rd.
near Avenue Rd.
964-0053
Closed Sun. L, D Mon to Sat. No cards.

Harbord Fish and Chips $
147 Harbord St. near Bathurst
925-2225
Closed Sun. L, D Mon to Sat. No cards.

Penrose Fish and Chips $
600 Mt. Pleasant Rd.
near Eglinton E.
483-6800
Closed Sun and Mon. L and early dinner Tues to Sat. Closes at 7 P.M. No cards.

STEAKS

Barberian's Steak House $$$
7 Elm St. near Yonge
597-0225
Traditional steakhouse menu. Outstanding Caesar salad and the creamiest crème caramel. L Mon to Fri, D daily. Major cards.

George Bigliardi's Steak, $$–$$$
Veal and Seafood Restaurant
463 Church St. near Carlton
922-9594
Top-quality steakhouse. Visiting celebrities often drop in from Maple Leaf Gardens for a late meal. Closed Sun. D Mon to Sat. Major cards.

VEGETARIAN

Annapurna Vegetarian $
Restaurant
1085 Bathurst St. at Dupont
537-8513
Full vegetarian selections: nondairy, macro-plates and South Indian specialties at reasonable prices. Unlicensed. Closed Sun. L, D Mon to Sat (closes Wed at 6:30 P.M.). No cards.

Jake's $$
406 Dupont St. near Bathurst
961-8341
Cozy room, well-prepared and colourful vegetarian dishes. Offers some meat choices. Closed Mon. D Tues to Sun. Some cards.

The Vegetarian Restaurant $
4 Dundonald St. near Yonge
961-9522
Cafeteria-style restaurant serves up wholesome, nutritious dishes and scrumptious desserts. One of Toronto's original veggies. L Mon to Sat, D daily. Some cards.

Yofi's $
19 Baldwin St. near University
977-1145
Very casual, and a nice patio in summertime. Frozen yogurt is a delight for dessert. Closed Sun. L, D Mon to Sat. Some cards.

WITH A VIEW

Fifty-Fourth   **$$$**
Toronto-Dominion Tower
54th floor
King St. at Bay
366-6575
Fabulous spot to enjoy Toronto sunsets
and the lights of the city afterwards.
Pleasant French cuisine. Closed Sun.
B (from 7:30 A.M.), L, D daily. Major
cards.

The Lighthouse   **$$–$$$**
Harbour Castle Westin
1 Harbour Square
at Queen's Quay E.
869-1600
Great vantage point for taking in
Toronto's bustling Harbourfront and
the islands. The revolving restaurant
specializes in continental dishes. L, D
daily. Major cards.

Holiday Inn Roof Garden   **$$$**
Restaurant
89 Chestnut St. near Dundas W.
977-0707
Enjoy continental cuisine and live
entertainment while overlooking
Toronto's City Hall. Closed Sun and
Mon. D Tues and Sat. Major cards.

Scaramouche   **$$–$$$**
1 Benvenuto Place near
Avenue Rd. and St. Clair W.
961-8011
One of the finest restaurants in the city.
Gorgeous French food and desserts to
match the spectacular view of
downtown Toronto. Scaramouche also
features one of the city's first, and still
one of the best, pasta bars. Highly recommended for those moments when
something light is called for. Closed Sun.
D Mon to Sat. Major cards.

Top of Toronto Restaurant   **$$$**
CN Tower
301 Front St. W. near John
362-5411
Without a doubt, the best view in the
city is from this revolving restaurant.
Continental cuisine. A great place to
have a drink. L, D daily. Major cards.

TRANSPORTATION   5

THE TORONTO TRANSIT COMMISSION SYSTEM

Toronto's public transit system is just one more good reason why Torontonians can be proud of their city. The international award-winning Toronto Transit Commission (TTC) is safe, clean, efficient and affordably priced.

More than 2500 subway and light rail transit cars, buses, trolley buses and streetcars carry almost 450 million passengers a year over 1340 km (835 mi.) of routes throughout Metro. The TTC has a ridership equal to more than 200 rides a year for every Metro resident.

FARES/DIRECTIONS

All TTC vehicles charge the same fares. Bus and streetcar operators do not carry change and require exact cash fare, tickets or tokens. Tickets and tokens are sold at all subway stations and at authorized stores throughout Metro, which display the TTC Ticket Agent sign. The adult one-way cash fare is $1.10. Eight tickets or tokens cost $7.50, and 24 tokens cost $22.50. Children's tickets are four for $1.10 or exact cash fare of 50¢. Second fares are required on all routes beyond Metro boundaries. Contact the TTC for specific second fare prices at 393-INFO.

A Sunday/holiday pass is good for unlimited travel on all TTC routes for one day. One pass may be used by one person or a group of up to five with a maximum of two adults. Passes are available at all subway stations and cost $4.

If you're staying for a month or more, consider buying a Metropass, a photo-ID card that lets you ride as often as you want during any one month. It costs $49 and is on sale from the 24th of the preceding month to the fourth working day of the month it's valid for. It's sold at all subway stations and at branches of the Canadian Imperial Bank of Commerce. The photo portion of the card is acquired at 33 Bloor St. E. (Bloor/Yonge subway station), Mon to Fri noon to 7 P.M., Sat 10 A.M. to 4 P.M., for $2.

If you are going to switch from one route to another (say, from the subway to a streetcar), you need a paper transfer—otherwise you'll have to pay a second fare. Transfers are free, but must be obtained when you pay your first fare. Automatic transfer dispensers are at ticket booth level in all subway stations. Transfers are good for travel in one direction only and for a limited time—stopovers aren't allowed.

Transit information is available at 393-INFO every day between 7 A.M. and 11:30 P.M. The TTC publishes the "Ride Guide," which shows subway routes and connecting services. These are free for the asking at subway stations. A map of the entire subway system is displayed in each subway car, and there are system maps, including bus routes, in each subway station and city bus shelter. In many subway stations maps of the immediate area are also found.

Subway hours are Mon to Sat 6 A.M. to 1:30 A.M. (half an hour after "last call"), Sun 9 A.M. to 1:30 A.M. In the downtown core, many bus and streetcar

We've got a good thing going.

Toronto Transit Commission

SUBWAY AND RT ROUTE MAP

LEGEND
BLOOR-DANFORTH ROUTE
YONGE UNIVERSITY SPADINA ROUTE
SUBWAY INTERCHANGE
SCARBOROUGH RT ROUTE
SUBWAY/RT INTERCHANGE

Toronto Transit Commission

routes operate 24 hours a day (the Blue Night Network).

There are 10 subway washrooms throughout the system. On the east/west Bloor-Danforth line these are found at Kipling, Islington, Bathurst, Warden and Kennedy. On the north/south Yonge-University line you will find them at Finch, York Mills, Eglinton, Yonge/Bloor and Wilson.

The subway is easy to use. There is one east/west line (Bloor-Danforth), which runs across the city at approximately the mid-way point. The north/south loop runs down Yonge St. to Union Station and then up University and Spadina.

Allow subway passengers off the train before you enter. Two whistles sound before the doors close.

Travel Hint: Avoid the Bloor/Yonge and St. George stations at the rush hours: 8 A.M. to 9:30 A.M. and 4:30 P.M. to 6:30 P.M. The volume of people passing through these stations at these times can make life in the fast lane a reality. Also avoid Wellesley station from 4 P.M. to 5:30 P.M.

WHEEL TRANS

The TTC's Wheel Trans service provides door-to-door transportation for people who are unable to board regular public transit vehicles. The service operates within the boundaries of Metro Toronto, Mon to Fri 7 A.M. to 11 P.M.; and Sat, Sun and holidays 8:30 A.M. to 11 P.M. You can register by calling administration Mon to Fri 8 A.M. to 4 P.M. at 393-4222 or the dispatch office evenings and weekends at 393-4333.

This service is also available to visitors. When you call in, you will be asked to provide certain information including

Toronto Transit Commission

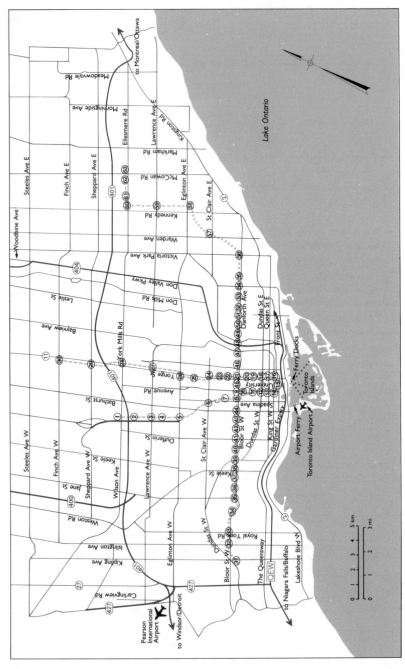

TRANSPORTATION

---- Yonge-University-Spadina
    Subway
•••• Bloor-Danforth Subway
–•–• Scarborough RT
—— Highway
③ Stations
◈ Bus Terminal
▲ Union Station
   (VIA Rail Terminal)
•••• Ferry
● CN Tower

1	Wilson	33	Royal York
2	Yorkdale	34	Old Mill
3	Lawrence W	35	Jane
4	Glencairn	36	Runnymede
5	Eglinton W	37	High Park
6	St Clair W	38	Keele
7	Dupont	39	Dundas W
8	Spadina	40	Lansdowne
9	St George	41	Dufferin
10	Museum	42	Ossington
11	Queen's Pk	43	Christie
12	St Patrick	44	Bathurst
13	Osgoode	45	Bay
14	St Andrew	46	Sherbourne
15	Union	47	Castle Frank
16	King	48	Broadview
17	Queen	49	Chester
18	Dundas	50	Pape
19	College	51	Donlands
20	Wellesley	52	Greenwood
21	Bloor/Yonge	53	Coxwell
22	Rosedale	54	Woodbine
23	Summerhill	55	Main St
24	St Clair	56	Victoria Pk
25	Davisville	57	Warden
26	Eglinton	58	Kennedy
27	Lawrence	59	Lawrence E
28	York Mills	60	Ellesmere
29	Sheppard	61	Midland
30	Finch	62	Scarborough
31	Kipling		Centre
32	Islington	63	McCowan

your type of disability, the duration of your visit and whether you are registered in another city. Fares differ for the disabled and their accompanying non-disabled assistant. Because of the demands on the system, your choice of pick-up times is limited. Also, if you're one of the first to board, you may have to wait while other passengers are picked up. This can make for a long trip.

THE BUS TERMINAL

All inter-city buses arrive at and depart from the bus terminal at 610 Bay St. at Dundas. The terminal is open daily 5:30 A.M. to 1 A.M. The closest subway stops are St. Patrick and Dundas.

The bus lines that operate from the bus terminal include: Gray Coach Lines (northern and western Ontario); Greyhound Coach Lines (west across Canada, western Ontario and the United States); Voyageur Colonial (east into Ontario and Quebec); Penetang Midland Coach Lines (north of Toronto), and Travelways (Lindsay/Haliburton and Kincardine). For information on all these bus lines, call 979-3511. (You need to be patient, since this number is very busy.)

You can catch some buses at the Yorkdale GO Terminal. Phone 979-3511 for information.

Hint: It's often faster to buy tickets at the terminal's Elizabeth St. ticket booth, since the main booth almost always has long line-ups.

CARS

CAR RENTALS

The major car rental companies are:

Avis
211 Adelaide St. W.
near University
598-5007
80 Bloor St. E. near Yonge
964-2051
Airport
676-3844

Budget Rent-a-Car
(44 Toronto locations)
5905 Campus Rd., Mississauga
676-1240
Airport
678-2198

Discount Car and Truck Rentals
980 Yonge St. near Davenport
961-8006
6415 Airport Rd. (near airport)
678-0556

Hertz Canada
Downtown locations:
620-9620
Airport
676-3241

Tilden
20 Metro locations:
925-4551
Airport
676-2647

Thrifty Rent-a-Car
124 Jarvis St. at Queen W.
868-0350

For a cheap car rental, call:

ANSA International Car
and Truck Rental
72 Lippincott St. near College
972-1705
27 Faskin Dr.
(near the airport)
674-9690

To rent a bus or camper:

Owasco Canadian Car and
Camper Rental
1425 Dundas St. E., Whitby
683-3235

Toronto RV Centre
7200 Hwy. 27 near Steeles
743-1021

PARKING

There are 27 city-run parking lots downtown. Free maps indicating their locations are available from the Parking Authority at 393-7275 or 33 Queen St. E., 2nd floor. Three of their major downtown lots are: Nathan Phillips Square Garage (underneath the new City Hall at the corner of Bay St. and Queen W.—reputed to be the world's largest underground parking lot); University Ave./York St. and Front St. Garage; Yorkville Ave./Cumberland St. Garage.

All Parking Authority lots are identified by a round sign with a white P on a green background. An arrow on the sign indicates the direction into the parking lot. In most cases, Parking Authority lots are less expensive than privately operated lots throughout downtown.

The Toronto green hornets strictly enforce all parking meters and limited-parking zones. Infringing cars are towed away, and this can be very expensive. Do not expect any leniency just because you have out-of-province licence plates. Please check the parking meter and parking signs for the times you can legally park in that zone. During the rush hour (before 9 A.M. and from 3:30 P.M. to 6 P.M.), parking is illegal throughout much of the downtown core. See also Essential Information (Automobiles).

TAXIS

Throughout Toronto, and particularly downtown, it is possible to hail a taxi. But if hailing a cab doesn't seem too productive when you try it, proceed to one of the downtown cab stands or to any large downtown hotel. Among other locations, cab stands are on both sides of the street between Union Station and the Royal York Hotel and on all four sides of the block bounded by Wellington, York, King and Bay. Among the several large taxi companies are:

Diamond Taxi Cab
366-6868
From our experience, the best of the bunch. Cabs are usually very clean and in good repair.

Metro Cabs, 363-5611
Beck Cabs, 449-6911
Co-op Cabs, 364-8161

LIMOUSINES

Whether you require a limousine or a chauffeur for an impression or a procession, limousine rental companies include:

Rosedale Livery, 677-9444
House of Limousines, 364-6199

TRAINS

All trains arrive at and depart from Union Station at the foot of Bay St. on Front St.

VIA RAIL

VIA Rail, the government-administered passenger rail service, links most major cities in the province and throughout the country and makes regular connections in the United States with Amtrak and other U.S. rail lines. For fares and schedules, call 366-8411.

The ticket office at Union Station is open Mon to Sat 6:45 A.M. to 11:35 P.M., Sun from 7 A.M. to 11:35 P.M. Tickets can also be bought at travel agents around town, wherever the "VIA Rail Tickets Sold Here" sign is displayed.

Even if you are not catching a train, Union Station is architecturally well worth seeing and is a terrific place to people-watch, especially on busy holidays and weekends. See Sightseeing (Great Buildings).

Union Station—a Toronto landmark.
(Metropolitan Toronto Library, T 33049)

TORONTO ISLANDS FERRIES

The Toronto Islands Ferry Boat Services offers a 10-minute ride to the Toronto Islands. In summer, ferries go to Wards Island, Centre Island and Hanlan's Point. All ferries depart from the ferry docks behind the Harbour Castle Westin Hotel. Ferries usually run until 11 P.M. The Centre Island ferry runs only in the summer. The prices are so reasonable you may wish to take a return trip simply for the sightseeing—even if you don't have time to visit the Toronto Islands. For times and fares, call 392-8193.

Ferries regularly ply the harbour between the mainland and the Toronto Islands. A great way to view the skyline. (Metropolitan Toronto Parks and Property Department)

LESTER B. PEARSON INTERNATIONAL AIRPORT

Terminal 2
Extension

Terminal
3

Terminal 2

Terminal 1

Transport Canada

LESTER B. PEARSON INTERNATIONAL AIRPORT

Many locals still call it by its old name, Toronto International Airport. Canada's busiest airport is a half-hour's drive from downtown, just north of Hwy. 401 and just west of Hwy. 427. It currently has two terminals, thoughtfully named Terminal 1 and Terminal 2. (Terminal 3 is under construction.) They are separated by a healthy walk, so whether you're flying out or picking up visitors, make sure you find out which terminal services your airline. Terminals 1 and 2 are linked by an underground walkway as well as by a shuttle bus service, which runs between the departures level of each terminal.

GETTING THERE

The cheapest way to the airport is by TTC. Buses leave from Lawrence West subway station frequently and go express directly to each terminal. Since the airport is in Mississauga, outside

Metro, you must pay two fares; the second fare is paid when you leave the bus.

The airport is served by an express bus operated by Gray Coach, which makes return trips to each terminal from the York Mills, Yorkdale and Islington subway stations. Call 979-3511 for departure times. Gray Coach also operates an airport link from downtown. This service leaves the Royal York Hotel every 20 minutes daily from 7 A.M. to midnight. It picks up at other major downtown hotels including Holiday Inn, Sheraton Centre, Delta Chelsea Inn, L'Hotel and Harbour Castle Westin, but it's better to get on at the Harbour Castle Westin (no service from here on Sat or Sun) or the Royal York, since these are the last stops before the airport. Fare is $8.50 per person. Phone 979-3511.

You can arrange for limousine service to the airport, or you can obtain a limousine at the airport on the arrivals level. Limousines charge flat rates depending on where they pick you up. A trip from the airport to downtown costs about $25, not much more than taxi fare. Taxis are also available on the arrivals level and charge on a time and mileage basis.

Limousines providing airport service include:

Airline, 676-3210
Aircab Limousine Service,
741-1114
Aeroport, 745-1555
Airlift, 222-2525

AIRPORT PARKING

Terminal 1 has an eight-level parking garage with more than 2000 parking spaces. Terminal 2 has a five-level structure, which is the largest covered parking facility in Canada with 4500 parking spaces. An uncovered car park on the airport grounds is linked to the terminals by a shuttle bus. In the immediate vicinity of the airport are several thousand private parking spaces, most of which provide private shuttle bus services to each terminal. One such lot is **Park 'n' Fly** at 677-9143.

AIRPORT SERVICES

Immigration and Customs are located in each terminal.

Transport Canada operates multilingual information counters on the arrivals level of each terminal. The Terminal 1 booth is open daily from noon to 10 P.M. The Terminal 2 booth is open daily from 2 P.M. to 8 P.M. It's best to start here with your questions about incoming and outgoing flights, delays, shuttle bus service or airport facilities. Or you can call 676-3506 from any airport phone for the airport's own multilingual Information Services, daily be-

tween 10 A.M. and 10 P.M. You can also monitor daily radio broadcasts on CFYZ (AM 530) for information on airport road conditions, delays, and arrivals and departures.

The airport provides certain facilities for the disabled, including wheelchair access to buildings, washrooms and drinking fountains. There are telephones equipped for the hard-of-hearing. Signs indicate the locations of these facilities.

Banking machines and currency exchanges are available at each terminal.

TORONTO ISLAND AIRPORT

This airport, which handles mostly private flights, can only be reached by a short ferry ride, leaving every 15 minutes from the foot of Bathurst St. Phone 868-6942 for Customs information and landing fees. City Express has scheduled flights to London, Montreal, Ottawa, Rochester and Newark. Phone 360-4444. City Express runs a shuttle bus to and from the Royal York Hotel.

TORONTO BUTTONVILLE AIRPORT

A very busy private airport, just north of Hwy. 7 off Woodbine Ave. In addition to private flights, there are executive air charters. Torontair offers scheduled flights daily. For information phone 477-8200.

SIGHTSEEING   6

SIGHTSEEING

THE SIGHTS

Canada's largest metropolis offers something for everyone. Whether you are a history buff, thrill-and-adventure seeker, or an admirer of architecture or natural beauty, the Toronto area has an abundance of attractions to keep you fully occupied. Many sights and attractions are described in this section and elsewhere in the book, but we recommend that you do not miss our Top 10:

1. Ontario Science Centre, see below
2. The Metro Toronto Zoo, see below
3. The McMichael Canadian Collection, see Museums/ Art Galleries
4. The Royal Ontario Museum, see Museums/Art Galleries
5. CN Tower, see below
6. The Art Gallery of Ontario, see Museums/Art Galleries
7. The Eaton Centre, see Shopping
8. The Parliament Buildings, see Great Buildings below
9. Harbourfront, see below
10. The Toronto Islands, see Parks/ Gardens

DOWNTOWN SIGHTS

1	Metropolitan Toronto Reference Library
2	Royal Ontario Museum
3	McLaughlin Planetarium
4	Ontario Parliament Buildings
5	Art Gallery of Ontario
6	The Grange
7	Church of the Holy Trinity
8	Eaton Centre
9	Mackenzie House
10	St Michael's Cathedral
11	New City Hall
12	Campbell House
13	Osgoode Hall
14	Old City Hall
15	Metropolitan United Church
16	Toronto Stock Exchange
17	St James' Cathedral
18	St Lawrence Hall
19	The Gooderham (Flatiron) Building
20	Union Station
21	Fort York
●	CN Tower
■	SkyDome
→	Traffic direction Not all one-way streets are shown

A hair-raising experience at the always stimulating Ontario Science Centre.

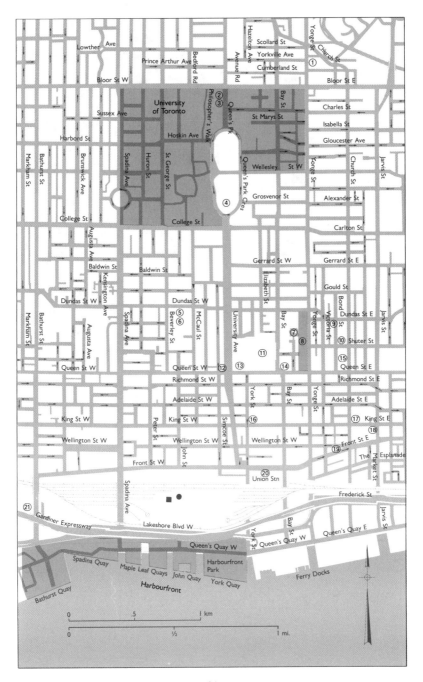

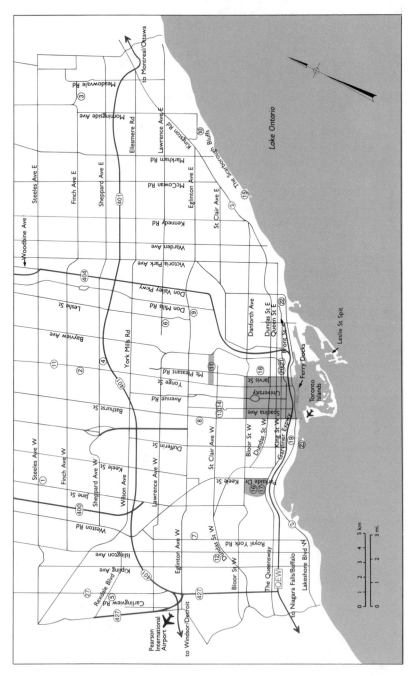

METRO ATTRACTIONS

1 Black Creek Pioneer Village
2 Gibson House
3 Metro Toronto Zoo
4 Puppet Centre
5 Woodbine Race Track
6 Edwards Gardens
7 James Gardens
8 Beth Tzedec Museum
9 Ontario Science Centre
10 Spencer Clark Collection of Historic Architecture
11 Mt Pleasant Cemetery
12 Montgomery's Inn
13 Casa Loma
14 Spadina
15 Bluffers Park
16 High Park
17 Colborne Lodge
18 Allan Gardens
19 Exhibition Place
   (with Hockey Hall of Fame and Museum, Canadian Sports Hall of Fame, and Marine Museum of Upper Canada)
20 Enoch Turner School House
21 Little Trinity Church
22 Greenwood Race Track
23 Ontario Place
   (with Canadian Baseball Hall of Fame)
▨ Downtown
–②– Highway

ATTRACTIONS

The Ontario Science Centre
770 Don Mills Rd.
near Eglinton E.
429-4100 or 429-0193 (recording)
Torontonians are justifiably proud of their Science Centre. Three connected buildings descending from Don Mills Rd. into the Don River ravine are the graceful, eye-pleasing design of architect Raymond Moriyama. Kids absolutely love the indoors, and adults find it amazing too: more than 800 exhibits plus workshops and changing demonstrations. Participation is the rule rather than the exception here. You could spend days exploring the 12 halls that cover everything from Exploring Earth to Exploring the Molecule, from the Hall of Life to the Hall of Technology. At the Science Centre you can stand at the edge of a black hole, walk away from your shadow, land on the moon, pedal your way onto television, race a world-class runner, try papermaking, measure your horsepower output, learn about holograms and lasers, and much, much more. The Science Centre always offers new exhibits, speakers and demonstrations.

By TTC take the Don Mills 25 bus from Pape subway station to St. Dennis Dr., or the Eglinton East 34 bus from Eglinton subway station to Don Mills Rd. at Eglinton Ave. E. Parking. Open every day but Christmas Day, 10 A.M. to 6 P.M., Fri to 9 P.M. Wheelchair accessible. Admission: adults $3, youths (13–17) $2, seniors and toddlers free.

10 SCIENCE CENTRE BESTS
Dr. Jim Parr
Former Director General,
Ontario Science Centre

1. **Choose a meal.** Pick a meal from a banquet table, then run your choice through a computer to discover its nutritional value.

2. **Driver reaction test.** Test your reaction time. Try to stop a simulated car—to a warning stimulus.

3. **Sparks.** See your hair stand on end as you get zapped by a million volts of electricity.

4. **Foundry demo.** Real sand moulds are made and bronze castings poured. Have a look inside a 650°C (1200°F) furnace.

5. **Cantilever bridge.** Walk on a 25-m (80-ft.) long bridge—and feel and measure its movement.

6. **Video wall.** Manipulate your own image on a wall of 180 TV monitors—the world's largest.

7. **Jacquard loom.** Discover the surprising similarities between Canada's oldest weaving loom and a modern-day computer.

8. **Reproduction exhibit.** Study the fascinating stages of human development before birth.

9. **Elephant heart.** A real 75-cm (2½-ft.) high elephant heart, beside hummingbird and human hearts.

10. **Tilt test.** Stand on a tilted floor in a dark bubble and try to level the floor perfectly.

Ontario Science Centre

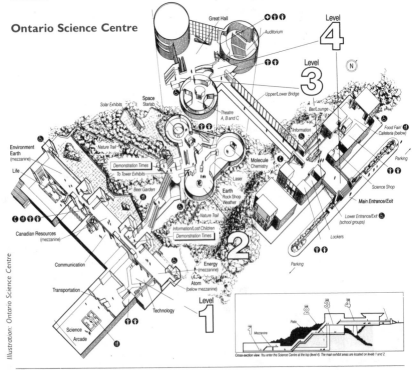

Cross-section view. You enter the Science Centre at the top (level 4). The main exhibit areas are located on levels 1 and 2.

Illustration: Ontario Science Centre

The Metro Toronto Zoo
Hwy. 401 at Meadowvale Rd.
Scarborough
392-5900 or 392-5901 (recording)
From the city that works, a zoo that works. Absolutely terrific and a must for visitors. Spread over 280 ha (710 acres), the Metro Toronto Zoo contains more than 4000 native and exotic animals and a huge botanical collection including, among other wonders, Canada's only living baobab tree. The zoo is divided into six zoogeographic regions—Africa, Eurasia, Australasia, Indo-Malaya, the Americas and the North Polar region. Eight pavilions throughout these regions recreate native ecological environments complete with living vegetation and, in some cases, free-flying tropical birds.

The zoo is home to many rare and endangered species including the jaguar, Siberian tiger, mountain gorilla and the orangutan. The polar bears are a must-see at feeding time, and the seals are always entertaining at the below-surface viewing area. There's even a "night exhibit" where you can view nocturnal creatures.

There are 10 km (15 mi.) of walking trails, with lots of picnic tables—so bring your own lunch. And if your feet get tired, there's the Monorail, Zoomobile or camel rides.

The zoo is in the Rouge River valley, Scarborough. From Hwy. 401 eastbound, exit on Meadowvale Rd. (Exit 389) north; westbound, exit on Sheppard Ave. (Exit 392) east. By TTC take the Scarborough 86A bus from Kennedy subway station or the Sheppard East 85B bus from Sheppard subway station. Plenty of parking. Open every day but Christmas Day from 9:30 A.M. until 7 P.M. in the summer and until 4:30 P.M. in the winter. Wheelchairs and strollers available. Admission: adults $6, youths (12–17) and seniors $3, children $1.50.

CN Tower
301 Front St. W.
360-8500
It's the world's tallest free-standing structure at 544.5 m (1815½ ft.)—the length of 5½ football fields—and it weighs more than 23,300 large elephants. Glass-faced elevators rush you—in 58 seconds—to the observation levels, and on a clear day you can see the mist rising above Niagara Falls. On the

The CN Tower, the world's tallest free-standing structure.

METRO TORONTO ZOO

Metro Toronto Zoo

🏕 Picnic Shelter	•••• Monorail
🚻 Washrooms	■ Restaurant
➕ Family Centre	△ Snack Bar
📞 Public Telephones	

10 ZOO BESTS
Calvin J. White
General Manager, Metro Toronto Zoo

1. Polar Bear exhibit
2. South American primate exhibit
3. Ghost tiger
4. Maya temple ruins
5. Elephants
6. Orangutans
7. Meerkats
8. African fur seals
9. Arctic wolf exhibit
10. Snow leopards

Part of the ever-changing scene at Harbourfront. (Harbourfront Corporation)

clearest days you can see for 150 km (100 mi.). There's an indoor/ outdoor observation deck at the 220-m (1100-ft.) level, a revolving restaurant, a night club, and the Space Deck for the brave at heart at the 440-m (1465-ft.) level. And, yes, there are stairs—the longest metal staircase in the world, with 1760 steps to the observation deck.

The CN Tower is entered from Front St. at the west end of the Metro Convention Centre complex. By subway exit at Union Station at Front St. and walk west two blocks to the convention centre and then the tower. Plenty of parking in convention centre or on north side of Front St. Open daily. Summer hours (from June 1 until Labour Day) are Mon to Sat 9 A.M. to midnight, Sun 9 A.M. to 11 P.M.; the rest of the year, Sun to Fri 10 A.M. to 10 P.M., Sat 9:30 A.M. to 10 P.M. Admission: adults

$7, seniors $4.50, children 12 and under $3.50.

Harbourfront
235 Queen's Quay W.
973-3000

So much to do at the waterfront— count on spending the whole day. This 37-ha (92-acre) complex offers year-round theatre, music, film, dance and craft presentations, numerous restaurants, an art gallery, lots of shopping, boating activities including five sailing schools, and playgrounds and a wading pool/skating rink for the kids. The water's edge promenade is especially popular and is without a doubt one of the greatest places to people-watch in Toronto. The antique market attracts

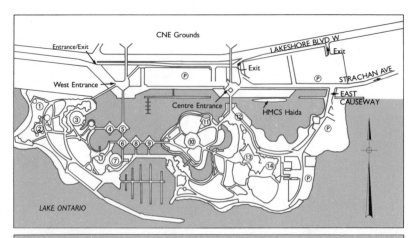

ONTARIO PLACE

1	Wilderness Adventure Ride
2	Ontario North Now
3	Waterfall Showplace
4	Trillium Restaurant
5	Pod 1
6	Theatre 1
7	Cinesphere
8	Theatre II
9	Canadian Baseball Hall of Fame & Museum
10	Forum
11	Administration Bldg
12	Brigantine Dock
13	Children's Village
14	Children's Theatre
Ⓟ	Parking

thousands, especially on weekends when there are more dealers. There's something to do here every day. Free admission to many events. For information on paid events call the box office at 973-4000.

By TTC take the Spadina 77B bus from either Union Station or Spadina subway station. Parking by York Quay on both the north and south sides of Queen's Quay W.

Ontario Place
955 Lakeshore Blvd. W.
965-7917 or 965-7711 (recording)
1-800-268-3735 toll free
Situated on three man-made islands on the Lake Ontario waterfront, Ontario Place is popular any time—particularly on hot summer weekends. An internationally acclaimed cultural, leisure and entertainment complex, Ontario Place puts the emphasis on fun. There are beer gardens, outdoor restaurants, waterslides, pedal boats, bumper boats, boat tours, a wilderness adventure ride, the World War II destroyer HMCS *Haida,* marinas, the Canadian Baseball Hall of Fame, a children's village, exhibits dealing with Ontario's achievements, and a variety of unique theatres. Especially popular is the huge Cinesphere, one of the world's most advanced film theatres. There is also a 3-D theatre. The Forum, a hugely popular outdoor entertainment centre, features a state-of-the-art sound system and seats about 10,000 under the canopy and on the surrounding grassy slopes. Summer concert programming covers the entire entertainment palette from rock to classical.

By TTC take the Dufferin 29 bus from Dufferin St. downtown or the 511 Exhibition streetcar from Bathurst sub-

way station. GO Transit trains stop at the nearby CNE grounds. Large parking lots on the mainland directly across from Ontario Place. Open daily from mid-May to mid-Sept, from 10 A.M. to 1 A.M., Sun to 11 P.M. Wheelchair accessible. Admission: adults $5, juniors (over 3) $5, children (accompanied) $1, seniors free.

Tour of the Universe
301 Front St. W.
364-2019
Blast off from the base of the CN Tower into the 21st century on a trip to Jupiter and back. This simulated space travel presentation is a unique experience for kids *and* adults. The children on our tour were absolutely spellbound by the state-of-the-art technology and mind-boggling special effects.

By subway exit at Union Station and walk west on Front St. Parking. Open every day of the year. Summer hours (from June 1 to Labour Day) are 10 A.M. to 10 P.M. Phone for operating hours at other times, admission prices and group rates.

Casa Loma
1 Austin Terrace at Spadina
923-1171
One of the city's most popular tourist attractions is Toronto's castle on the hill. Millionaire financier Sir Henry Pellatt had this incredible 98-room castle built at a cost of $3 million; construction began in 1911 and took three years. It's said he paid local children $1 for each stone in the huge wall surrounding the property. By 1923 Sir Henry's financial fortunes had reversed, and he could no longer afford to live in his castle. He died a pauper. Make sure you take the tunnel from the main house to the

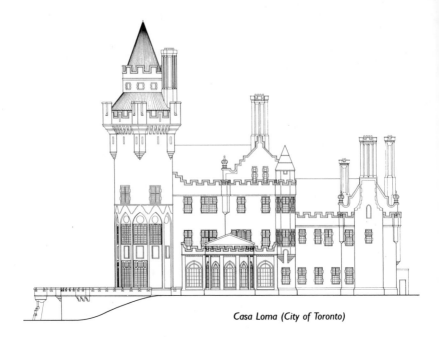

Casa Loma (City of Toronto)

"stables." By the way, Casa Loma is built on a ridge that marks the shoreline of Lake Iroquois, which existed before the last ice age.

By TTC exit at Dupont subway station and walk (or take the 127 Davenport bus) north up Spadina Rd. to Davenport. Walk up the historic Baldwin Staircase to Austin Terrace. Free parking on the castle grounds. Open daily 10 A.M. to 4 P.M., but closed weekdays in Jan and Feb. Admission: adults $4, children (5–18) $2, children under 5 free, seniors $1.

Also
McLaughlin Planetarium, see Museums/Art Galleries
Scarborough Bluffs, see Parks/ Gardens

HISTORIC SITES

History buffs should seek out the following sites. Additionally, dozens of historical plaques throughout Toronto commemorate famous people, famous events and famous buildings that are no longer standing.

Black Creek Pioneer Village
1000 Murray Ross Pkwy.
(Jane St. and Steeles)
736-1733 or 661-6610 (recording)
One of the most extensive historic village recreations in Canada, Black Creek is the site of more than 40 faithfully restored pre-Confederation (1867) buildings, from the Mennonite Meeting House to the Limehouse Backhouse. Villagers in period costume not only answer everybody's questions but also expertly demonstrate tin-smithing, black-

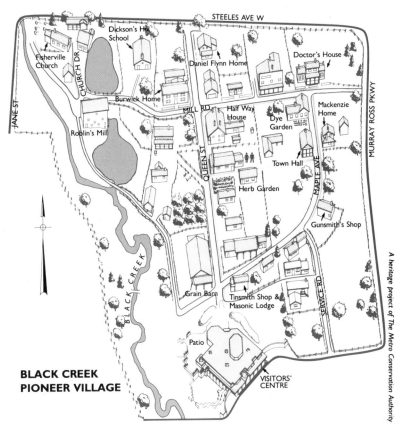

STEELES AVE W

Dickson's Hill School

Fisherville Church

CHURCH DR

Daniel Flynn Home

Doctor's House

Burwick Home

MILL RD

Half Way House

Dye Garden

Mackenzie Home

JANE ST

Roblin's Mill

QUEEN ST

Town Hall

MAPLE AVE

MURRAY ROSS PKWY

Herb Garden

Gunsmith's Shop

BLACK CREEK

Grain Barn

Tinsmith Shop & Masonic Lodge

SERVICE RD

Patio

BLACK CREEK PIONEER VILLAGE

VISITORS' CENTRE

A heritage project of The Metro Conservation Authority

smithing, broom-making, weaving and cabinet making among other arts, while the grist mill grinds, the printshop prints and pigs wallow in the piggery.

By TTC take the Jane 35B bus from Jane subway station straight to Black Creek. Parking. Open year-round. Hours in July and Aug are 10 A.M. to 6 P.M. Phone for hours at other times. Admission: adults $4.50, children, seniors and students $2.25.

Authentically restored buildings at Black Creek Pioneer Village recreate the feel of pioneer days.

Fort York
Garrison Rd. at Fleet St.
392-6907

The original Fort York was built in 1793 on the orders of the founder of Toronto, Governor General John Graves Simcoe. The fort you now see is a restoration of the structure that saw action during the War of 1812. Authentically costumed staff recreate the daily life of an early 19th-century British garrison. Seven original buildings within the fort contain presentations and displays of period furniture and artifacts.

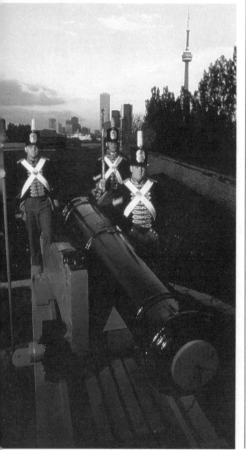

Fort York is on Garrison Rd. off Fleet St. between Bathurst St. and Strachan Ave. By TCC take the 511 streetcar from Bathurst subway station. Free parking. Open Mon to Sat 9:30 A.M. to 5 P.M. all year, Sun and holidays 9:30 A.M. to 5 P.M. from May to Sept and noon to 5 P.M. from Oct to April.

Colborne Lodge
south entrance of High Park
392-6916

Built in 1836 by Toronto resident John G. Howard, this Regency-style house has been restored to the 1870s and contains original furnishings and an important collection of Howard's own artwork. Costumed "residents" demonstrate cooking and crafts daily. Howard, a highly respected architect from England, held the posts of city surveyor, city architect and city engineer. He was also drawing master at Upper Canada College. He donated his property, much of which now comprises High Park, to the City of Toronto in 1873. Both he and his wife are buried in the park near their house.

The lodge is at the south end of High Park on Colborne Lodge Dr. at the Queensway. By TTC take the 501 streetcar west from Queen or Osgoode subway stations to Colborne Lodge Dr. Free parking. Open Mon to Sat 9:30 A.M. to 5 P.M., Sun and holidays noon to 5 P.M. Admission: adults $2.50, children and seniors $1.50, family $7.

Members of the Fort York garrison, uniformed as they would have been in 1813, prepare to fire one of the fort's historic cannons.

Colborne Lodge, built in 1836 by architect J. G. Howard, crowns the hilltop overlooking Grenadier Pond in High Park. (Toronto Historical Board)

Mackenzie House
82 Bond St. near Dundas E.
392-6915

The home of William Lyon Mackenzie, the first mayor of Toronto and leader of the 1837 Rebellion of Upper Canada. The house has been refurbished to the Victorian 1860s when Mackenzie lived there, with period furnishings and artifacts including many of Mackenzie's own mementos. There is also a historic printshop. Ask about the ghost who haunts the premises. By subway exit at Dundas, walk east on Dundas St. and turn south onto Bond St.

Open Mon to Sat 9:30 A.M. to 5 P.M., Sun and holidays noon to 5 P.M. Admission: adults $2.50, children and seniors $1.50, family $7.

Spadina
285 Spadina Rd. near Davenport
392-6910

Spadina (pronounced "Spadeena") is a next-door neighbour to Casa Loma. It was the grand estate of prominent

Mackenzie House (Toronto Historical Board)

Spadina (Toronto Historical Board)

Toronto businessman James Austin, who had it built in 1866. The home contains original Victorian and Edwardian furnishings and art and is surrounded by 2.5 ha (6 acres) of restored historic gardens.

By TTC exit at Dupont subway station and walk (or take the 127 Davenport bus) north to Davenport. Walk up the historic Baldwin Staircase to Austin Terrace and Spadina. Free parking next door at Casa Loma. Open Mon to Sat 9:30 A.M. to 5 P.M., Sun and holidays noon to 5 P.M. Admission: adults $4, seniors and children $2, family $10.

The Gibson House
5172 Yonge St., North York
225-0146

This fine example of a Georgian-style home was built by David Gibson, a Scottish land surveyor and local politician, who obtained some notoriety as a supporter of William Lyon Mackenzie in the 1837 Rebellion. Superbly restored to the affluent 1850s, the house offers displays, demonstrations and guided tours. By subway exit at Sheppard and walk north 10 minutes. Gibson House is behind the Willowdale Post Office. Free parking. Open weekdays 9:30 A.M. to 5 P.M., weekends and holidays noon to 5 P.M. Admission: adults $1.50, students $1.25, children and seniors 75¢, family $3.50.

Enoch Turner School House
106 Trinity St. near King E.
863-0010

Until the Common School Act of 1846, only the rich had access to schooling in Upper Canada, because schools were private and charged a fee. Even then, Toronto's thrifty school trustees refused to levy the taxes allowed by the 1846 act, which would have built

The Enoch Turner Schoolhouse Foundation

schools for the children of the poor. Enter Enoch Turner, brewer and benefactor. In 1848 he paid for Toronto's first free school for the city's poor out of his own pocket. In the restored schoolhouse, discover what schooling was like in the 19th century. By TTC from King subway station take the King 504 streetcar east to Trinity St. Open Mon to Fri 10 A.M. to 4 P.M. Free admission.

Montgomery's Inn
4709 Dundas St. W. at Islington
394-8113

Built in 1830, this handsome Georgian inn has been restored to the late 1840s. Historical demonstrations and guided tours are available. Afternoon tea is served daily from 2 P.M. to 4:30 P.M. By TTC take the Islington 37 bus north from Islington subway station to Dundas St. Open Mon to Fri 9:30 A.M. to 4:30 P.M., weekends and holidays 1 P.M. to 5 P.M. Admission: adults $1.50, seniors and students $1, children 50¢.

Campbell House
160 Queen St. W. at University
597-0227

Sir William Campbell, a Scot who fought in the Revolutionary War, became the sixth chief justice of Upper Canada and the first judge in Upper Canada to receive a knighthood. He built this home on Adelaide St. E. near Jarvis in 1822; it was moved to its present site in 1972. It has been carefully restored to its Georgian elegance and refurbished to portray Campbell's affluent lifestyle. The house is run by and is the current home of the Advocates' Society. At the northwest corner of University and Queen at the Osgoode subway station. Open Mon to Fri 9:30 A.M. to 11:30 A.M., 2:30 P.M. to 4:30 P.M.; weekends noon to 4:30 P.M. Admission: adults $1.50, seniors, students and children 75¢.

The Grange
Grange Park at John St.

Toronto's oldest surviving brick residence and the original home of the Art Gallery of Ontario. Built in 1817 by D'Arcy Boulton, Jr., who named the Georgian-style house after the home he had left in England. Fully restored, and staffed by authentically costumed guides. Enter from inside the Art Gallery of Ontario. For hours and prices, see AGO in Museums/Art Galleries. By TTC exit at St. Patrick subway station and take the 505 streetcar west to Beverley.

The Church of the Holy Trinity
Trinity Square
(beside the Eaton Centre)

The story has it that this Anglican church, built in 1847, was funded by an anonymous woman smitten with Toronto's Bishop Strachan. It did not charge pew rentals, a rarity in that day. The beautiful landscaped space next door, Trinity Square, is a peaceful oasis in the midst of a busy city block.

Little Trinity Church
425 King St. E. at Trinity

A treasure. The city's oldest surviving church was built by Anglicans in 1843–45 who resisted the pew rents then charged at St. James' Cathedral.

Metropolitan United Church
Queen St. E. at Church

Originally built in 1870–72 and rebuilt, after a fire, in 1928–29, this magnificent cathedral has a commanding presence, sitting as it does in the middle of its expansive grounds, which take up an entire city block.

St. Michael's Cathedral
Bond St. at Shuter

Construction was started in 1845 at the urging of the first Roman Catholic bishop of Toronto, and St. Michael's is still the principal church of Canada's largest English-speaking Catholic archdiocese. Glorious stained-glass chancel window. Most Sundays during the summer until Thanksgiving weekend tours are given after noon mass. Phone 364-0234 to confirm.

GREAT BUILDINGS

We highly recommend the excellent in-depth guide, *Toronto Architecture: A City Guide* by Patricia McHugh.

The Ontario Parliament Buildings
1 Queen's Park
965-4028

The oldest sections of the provincial parliament buildings were begun in 1886. Designed by American architect Richard Waite, the Romanesque sandstone exterior is especially notable for its carved detail. The interior features

Formal gardens and statuary provide a distinctive setting for the Ontario Parliament Buildings.

works of art in carved mahogany and sycamore detailing by Scottish master carver William McCormack. The ceremonial staircase in the lobby is truly grand. The buildings also contain an impressive collection of Canadian art, and Canadian history buffs will find a walk past the garden statuary worthwhile. Rumour has it that the legislature was built on the site of a madhouse, which may explain some of the goings-on there today.

By subway exit at Queen's Park and walk north. Parking at the front of the building (2-hour max.). Free tours Mon to Fri 8:30 A.M. to 3:30 P.M. You may visit the legislative chamber when it's in session. Wheelchair accessible.

University of Toronto
Bounded by College, Bloor, Bay and Spadina
978-4111 or 978-6564

Canada's largest university, founded in 1827. Although the city has now grown up around it, U of T remains an academic enclave with cloistered courtyards, a rich variety of stone architecture and a beautifully treed campus. Croft Chapter House of University College even has a claim to a ghostly inhabitant. The ghost of a stonemason killed in a love triangle in the 1850s has reputedly spooked the tower for decades. Free campus tours are given in June, July and Aug, Mon to Fri 10:30 A.M., 12:30 P.M. and 2:30 P.M. Phone for details. Free campus maps can be picked up in Rm. 133, Simcoe Hall, 27 King's College Circle.

With its hammerbeam roof and splendid stained glass windows, Hart House's Great Hall is one of the university's architectural treasures. (Photo by Marc Rochette)

Old City Hall still maintains a position of prominence across the street from the popular Nathan Phillips Square. (Metropolitan Toronto Library, T 11804)

St. Lawrence Hall
151 King St. E. at Jarvis
392-7986

Built in 1850 by Toronto architect William Thomas, St. Lawrence Hall is a prominent example of Victorian classicism. Especially remarkable is the 30-m (100-ft.) long third-floor Great Hall with its tall windows, gaslit crystal chandelier and gilt trim. It was, in the last half of the 19th century and the first part of this century, the principal venue for Toronto's most noteworthy cultural events. Jenny Lind (the Swedish Nightingale) sang here in October 1851; tickets cost $3 and $4, extortionate prices in that day. St. Lawrence Hall is also the home of the National Ballet of Canada.

Old City Hall
60 Queen St. W. at Bay
965-7523

Built from 1889 to 1899, this Romanesque sandstone structure was designed by well-known Toronto architect E. J. Lennox. An abundance of carved detail graces the exterior. Its architectural appeal has made it very popular as a set for feature-length films. No inside tours, but there's lots to see from the outside. By subway exit at Queen and walk 1 block west to Bay. Parking below New City Hall off Queen.

The new City Hall with Nathan Phillips Square in the foreground. (Photo by Brian Pel)

Summertime concerts are often performed in the bandshell beside St. James' Cathedral. (Photo by Brian Pel)

New City Hall
100 Queen St. W. at Bay
392-7341

The two tall, curved towers in the design submitted by Finnish architect Viljo Revell placed first in an international competition of 520 entries. The innovative building was completed in 1965, and its clean lines, coupled with the expansive plaza of Nathan Phillips Square and its large reflecting pool, make it as popular with residents as it is with visitors. A great place to people-watch. Free tours Mon to Fri at 3:15 P.M. year-round.

St. James' Cathedral
106 King St. E. at Church
364-7865

The church you see today was completed in 1853 and is the fourth St. James on the site. Its immediate predecessor was destroyed in the great fire of 1849. The existing version was designed by Frederick Cumberland, who also designed Osgoode Hall and U of T's University College. The interior is well worth a look, especially for its intricately carved woodwork (ceiling, choir stalls and pulpits) and the stained-glass windows, particularly the one by the Lady Altar made by Tiffany of New York, c.1900. The 92-m (306-ft.) spire is the tallest in Canada and in the past was often used as a landmark by ships on Lake Ontario.

One of Toronto's best-loved landmarks—the Gooderham Flatiron building at the corner of Wellington and Church.

The Gooderham Building
(The Flatiron Building)
49 Wellington St. E. at Church

This rare example of flatiron architecture (so-called because of its shape) was built for financier George Gooderham in 1892 as the administrative offices of Gooderham and Worts Distillery. The grassy knolls of Berczy Park next door are a great place from which to view Derek Besant's famous flatiron mural.

Union Station
65–75 Front St. W. at Bay

This truly monumental Classical Revival building was erected between 1915 and 1920. At 255 m (850 ft.) in length, it still manages to dominate the streetscape despite its proximity to much taller towers in the financial district. Enter the building between the rows of impressive pillars and view the cathedral-like Great Hall with its 26.6-m (88-ft.) ceiling. What an institution should look like.

Osgoode Hall
116–138 Queen St. W.
at University
363-4101

The East Wing was constructed between 1829 and 1832; the Centre Block and the West Wing were raised in 1844. There have been numerous additions and renovations since. Named after the first chief justice of the province, William Osgoode, Osgoode Hall was built as the headquarters of the Law Society of Upper Canada. It was situated just north of the city limits at that time, marked by Queen St. To prevent intrusions from nearby cattle, the wrought-iron fence, complete with its cow gates, was added in 1866. The building today houses not only the Law Society of Up-

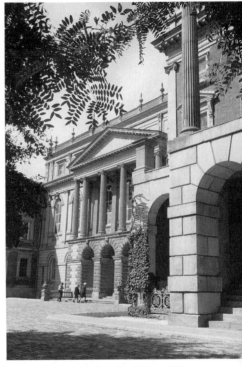

Osgoode Hall, home of the Law Society of Upper Canada and the Supreme Court of Ontario. (Photo by Brian Pel)

Courtesy of David Crighton © 1989

109

per Canada but also the Supreme Court of Ontario. As a centennial project, one of the early courtrooms was completely refurbished to its 1867 period. Visitors are welcome to wander. (Guards will tell you where you can't go.)

By subway exit at Osgoode onto the northeast corner of the Queen St. W./University Ave. intersection. Parking below New City Hall off Queen.

Spencer Clark Collection of Historic Architecture
The Guild Inn
191 Guildwood Pkwy.
Scarborough
266-4449

A unique collection of important architectural pieces from more than 60 Toronto landmarks and great buildings long since fallen to "progress" and the wrecker's ball. The stone-carved panels from the original Globe and Mail building, the original Osgoode Hall steps, the original Bank of Toronto columns, plus others. A must for nostalgia and architecture buffs.

By TTC exit at Kennedy subway station and take the 34A Morningside bus, which stops directly in front of the Guild Inn. Or take the GO train from Union Station to Guildwood station and walk 1 km (half a mile) to the inn. The collection is on the Guild Inn grounds and is open every day during the daylight hours. Free.

The Metropolitan Toronto Reference Library
789 Yonge St. near Bloor
393-7196 (recording)

Designed by Raymond Moriyama (who also designed the Ontario Science Centre), the massive reference library has found a warm place in the hearts of Torontonians. The throng gathered before the doors open on weekends reminds you of a Boxing Day sale. You have to enter the building to really appreciate it, though. The soaring central space, the ponds complete with running water, the use of natural light, banners and warm colours all add to its considerable appeal. Open Mon to Thurs 10 A.M. to 9 P.M., Fri and Sat 10 A.M. to 6 P.M., Sun 1:30 P.M. to 5 P.M. By subway exit at Bloor and walk 1 block north on Yonge.

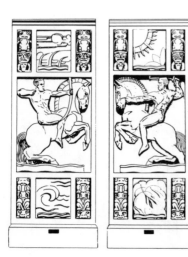

These carved stone panels from Toronto's old Globe and Mail building are on display at the unique Spencer Clark Collection. (The Guild)

The Toronto Stock Exchange
2 First Canadian Place
King St. and York
947-4676 (recording)
One of the city's shrines to commerce.
From the visitors' gallery you can view
the activity on the trading floor below.
There's a visitors' centre, and free tours
are conducted. By subway exit at St.
Andrew and walk a short distance east
on King St. Open Mon to Fri 9 A.M. to
4:30 P.M.

Exhibition Place
393-6000
This 140-ha (350-acre) site is the home
of the Canadian National Exhibition, the
Royal Winter Fair, the Molson Indy and
many of Toronto's consumer shows
such as the Boat Show, the Home Show
and the Sportsmen's Show. The older
buildings, such as the Arts Crafts Hob-
bies Building, the Automotive Building
and the Horticultural Building, are city
landmarks in their own right. Open for
exhibits and events year-round. South of
the Gardiner Expressway at the foot of
Dufferin St. By TTC exit at Bathurst
subway station and take the 511
streetcar into the Exhibition grounds.
Large parking lots; parking is free when
no events are on, but you have to pay
when something's happening.

Also
Casa Loma, see Attractions
CN Tower, see Attractions
Roy Thomson Hall, see Entertain-
ment/Culture
Royal Alexandra Theatre, see
Entertainment/Culture

TOURING TORONTO

You can experience the sights of
Toronto by bus, a variety of boats, trolley car, hot air balloon or on foot.

IN THE AIR

Central Airways
Toronto Island Airport
363-2424
Half-hour or one-hour sightseeing
flights over Toronto by Cessna. Three
passenger maximum. Flights are year-
round, daily dawn to dusk. The half-hour
flight is $52.50 divided among the num-
ber of passengers. Also available is a 1½-
hour sightseeing flight to Niagara Falls.
To reach the Island Airport take the airport ferry from the foot of Bathurst St.
By TTC take the 511 streetcar from
Bathurst subway station south to
Lakeshore Blvd. and walk south on
Bathurst to the ferry dock.

Cameron Balloons
Stouffville
1-640-1414
Not exactly a tour of Toronto. This
outfit offers hot air balloon flights over
rural Ontario in the Stouffville area—
the prevailing winds determine the
direction of your trip. The two balloons
each carry eight people and flights last 1
to 1½ hours. Each flight concludes with
a linen and crystal service picnic including champagne and pâté. The cost for a
group of six or more is $125 per per-
son, or $150 per person for fewer than
six. You must phone for reservations.

BY WATER

Gray Line Harbour and Island Tours
364-2412

Using those sleek and comfortable Amsterdam-style glass-top tour boats, this company provides enjoyable and informative 60-minute trips through the Toronto harbour and island lagoons. They also offer a separate tour of the Ontario Place waterways. The tours are fully narrated and there are lots of photo opportunities. Boats depart from two locations: Queen's Quay Terminal Dock at the foot of York St. and the Harbour Castle Westin Dock at the foot of Bay St. The Queen's Quay boats leave on the quarter-hour from 10:15 A.M. to 8:15 P.M., and the Harbour Castle boats leave on the hour from 10 A.M. to 8 P.M.

By transit take the Queen's Quay free shuttle bus from the front of Union Station. It leaves every 10 minutes. Or walk south on Bay St. from Union Station to the Harbour Castle Westin Hotel. Parking across the street from the nearby Toronto Star building. Tours operate from late April to mid-Oct. Adults $8.95, seniors $6.95, children $4.95.

Toronto Harbour Tours
145 Queen's Quay W.
(foot of York St.)
869-1372

Toronto Tours' 51-passenger sightseeing vessel offers indoor and outdoor seating on pleasant one-hour tours of the Toronto harbour and waterfront and the busy Port of Toronto. By TTC take the Spadina 77B bus from Union or Spadina subway stations. Parking opposite Queen's Quay Terminal Building. Tours run from mid-April to the end of Oct. Phone for sailing times. Adults $9.95, children 12 and under $4.95.

Toronto Islands Ferries
Entrance on west side of
Harbour Castle Westin Hotel
392-8193 (recording)

The cheapest tour available. Short, but a good way to introduce yourself to Toronto. Ferries leave every 20 minutes. Prices, times and destinations vary with the season, so call ahead for details.

PMCL Boat Tours
York Quay (foot of York St.)
861-1996

Ninety-minute narrated cruises aboard the 72-passenger *Ste. Marie I*. Fully licensed with cold snack bar. Tours run five times a day from May to Oct. Phone for departure times. Adults $9, seniors $8, children (2–12) $5.

BY BUS

Gray Coach Lines
610 Bay St. at Dundas
979-3511

City tours and tours beyond the metro area, such as to Niagara Falls and Canada's Wonderland. Buses depart from the main bus terminal at Bay St. and Dundas as well as from major downtown and midtown hotels. Call for times and prices.

Happy Day Tours
220 Yonge St. S., Aurora
593-6220

A city tour of Toronto and Black Creek Pioneer Village. This four-hour tour runs twice daily from all airport hotels, east end hotels and many downtown hotels. Adults $24.95, children 12 and under $12.50. Also offered once a day is a tour to Niagara Falls. Adults $49.95, children 12 and under $29.95 (includes lunch). Phone for reservations and pick-up times.

BY TROLLEY CAR

Toronto Tours
869-1372

A very popular 1½-hour guided tour of Toronto aboard a restored 1920s Peter Witt trolley car. The tour collects passengers at the Royal York Hotel (York at Wellington) and the Sheraton Centre Hotel (York at Queen). Departure times change with the season, so phone for details. Adults $12.95, children 12 and under $8.

INDUSTRIAL TOURS

The R. C. Harris Filtration Plant
2701 Queen St. E.
at Victoria Park
392-8209

Built between 1932 and 1941. The beaux-arts façade and interior detailing in terrazzo, brass and imported marble belies the fact that this immense building is in fact a waterworks that treats up to 225 million gallons of water each day. By TTC exit at Queen subway station and take the 501 streetcar east to Victoria Park. Tours on Sat and Sun at 10 A.M., 11:30 A.M., 1:30 P.M. and 3 P.M. year-round.

Upper Canada Brewing
2 Atlantic Ave. near King
534-9281

Tours year-round of their cottage brewing facilities. Mon to Fri 4 P.M., Sat 12:30, 1:30 and 2:30 P.M. If you're over 19, you even get to sample the beer.

Several wineries in the Niagara region offer tours. At the end of the tour, free samples of their wines are provided (to those over 19).

Inniskillin Wines
Niagara Pkwy.
1-468-3554

Château des Charmes Wines
Niagara-on-the-Lake
1-262-4219

Reif Winery
Niagara-on-the-Lake
1-468-7738

OUT-OF-TOWN ATTRACTIONS

Niagara Falls

In 1988 more than 15 million visitors came to see one of the seven wonders of the world. The 53-m (176-ft.) falls are spectacular in any season and are now illuminated for most of the evening year-round. In winter the ice bridges and the nearby ice-covered trees present a fairyland to the viewer. More than 100 years of tourism means that you will have lots to do whether you come for the day or for a longer stay. Attractions include a Spanish Aerocar trip over the whirlpool gorge; the *Maid of the Mist* boat tours to the foot of the falls; wax museums; the scenic tunnels; the Skylon observation tower; the Minolta Tower; Ripley's Believe It or Not Museum; historic sites such as Brock's Monument and the Laura Secord homestead; and golf courses, restaurants and gift shops galore. The Niagara Pkwy., a beautifully tended acreage running the full 56 km (35 mi.) beside the highway that follows the Niagara River from Niagara-on-the-Lake to Fort Erie, is one of the most scenic parklands in North America.

From Toronto take the Gardiner Expressway westbound until it turns into the Queen Elizabeth Way, and continue on the QEW for approximately one hour to the Niagara Falls exits.

Marineland
7657 Portage Rd., Niagara Falls
1-356-9565 (recording)

A top-notch aquatic show including performing killer whales, dolphins and sea lions. Also home of the world's largest steel roller coaster at Dragon Mountain.

The killer whales perform daily at Marineland, Niagara Falls.

From Toronto take the Queen Elizabeth Way to Exit 27 (McLeod Road) and follow the signs along McLeod Road to Marineland Pkwy. and Marineland. Summer hours are 9 A.M. to 6 P.M., off-season hours are 10 A.M. to 4 P.M. The rides are open 16 May to mid-Oct. Phone for information and rates.

Canada's Wonderland
Maple
832-2205 (recording) or
691-6335 (outside Toronto)

A spectacular theme park, and very popular with families, Wonderland features more than 30 rides, including White Water Canyon, Thunder Run, Mine Buster, Racing River and Canada's only looping stand-up roller coaster. There are also a Smurf Forest and a Hanna Barbera cartoon land for children. The park provides international shopping, a variety of dining facilities and live stage shows—the Kingswood Music Theatre presents top international concerts.

Canada's Wonderland is approximately 10 minutes north of Hwy. 401. Take Hwy. 400 north and exit at Rutherford Rd. You can't miss the Wonderland entrance. Plenty of parking. By public transit take the GO express bus from York Mills or Yorkdale subway stations. Open daily June, July and Aug; weekends only in May and Sept. (Some days they're closed, so phone ahead.) Hours are 10 A.M. to 10 P.M. There are a variety of admission packages. The Pay-One-Price Passport in 1988 cost $19.95 for the whole day and included regular live shows and unlimited use of all rides.

African Lion Safari
R.R. #1, Cambridge
(519) 623-2620

The Toronto area's most extensive wildlife park (200 ha/495 acres) features both a drive-through park and exotic animal and bird shows. On six large game reserves, more than 900 animals and birds live much as they would in their wild habitats. Among the exhibits, a birds of prey show provides a chance to see falconers giving flying demonstrations. Camping facilities are available.

From Toronto take Hwy. 401 westbound and exit on Hwy. 6 (Exit 299) south to Safari Rd., which leads straight to the wildlife park. Open from early April until late Oct. Phone for hours. Admission (by private car only): adults $8.95, youth and seniors $7.95, children 12 and under $6.95. Or you can take the Safari Tram, with a guided tour: adults $10.95, seniors $9.45, children 12 and under $7.95.

Algonquin Provincial Park

Ontario's favourite and one of Canada's largest parks. Algonquin Provincial Park covers 7655 km² (2955 sq. mi.) of dense mixed forest and contains thousands of Canadian Shield lakes. The Hwy. 60 corridor through the south of the park provides easy access to a true natural environment, and there's always the chance you'll see black bears, white-tailed deer and moose. Thankfully, most of the park is inaccessible by road and is therefore a haven for backpackers and canoeists. There are full camping facilities within the park. There are also three excellent lodges if you desire a somewhat more refined existence. For information on the park season, admission charges, camping, and fishing permits, write to the Superintendent, Algonquin Provincial Park, Ministry of Natural Resources, Box 219, Whitney, ON K0J 2M0. Call (705) 633-5572. You can also obtain information, including maps, from Provincial Parks Information, Whitney Block, Queen's Park, Toronto M7A 1W3.

From Toronto take Hwy. 400, then Hwy. 11 north to Hwy. 60 at Huntsville. Take Hwy. 60 east to the Park entrance.

Georgian Bay Islands National Park
Located on 77 islands or parts of islands in southern Georgian Bay (part of Lake Huron), north of Toronto, this park provides opportunities for excellent fishing, wildlife sightings and scuba diving. Access points are from Tobermory on the Bruce Peninsula and from Honey Harbour, approximately 210 km (130 mi.) from Toronto. For information on admission and permits, contact Parks Canada—Ontario Region, Box 1359, Cornwall, ON K6H 5V4; phone (613) 938-5866.

Point Pelee National Park
Because of its location on the principal North American migratory flyways, this small (15.5 km²/6 sq.mi.) park is world-famous with the birdwatching crowd. It is also the southernmost point in Canada, on the same latitude as northern California. About 400 km (240 mi.) from Toronto. Take Hwy. 401 westbound towards Windsor. The Point Pelee exit is marked Exit 48. Phone (519) 322-2365 or (519) 322-2371 (recording). Nearby campgrounds.

Cullen Gardens and Miniature Village
R.R. #2, Taunton Rd., Whitby
294-7965 or 1-668-6606
A 9-ha (22-acre) miniature village, where all buildings are one-twelfth scale. Full-size lush botanical gardens, topiary and seasonal flower exhibits. There are also four restaurants and daily musical performances and fireworks. Cullen Gardens is east of Toronto 5 km (3 mi.) north of Hwy. 401 off Hwy. 12. Open from mid-April to early Jan. Hours are variable, so phone before you go. Admission: adults $6.50, seniors and students $5.50, children $3.

Canadian Automotive Museum
99 Simcoe St., Oshawa
1-576-1222
This is one of Canada's foremost collections of historic and classic automobiles. In downtown Oshawa, 1 hour east of Toronto on Hwy. 401. Open Mon to Fri 9 A.M. to 5 P.M., weekends and holidays 10 A.M. to 6 P.M. Admission: adults $3.50, seniors and students $3, children $2.

Sharon Temple
Leslie St., Sharon
1-478-2389
Built between 1825 and 1832 by the Children of Peace, a Quaker splinter group, the Sharon Temple was in use until 1889. It has been completely restored and is a unique architectural gem; many of its architectural features have symbolic religious significance. In the July festival, Music at Sharon, excellent professional concerts are performed here. Phone for information. The town of Sharon is 40 km (25 mi.) north of Toronto. By car drive north on Hwy. 11 (Yonge St.) to Hwy. 9, then east to Les-

lie St., then north to the village of Sharon. Open 11 A.M. to 5 P.M. May through Oct; closed Fri except in July and Aug. Admission: adults $2, seniors and teens $1, children 50¢.

The RMS Segwun
Gravenhurst
(705) 687-6667
The 1887 *Segwun* is North America's oldest operating steamship and has been fully restored. A package by Tally Ho Tours (224-2585) combines a flight from Toronto Island Airport to Muskoka with a luncheon cruise on the *Segwun*. Offered July through to Sept, weekends only. Cost is $135 per person.

Historic Huronia/Martyrs' Shrine
Midland
A complete recreation of Sainte-Marie Among the Hurons, the Jesuit missionaries' 1639 mission in Huronia, near Midland. Sainte-Marie was totally destroyed by the Iroquois in their near extermination of the Hurons in the late 17th century. It was here that several French missionaries, including Jean de Brébeuf, met their deaths by torture at the stake. Now canonized, they are revered in the Catholic pilgrimage of Martyrs' Shrine just up the hill from Sainte-Marie Among the Hurons. Pope John Paul II paid homage at the shrine in 1986. The site is 113 km (70 mi.) north of Toronto in the town of Midland and is well worth a visit.

Also
Kortright Centre for Conservation, see Parks/Gardens
The McMichael Canadian Collection, see Museums/Art Galleries
Ontario Agricultural Museum, see Museums/Art Galleries
The Royal Botanical Gardens, see Parks/Gardens
The Shaw Festival, see Entertainment/Culture
The Stratford Shakespearean Festival, see Entertainment/Culture

The Sharon Temple's unique architecture and beautiful setting attract many visitors every year. (Photo by Anne J. Grieve)

CALENDAR OF EVENTS

Mid-Jan Toronto International Boat Show, indoors at Exhibition Place, 593-7333.

Late Jan TropiCanada, annual festival with concerts, skating, ice canoe race, barrel jumping and children's activities, at Harbourfront, 973-3000.

Early Feb The National Ballet of Canada begins its winter season at the O'Keefe Centre, 393-7469.

Mid-Feb Toronto Auto Show. Speed, chrome and femmes fatales, at the Metro Toronto Convention Centre, 493-6863.

Mid-March Toronto Sportsmen's Show. The latest in equipment plus demonstrations and exhibits, at Exhibition Place, 593-7333.

Late March The One-of-a-Kind Springtime Craft Show sale at Exhibition Place, 960-3680.

Early April National Home Show at Exhibition Place, 445-6641.

Late April The National Ballet of Canada begins its spring season at the O'Keefe Centre, 393-7469.

May–June Guelph Spring Festival, a Canadian music tradition for more than 20 years, noted for new Canadian operas and the works of Canadian composers, (519) 821-3210.

Mid-May Ontario Place opens for the season, 965-7711. ► International Children's Festival at Harbourfront, 973-3000.

Late May Victoria Day fireworks (on or around 24 May), on the waterfront.

Mid-June Canadian Open at Glen Abbey Golf Course, Oakville, 844-1800. ► Metro International Caravan, a colourful celebration of the city's diverse cultural heritage featuring ethnic "pavilions'" throughout Toronto, 977-0466.

Late June Mariposa Folk Festival at Molson's Park, Barrie, (705) 737-0013. ► Downtown Jazz Festival sees international artists at several venues, 593-4828.

July–Sept The Toronto *Star*'s Annual Great Salmon Hunt, see Sports/ Recreation.

July Music at Sharon: classical music each July weekend at the historic Sharon Temple, 1-478-2389.

Ice canoe racing—a popular spectator event at Harbourfront's TropiCanada festival. (Harbourfront Corporation)

1 July Canada Day celebrations all over town include spectacular fireworks displays at Ontario Place, Canada's Wonderland and Harbourfront.

Early July The CHIN International Picnic: Guinness Records says it's the world's biggest free picnic, at Exhibition Place, 531-9991. ▶ International Balloon Meet at Molson's Park, Barrie, (705) 737-0013.

Mid-July Queen's Plate at Woodbine, the oldest stakes race in North America, 675-6110. ▶ The Molson Indy Car Race, a 300-km (185-mi.) race through Toronto streets for $850,000 prize money, 869-8538. ▶ Annual Outdoor Art Exhibition, with showings by more than 500 artists from around the world, at Nathan Phillips Square, City Hall, 392-9111.

Late July Soul and Blues Festival—Canada's only—at Harbourfront, 973-3000. ▶ Caribana: one of North America's largest West Indian festivals, with a

The Kiev dancers always provide highly athletic performances during the Metro International Caravan festival.

Caribana's popularity is due in no small part to the tempo of its music and the extravagance of its costumes.

lively, colourful parade down University Ave. followed by Centre Island celebrations, 925-5435.

Early Aug WOMAD (World of Music, Art and Dance), an international festival at Harbourfront, 973-3000.

Mid-Aug The Canadian National Exhibition opens, 393-6000. ► Player's tennis championship, see Sports/Recreation.

Early Sept Festival of Festivals, one of the world's best film festivals, 967-7371. ► Toronto Symphony Orchestra begins its season at Roy Thomson Hall, through to late May, 598-3375. ► The Binder Twine Festival in Kleinburg: games, performances, home baking and lots of crafts.

Mid-Sept Pioneer Festival at Black Creek Pioneer Village, one of Ontario's best fall fairs, 661-6610.

Roblin's Mill at Black Creek Pioneer Village. (A heritage project of the Metro Conservation Authority)

Early Oct The Canadian Opera Company's season begins at the O'Keefe Centre, 363-6671.
► Octoberfest in Kitchener, the biggest Bavarian beerfest in North America, (519) 744-1555.

Mid-Oct International Festival of Authors: North America's most prestigious gathering of international writers, at Harbourfront, 973-4000.

Late Oct The Rothman's International at Woodbine Race Track, *the* thoroughbred race of the year, 675-6110. ► Hadassah-Wizo Bazaar, the bargain hunt of the year, at Exhibition Place, 789-4373.

Early Nov The Royal Agricultural Winter Fair, the world's largest agricultural fair under one roof, is great for kids as well as adults; at the CNE Coliseum, 393-6400. ► The National Ballet of Canada begins its fall season at the O'Keefe Centre, 393-7469. ► The Santa Claus Parade, the one every child waits for.

Late Nov Toronto Antique Show, at the Metro Toronto Convention Centre, 461-8171. ► The One-of-a-Kind Canadian Craft Show and Sale, with items by top designers and artisans, at Exhibition Place, 960-3680.

Mid-Dec *The Nutcracker* by the National Ballet of Canada at the O'Keefe Centre, 362-1041. ► The *Messiah* by the Mendelssohn Choir at Roy Thomson Hall, 593-4828.

31 Dec New Year's celebrations at Nathan Phillips Square.

The Princes' Gates. (CNE Archives)

THE CANADIAN NATIONAL EXHIBITION

The Ex opens mid-Aug and closes on Labour Day. The world's largest and longest-running fair (according to the *Guinness Book of World Records*) is everything a fair should be and more. As well as the multitude of displays and exhibits, there's a large midway with rides and carny games, an air show, a boat show, horse shows and cat shows, fireworks, food, and concerts at the Grandstand. A recent Grandstand line-up included Huey Lewis, George Michael, Hall and Oates, Rod Stewart and Bob Dylan. The grounds are open daily 8 A.M. to midnight—buildings are open 10 A.M. to 10 P.M. Adults $6, seniors $2 (free before 1 P.M.), children 13 and under $2. By TTC exit at Bathurst subway station and take the 511 Exhibition streetcar into the Exhibition grounds. Large parking lots and large traffic jams.

The CNE midway has been drawing huge crowds for over a century. (CNE Archives)

10 BEST VIEWS OF THE CITY

1. CN Tower
2. Casa Loma
3. Café Terrace rooftop lounge, Park Plaza Hotel
4. The Lighthouse revolving restaurant, Toronto Harbour Castle Westin
5. The Winter Palace, Sheraton Centre
6. Scaramouche Restaurant, Avenue Rd.
7. The Toronto Islands Ferries
8. Riverdale Park
9. Fifty-Fourth restaurant, Toronto-Dominion Centre
10. The Fitness Institute restaurant, IBM Tower, Toronto-Dominion Centre

The skyline of Toronto seen from the Toronto Islands. (Metropolitan Toronto Parks and Property Department)

PARKS/GARDENS 7

A CITY OF TREES

Over the years Toronto has borne epithets ranging from "Muddy York" to "Hogtown" to "Toronto the Good," but "Toronto the Green" would be far more appropriate. Visitors are always impressed with the city's verdant quality. And Torontonians tend to take it for granted until they visit other cities and become aware of their own good fortune. Look down from any of the high vantage points listed under 10 Best Views of the City (see Sightseeing) and you too will be struck by the blanket of foliage.

Much is owed to the municipalities, which planned and now maintain a great deal of the green space in the city. (The motto in Toronto parks is "Please walk on the grass.") But perhaps more has to do with a fortunate topography. The region's many rivers and large creeks, including the Credit, the Humber and the Don, carved extensive ravine valleys after the last ice age. These ravines have been saved from development and now offer Torontonians miles of lush, peaceful greenscape.

An excellent guidebook to these ravines is *Toronto's Backyard: A Guide to Selected Nature Walks,* by Gregory and MacKenzie, available in most bookstores.

WATERFRONT PARKS

THE SCARBOROUGH BLUFFS

These lakeshore cliffs dominate the waterfronts of seven city parks in Scarborough. From west to east these are: Rosetta McLain Park, Bluffers Park, Cathedral Bluffs Park, Cudia Park, Sylvan Park, Guildwood Park and East Point Park. From their 27-m (90-ft.) heights you have panoramic views of Lake Ontario and the Toronto skyline. All the parks are of interest, though our favourites are the Needles Bluffs area of Rosetta McLain Park and Cathedral Bluffs Park. Please note that, while beautiful, the Bluffs are high, windswept and in places weakened by erosion. Take care not to stray too near the edge.

To reach the Needles Bluffs area from downtown, proceed east on Kingston Rd. (Hwy. 2), turn south onto Scar-

Cross-section of Scarborough Bluffs (Source: D. R. Sharpe, Quaternary Geology of Toronto and Surrounding Area)

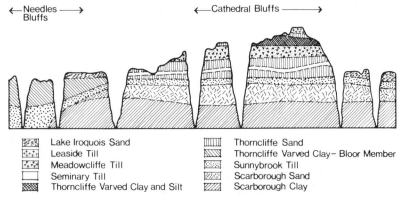

←—Needles—→ Bluffs

←—Cathedral Bluffs—→

Lake Iroquois Sand	Thorncliffe Sand
Leaside Till	Thorncliffe Varved Clay– Bloor Member
Meadowcliffe Till	Sunnybrook Till
Seminary Till	Scarborough Sand
Thorncliffe Varved Clay and Silt	Scarborough Clay

Bluffers Park Marina, one of the many along Toronto's waterfront. (Metropolitan Toronto Parks and Property Department)

boro Cres. to Drake Cres. Park here and walk to the Bluffs. By TTC exit at Victoria Park subway station and take the Kingston Rd. 12 bus to Scarboro Cres. Walk south to the Bluffs. The exotic forms of Needles Bluffs are the result of constant erosion by wind and water. Look below you to see the sailors and picnickers at Bluffers Park. You can reach Bluffers Park by driving farther east on Kingston Rd. and turning south onto Brimley Rd. Bluffers Park offers scenic views of the Bluffs, beachfront and an extensive family picnic area with washrooms.

To reach Cathedral Bluffs Park, drive even farther east on Kingston Rd. and turn south on Cathedral Bluffs Dr. Rising to heights of 98 m (320 ft.), they afford spectacular vistas.

Farther east on Hwy. 2, you can turn onto Guildwood Pkwy. to Guildwood Park. Both the impressive Guild Inn (see Where to Stay) and the Spencer Clark Collection of Historic Architecture (see Sightseeing/Great Buildings) are found in a formal garden setting. Fortunately,

the previous owners of the Guild Inn preserved much of the surrounding hardwood forests and wildflower meadows. The inn is an excellent place to stop for lunch or tea.

An interesting landscape feature to look for while at the Bluffs is the remains of the shoreline of Lake Ontario's predecessor, Lake Iroquois. It's evident in several places in the city, such as at the Casa Loma hill, but at the Scarborough Bluffs the ancient lakeshore can be readily seen close to Lake Ontario—it's the small but distinct rise in the land at the top of the Brimley Rd. Ravine.

For an excellent look at part of Toronto's glacial history, walk along the base of the Bluffs. Glacial deposits laid down over the centuries can be distinguished on the face of the Cathedral Bluffs, which geologists say are 90,000 years old at the base and 13,000–20,000 years old at the top. A note to amateurs: groundwater seepage at points up the Bluffs is your clue to the various geological layers.

LESLIE ST. SPIT

The Leslie St. Spit was initially a landfill project started in 1959 to support increased shipping traffic in the Port of Toronto. The increase never materialized, and Torontonians are fortunate to now have an urban wilderness peninsula that not only provides excellent views of the city's skyline but also offers unparalleled bird watching.

The Leslie St. Spit (now known as Tommy Thomson Park) is open throughout the year on weekends and on all holidays with the exception of Christmas Day and Boxing Day, from 9 A.M. to 6 P.M. Interpretive tours are held throughout the summer. Check the bulletin board at the entrance gate for tour schedule.

To reach the park, take Lakeshore Blvd. east to Leslie St. Proceed south on Leslie until it turns west and becomes Unwin Ave. To the south is the gate to the Spit. Park at the side of the road and walk, cycle or take the special TTC bus (see below). The Spit is 5 km (3 mi.) long, and a paved road runs this length, although it is gated to keep cars off it.

By TTC exit at Queen subway station and take the 501 streetcar eastbound to Berkshire Ave. On weekends from June through to Labour Day, transfer to a special TTC bus, which runs hourly right out to the end of the Spit. At other times of the year when the Spit is open, at Berkshire Ave. transfer to the Jones 83 bus southbound and continue to the intersection of Leslie St. and Commissioners St. Walk south down Leslie St. to the Spit (a fair hike).

A walk down the Spit will provide (besides fresh air and great views) proof of nature's adaptability. You'll be surprised at the high diversity of plant and bird life on this foundation of coarse concrete rubble and other waste. The plants you see are "colonizing" plants—those that first take hold in inadequate soil.

BIRD WATCHING ON THE SPIT

The entire Leslie St. Spit shoreline provides perfect habitat for both waterfowl and shore birds. The life list for the Spit now numbers more than 260 species (a larger life list than Algonquin Park's), among them ring-billed gulls, heron gulls, common terns, Caspian terns and black-crowned night herons. Only one other Caspian tern colony is on Lake Ontario and only one other black-crowned night heron colony is in the entire region. The ring-billed gull population, in the order of nearly 80,000 nesting pairs, is one of the largest such colonies in the world. The Spit also has the largest concentration on the Great Lakes of nesting common terns. You may also see marsh hawks, great black-backed gulls, California gulls and Wilson's phalaropes. Because the Spit is so close to the nearest North American flyway, migratory birds such as water pipits, horned larks, Lapland longspurs, snow buntings, shoreared owls and snowy owls frequently drop in, and there are lots of hawks to be seen in the fall. In the last few years, 30–50 per cent of all exceptional rarities in the region have been sighted on the Leslie St. Spit.

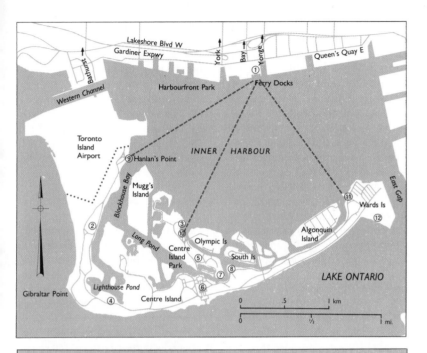

THE TORONTO ISLANDS

1 Harbour Castle Westin Hotel
2 Hanlan's Point Tennis Courts
   (public with lights)
3 Island Paradise Restaurant
4 Old Gibraltar Lighthouse
   (built 1808)
5 Centreville
   (children's amusement park)
6 Avenue of the Islands
   (formal gardens)

7 Far Enough Farm
   (farm animals)
8 The Island Church
   (St Andrew-by-the-Lake,
   built 1884)
9 Hanlan's Point Ferry Docks
10 Centre Island Ferry Docks
11 Wards Island Ferry Docks
12 Wards Island Park and Beach

THE TORONTO ISLANDS

The Toronto Islands are just a ferry ride away from downtown Toronto. With their beaches, parkland, mature trees and interconnecting lagoons, they provide a welcome contrast to the built-up city core. The main island—Centre Island—was once joined to the mainland at its easternmost end, now known as Wards Island. A terrific storm in the mid-1800s opened up the gap, and we have had the "Islands" ever since.

Taking the ferry is part of the islands experience, mainly for the panoramic views. There are three ferry routes, to Hanlan's Point, Centre Island and Wards Island. All leave from behind the Harbour Castle Westin Hotel at the foot of Bay St. The Centre Island ferry runs in summer only. For recorded schedules and fares, phone 392-8193.

The Toronto Islands offer picnic facilities, playgrounds for children, miles of sandy beaches for sunbathers and miles of trails for walking or cycling. You can fish at the stocked trout pond near the Gibraltar Point Lighthouse (catch limit of two per person). In Centreville, on Centre Island, there are rides, general stores, eating places, boat rentals and a children's petting farm. Several large, well-heeled marinas and yacht clubs are spotted along the island shorelines. There is even a frisbee golf course.

LAKESHORE PARKS

The Lakeshore parks, concentrated around Exhibition Place, are Gore Park, Battery Park and Coronation Park. The Martin Goodman Trail (see Sports/Fitness) runs through the heart of these parks and is ideal for walking, jogging and bicycling. You can stroll along the waterfront and watch the boating activity on the lake, and you can stop at Ontario Place or Exhibition Place, where there's always something going on.

By car follow Lakeshore Blvd. west from downtown. Park at Ontario Place. By TTC take the Dufferin 29 bus from Dufferin St. downtown or the 511 Exhibition streetcar from Bathurst subway station.

MT. PLEASANT CEMETERY

Mt. Pleasant Cemetery, just north of St. Clair Ave. E. at Yonge and divided through the middle by Mt. Pleasant Rd., is home to one of the finest tree collections in North America, with more than 1000 varieties of native and introduced trees and shrubs on the 80-ha (200-acre) site. Many of the trees bear small plaques with their botanical and common names. As well, the Toronto Trust Cemeteries office in the centre of the cemetery provides detailed arboretum maps. Public use of this beautiful re-

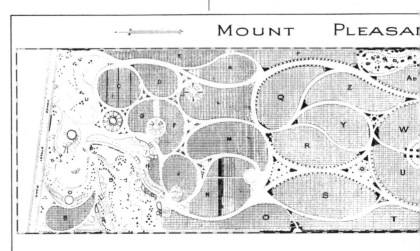

MOUNT PLEASAI

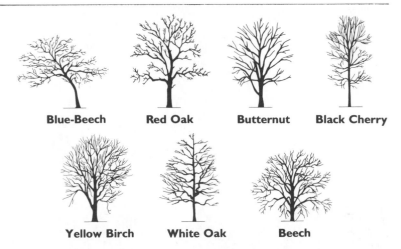

Blue-Beech   Red Oak   Butternut   Black Cherry

Yellow Birch   White Oak   Beech

The trees shown here are but a small sampling of the more than 1000 varieties of trees and shrubs at Mt. Pleasant Cemetery. The arboretum guide available at the cemetery office lists tree species by their botanical and common names as well as by their location in the grounds.

source is encouraged, and if you visit the cemetery you need not worry about being alone among the monuments. Many walkers, joggers and cyclists find it a welcome retreat from the fast pace of city life.

The office will also provide you with a list of notables who are buried here

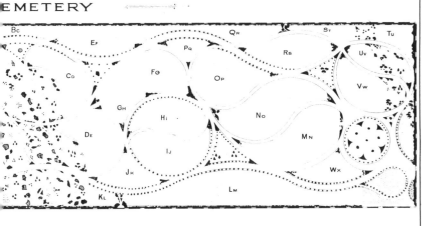

EMETERY

An afternoon's solitude in High Park. (Photo by Ottmar Bierwagen)

complete with a map for finding their memorials. Mt. Pleasant Cemetery is the resting place of William Lyon Mackenzie King, Sir Oliver Mowat, Sir Frederick Banting, Dr. Charles Best, Glenn Gould and the Eaton and Massey families, among others. Open daily 8 A.M. to a half-hour before dusk.

HIGH PARK

The first land for High Park was donated by J. G. Howard (of Colborne Lodge fame) in 1873. Subsequent acquisitions have expanded it to more than 160 ha (400 acres), making it Toronto's largest park. It's an extremely popular place with the denizens of downtown Toronto, and well it should be, since it has something for everyone—playgrounds, tennis courts, floral displays, boating, sports fields, a large restaurant, refreshment booths, animal paddocks and lots of old trees. High Park just wouldn't be High Park without the multitude of bicyclers, joggers, sunbathers, picnickers and fishermen. It's always busy but seldom overcrowded. On most summer nights there are also very good outdoor theatre performances, for free.

High Park stretches between Bloor St. and The Queensway along Parkside Dr. By subway exit at High Park station and walk south into the park. For an enjoyable afternoon outing, leave your car at the south end of the park off Colborne Lodge Dr. and walk north along the shore of Grenadier Pond. Turn up the slope and have a bite at the Grenadier Restaurant before returning south to either the greenhouse or Colborne Lodge.

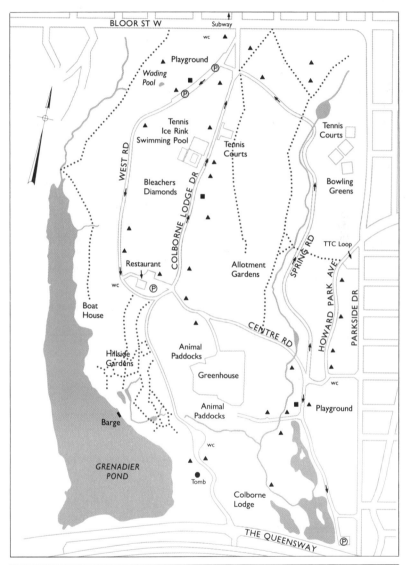

BLOOR ST W

Subway

Playground

Wading Pool

Tennis
Ice Rink
Swimming Pool

WEST RD

Tennis
Courts

Bleachers
Diamonds

COLBORNE LODGE DR

Tennis
Courts

Bowling
Greens

TTC Loop

Restaurant

Allotment
Gardens

SPRING RD

HOWARD PARK AVE

PARKSIDE DR

Boat
House

wc

CENTRE RD

Hillside
Gardens

Animal
Paddocks

Greenhouse

wc

Playground

Animal
Paddocks

Barge

wc

GRENADIER
POND

Tomb

Colborne
Lodge

THE QUEENSWAY

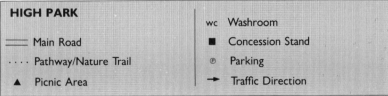

HIGH PARK

——— Main Road

···· Pathway/Nature Trail

▲ Picnic Area

wc Washroom

■ Concession Stand

℗ Parking

→ Traffic Direction

CONSERVATION AREAS

The Metropolitan Toronto and Region Conservation Authority maintains 13 conservation areas. For general information call 661-6600.

For nature buffs, one of the most interesting is the Kortright Centre for Conservation, near Kleinburg, about half an hour from downtown. This centre has 12 km (7½ mi.) of trails suitable for hiking and cross-country skiing and is famous for its Owl Prowls and Moccasin Walks. At the Kortright's central building are a theatre, a nature book and gift shop, café and exhibits. A sugar shack, a wildlife pond and a bee house are also on the property.

By car take Hwy. 400 north to Major Mackenzie Dr. Go west along Major Mackenzie 3 km (5 mi.) to Pine Valley Dr. Turn south to the well-marked entrance. Open all year except Christmas Day, 10 A.M. to 4 P.M. Extended hours for some special programs, such as Owl Prowls.

FORMAL GARDENS

EDWARDS GARDENS

It's a toss-up between Edwards Gardens and James Gardens as to which is the prettiest formal garden park in the city. Edwards Gardens is a favourite with photographers because of its abundance of colourful floral displays, rock gardens and secluded pathways. The Civic Garden Centre, in the northeast corner beside the parking lot, contains a garden shop, an outstanding horticultural library and an intriguing garden-oriented bookstore. For an extended nature walk, you can walk south out of Edwards Gardens into Wilket Creek Park and follow Wilket Creek as it winds its way to meet the Don River.

Edwards Gardens is at the intersection of Lawrence Ave. E. and Leslie St. By car take the Don Valley Pkwy. north from downtown and turn west onto Eglinton Ave. Turn north on Leslie St. until you see the gardens' parking lot entrance. By TTC Mon to Fri exit at York Mills subway station and take the Edwards Gardens 101 bus to the gardens. On weekends exit at Eglinton subway station and take either the Leslie bus or the Lawrence bus to the corner of Leslie and Lawrence.

Open Mon to Fri 9:30 A.M. to 5 P.M. (May to Oct), Mon to Fri 9:30 A.M. to 4 P.M. (Nov to April), weekends all year, noon to 5 P.M.

JAMES GARDENS

Don't forget your camera. James Gardens is a beautiful formal garden with a tremendous diversity of floral displays and picturesque bridges over spring-fed ponds. Lambton Woods, just south of the gardens and connected by an asphalt trail, is one of the most scenic natural woodlands left in the city, featuring such trees as black cherry, butternut, beech, white oak, yellow birch, red oak and blue beech. Year-round parking. The garden is just east of Royal York Rd. between Dundas and Eglinton. By car from the intersection of Bloor St. W. and Royal York Rd., drive north on Royal York Rd. for 2.8 km (1.7 mi.) to Edenbridge Rd. Follow Edenbridge east to the free parking lot at the entrance to the gardens. By TTC exit at Royal York subway station and take the Royal York Rd. 73 bus north to Edenbridge Rd. Walk east to the entrance. Open daily 9 A.M. to 9 P.M.

ALLAN GARDENS

Allan Gardens, formally opened in 1860, is Toronto's oldest botanical garden. The greenhouse in the middle of the park features an elegant glass-domed Palm House designed in 1910 by the city architect Robert McCallum. It is one of the few remaining examples of traditional British Palm House architecture in North America. The greenhouse is filled with tropical plants and seasonal flowers, and a visit there may be just the pick-up you need on a chilly winter day. (It's open daily 10 A.M. to 5 P.M.) The rest of the year the formal grounds surrounding the greenhouse are the perfect place for relaxed strolls in the heart of downtown.

The garden is at the corner of Carlton St. at Sherbourne. By TTC exit at either Queen's Park or College subway stations and take the 506 streetcar east to Sherbourne St.

The glass-domed Palm House at Allan Gardens. (Photo by Ottmar Bierwagen)

THE ROYAL BOTANICAL GARDENS

The Royal Botanical Gardens must be the most extensive and most beautiful botanical gardens in North America. You need at least a day to see the entire display of formal gardens, greenhouses, an arboretum and nature trails. Your visit could include a leisurely walk through any number of specialty gardens. Popular ones are the Rose Garden; the Medicinal Garden featuring plants used to cure various ailments; the Woodland Garden; the Clematis Collection, and the Laking Garden, which features one of North America's major iris displays. Take a break at the tea house restaurant in the Rock Garden.

The arboretum overlooks a bird sanctuary and features, as well as the world-famous Katie Osborne lilac garden, an incredible variety of flowering trees, shrubs and native trees—so many in fact that local universities and colleges send their student botanists, foresters and landscape architects on field trips here to sharpen their plant identification skills. The RBG also has a unique Mediterranean garden greenhouse complex, which exhibits a rich variety of aromatic flora including orange, lemon, fig and olive trees. These greenhouses also contain plants from southern Italy, South Africa, the chaparral of California and the Outback of southwestern Australia (where a visit may bring you face to face with a strange "kangaroo paw").

The RBG Centre is at 680 Plains Rd. W., in Burlington, and is open year-round. For information call 1-800-263-8450 toll free. From Toronto take the QEW west onto Hwy. 403, then go north on Hwy. 6 and follow the RBG signs.

RAVINES/PARKS

The ravine valleys of the Humber River, Don River, Highland Creek, Rouge River, Credit River, Etobicoke Creek and many others are lovely settings for nature walks, bicycling, picnicking, fishing, kayaking, bird watching and cross-country skiing. As well, the region's huge park system caters to a range of activities and interests from formal gardens to picnic grounds to municipal golf courses.

For information on the park nearest to you, phone City of Toronto Parks and Recreation (392-7286 or 392-7259), Metro Toronto Parks (392-8186) or the Metropolitan Toronto and Region Conservation Authority (661-6600).

MUSEUMS/ART GALLERIES 8

MAJOR MUSEUMS

The Royal Ontario Museum
100 Queen's Park at Bloor W.
586-5549

Absolutely amazing! The Royal Ontario Museum (or "ROM" as it's known by the natives) is yet one more reason why Toronto has acquired a truly international stature. Every visitor should ensure that the ROM is near the top of their must-see list. Where else can you tour a Jamaican bat cave, walk through a Ming tomb, come face to face with a mastodon, peer into an Iroquois longhouse and stand in awe of a crested parasaurolophus—all in one afternoon? If your time is limited, make sure you at least see the world-renowned Chinese, dinosaur, textile, Greek and Roman exhibits.

Opened in 1912, the ROM, with more than 6 million objects in its collections, is Canada's largest museum and one of the busiest in North America. When the current expansions and renovations are completed in the early 1990s, the ROM will be second in size only to New York's Metropolitan

DOWNTOWN MUSEUMS/ GALLERIES/THEATRES

1. Museum of the History of Medicine
2. William Ashley Crystal Museum
3. Royal Ontario Museum
4. McLaughlin Planetarium
5. George R Gardiner Museum of Ceramic Art
6. Sigmund Samuel Building
7. Osborne Collection of Early Children's Books
8. Art Gallery of Ontario
9. The Grange
10. Pantages Theatre
11. Massey Hall
12. Elgin and Winter Garden Theatres
13. Post Office Museum
14. Royal Alexandra Theatre
15. Roy Thomson Hall
16. Toronto Sculpture Garden
17. Market Gallery
18. O'Keefe Centre
19. St Lawrence Centre
20. The Power Plant
21. Premiere Dance Theatre
22. Redpath Sugar Museum
- ●   CN Tower
- ■   SkyDome
- →   Traffic direction
    Not all one-way streets are shown

The Mankind Discovering Gallery.

Illustrations and photographs courtesy of The Royal Ontario Museum

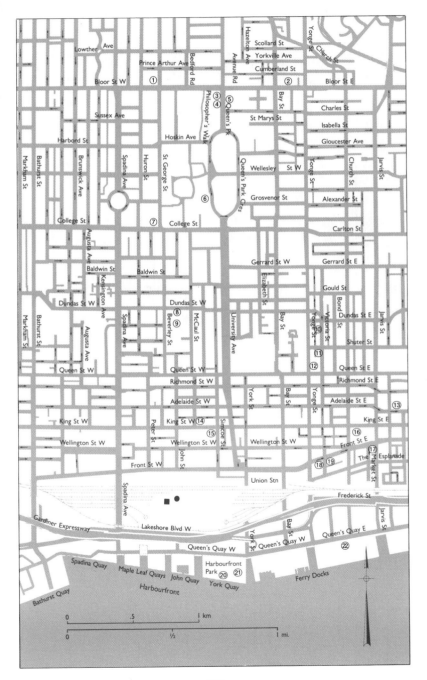

Royal Ontario Museum

GROUND FLOOR

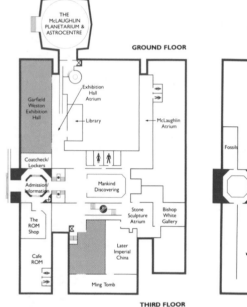

THE McLAUGHLIN PLANETARIUM & ASTROCENTRE

- Garfield Weston Exhibition Hall
- Exhibition Hall Atrium
- Library
- McLaughlin Atrium
- Coatcheck/ Lockers
- Admission/ Information
- Mankind Discovering
- The ROM Shop
- Stone Sculpture Atrium
- Bishop White Gallery
- Cafe ROM
- Later Imperial China
- Ming Tomb

SECOND FLOOR

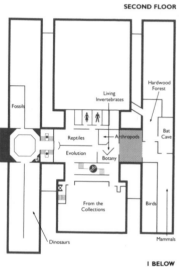

- Fossils
- Living Invertebrates
- Hardwood Forest
- Reptiles
- Arthropods
- Bat Cave
- Evolution
- Botany
- From the Collections
- Birds
- Dinosaurs
- Mammals

THIRD FLOOR

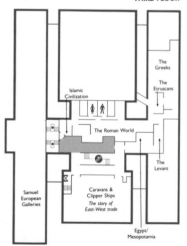

- The Greeks
- The Etruscans
- Islamic Civilization
- The Roman World
- The Levant
- Samuel European Galleries
- Caravans & Clipper Ships
  The story of East-West trade
- Egypt/ Mesopotamia

I BELOW

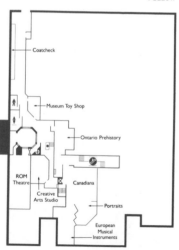

- Coatcheck
- Museum Toy Shop
- Ontario Prehistory
- ROM Theatre
- Creative Arts Studio
- Canadiana
- Portraits
- European Musical Instruments

Part of the Bishop White Gallery display.

Illustrations and photographs courtesy of The Royal Ontario Museum

Museum of Art. This multidisciplined museum displays collections focussed on the arts and sciences as well as on history and archaeology. Lectures, shows, hands-on workshops, concerts and plays emphasize interactive participation.

In addition to the main building at the corner of Bloor St. and Queen's Park, the ROM includes the McLaughlin Planetarium in a connected building, The George R. Gardiner Museum of Ceramic Art just across the street and the Canadiana Collection in the Sigmund Samuel Building—a 10-minute walk south on Queen's Park.

Galleries at the ROM include:

• The Bat Cave. This scaled-down version of a Jamaican original features 3000 model bats and a state-of-the-art audio and light tour of the cave. You'll come away with an understanding of echolocation and why bats do not end up in your hair.

• The world-famous Bishop White Gallery. Features Buddhist and Taoist paintings and sculptures including three Chinese wall paintings that are among the finest of their kind.

• The Ming Tomb. This recreation of a monumental tomb complex, with its gargantuan stone figures, is representative of the late Ming dynasty.

• Dinosaur Gallery. One of the ROM's most popular attractions. Dinosaur skeletons exhibited in simulated natural habitats include the stegosaurus, the carnivorous allosaurus and the rare crested parasaurolophus (the most complete of only three specimens in the world). Dioramas include the Le Brea tar pit, the evolution of the horse and the mastodon display.

• Ontario Prehistory Gallery. See what life was like in Ontario hundreds of

Artifacts on display in the Greek World Gallery.

Illustrations and photographs courtesy of
The Royal Ontario Museum

10 ROM BESTS
Dr. T. Cuyler Young, Jr.
Director, Royal Ontario Museum

1. **The Metjetjy Relief,** Egypt, Sakkara, Dynasty V, c.2420 B.C.
2. **A Lion Relief in Glazed Brick,** Mesopotamia, neo-Babylonian, c.600 B.C.
3. **A Polychrome Velvet Embroidery on a Gold Ground,** Iran, Safavid, early 17th century
4. **Buddhist Frescoes,** China, Yuan Dynasty, c.1300
5. **Mortuary Model of a Residential Compound,** China, Ming Dynasty, 16th century. Partially glazed pottery.
6. **Imperial Poetry Cabinet,** China, Ch'ing Dynasty, 1736–96. Red, green and yellow lacquer.
7. **Double Handled Ceramic Bowl (Crater),** Thebes, c.800 B.C. Geometric.
8. **Madonna and Child,** France, 14th century (School of Paris). Ivory.
9. **Virginal,** Italy, c.1560
10. **The Death of Wolfe,** Benjamin West (1738–1820), London, 1776

Children of all ages are fascinated by the exhibits in the Dinosaur Gallery.

thousands of years ago. Displays feature the butchering of a woolly mammoth, an Early Palaeo-Indian hunting camp and an Iroquois village of 400 years ago complete with stockade.
• Life Sciences galleries. Exhibits encompass evolution, botany, invertebrates, arthropods, reptiles, mammals and one of the best mineral collections in the world.

The ROM is easily reached by subway: exit at the Museum station. (Parking is at a premium, so TTC travel is recommended.) Facilities include a cafeteria and three gift shops. Wheelchair accessible. Open daily 10 A.M. to 6 P.M., Tues and Thurs until 8 P.M. Admission: adults $5, seniors, students and children $2.50, family $10. Seniors are free Tues and everyone is free Thurs after 4:30 P.M. except during special ticketed exhibitions. Discount with Planetarium admission and free with Gardiner Museum of Ceramic Art admission.

The McLaughlin Planetarium
100 Queen's Park
586-5736

The Planetarium opens the door on the wonders of the universe. The Theatre of the Stars runs 45-minute shows complete with special effects at least twice daily (except Mon). A hi-tech projection system produces incredible astronomical images on the inside curve of the Planetarium dome. Shows change four times a year.

Planetarium staff give star-gazing workshops and star talks to explain each season's sky.

The Astrocentre features a permanent astronomical display including interactive computerized exhibits, blown-up photographs of cosmic phenomena, a 3-D stellarium and a solar telescope.

And if your big business deal depends on Jupiter aligning with Mars, call the Astronomical Information Line at 586-5751.

The Planetarium is immediately south of and connected to the main ROM building. The Astrocentre is open daily 10 A.M. to 6 P.M., Tues and Thurs till 8 P.M. Star Theatre Box Office is open Tues to Fri 10 A.M. to 5 P.M., weekends and holidays noon to 5 P.M. Star show admission: adults $4, seniors, students and children $2.25. Astrocentre admission is free with ROM or Gardiner Museum of Ceramic Art admission.

The Sigmund Samuel Building— Canadian Decorative Arts Department
14 Queen's Park Cres.
586-5549

The Canadiana collection contains outstanding examples of early Canadian craftsmanship from Ontario, Quebec and the Maritimes. In addition to room settings centred around 18th- and 19th-century furniture, Canadian-made glass, silver and wooden-ware are also on display. Upstairs is the famous McCrae collection of miniature models of early Ontario buildings and tools. Exhibited paintings, prints and maps from the extensive collection are changed regularly.

By TTC, exit at Museum subway station and walk south along Queen's Park to just opposite the Ontario Legislative Buildings (about 10 min.). Open Mon to Sat 10 A.M. to 5 P.M., Sun 1 P.M. to 5 P.M. Free admission.

The George R. Gardiner Museum of Ceramic Art
111 Queen's Park
(across from ROM)
593-9300

More than 2000 pieces, ranging from Italian Majolica to English Delftware and 18th-century European porcelain, are on display in North America's only ceramics museum. Combined with the ROM's extensive holdings, it is one of the world's finest collections of European ceramics.

The Greeting Harlequin, Meissen c.1740

10 FAVOURITE PIECES
Mr. and Mrs. George R. Gardiner
Founders, The George R. Gardiner Museum of Ceramic Art

1. **Bow owl,** English c.1760
2. **Yellow ground tea and chocolate service with fitted leather travelling case,** Meissen c.1740–45
3. **Covered wall vase,** Du Paquier c.1730
4. **Model of a cat with a mouse,** St. Cloud c.1745
5. **Bourdaloue,** Meissen c.1725–30
6. **Scent bottle depicting "Monk carrying provisions to the Monastery,"** Frankenthal c.1758
7. **Figure of seated Oriental (called a Maggot),** Chantilly c.1740
8. **Harlequin family,** Meissen c.1740
9. **Madonna and Child,** Italian Majolica, late 15th century
10. **Watering can,** Sèvres c.1753

The "Harlequin"-theme porcelains are perennial favourites. Yes, there is a predominance of yellow pieces. The museum's benefactors concentrated on the rare yellow, the most difficult colour to produce with then-existing technology.

And do visit the gift shop, which features the work of some fine contemporary ceramicists.

Open Tues to Sun 10 A.M. to 5 P.M. Admission: adults $5, seniors, students and children $2.50, family $10. Discount with Planetarium admission and free with ROM admission.

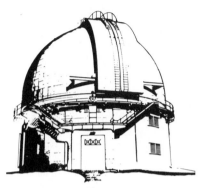

The David Dunlap Observatory

The David Dunlap Observatory Richmond Hill
884-2112

The main telescope was the second largest in the world when the observatory was built in 1935 and is still the largest in Canada with a diameter of 188 cm (74 in.). The observatory's impressive collection of stellar photographs is on display in the administration building. Open Sat evenings from mid-April to Oct. Tues morning tours are given all year. Admission is free, but you must phone for reservations and to confirm hours as they change seasonally. The nights can be cool even in summer, so bring warm clothes. From Toronto take Bayview Ave. north to Hillsview Dr. (just north of 16th Ave.). Proceed west to the gates on the south side of the road.

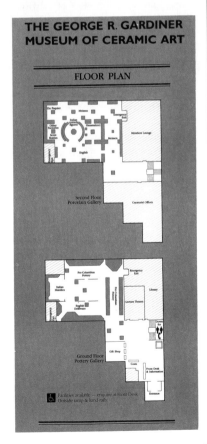

THE GEORGE R. GARDINER MUSEUM OF CERAMIC ART

FLOOR PLAN

The George R. Gardiner Museum of Ceramic Art

Canada Sports Hall of Fame Exhibition Place 595-1046

Two exhibit halls packed with memorabilia and videos. All major Canadian sports except hockey are represented. Tom Longboat, Jake Gaudaur, Ned Hanlan, Marilyn Bell, Capt. Angus Walters, Sylvia Burka and Terry Fox are among the many great Canadian sports figures with whom you will become acquainted. By TTC take the 511 streetcar from Bathurst subway station to Exhibition Place. Open daily 10 A.M. to 4:30 P.M. Free admission.

Hockey Hall of Fame and Museum Exhibition Place 595-1345

If you've always wanted to see Jacques Plante's mask, Bobby Hull's stick or hockey's most coveted trophy—the Stanley Cup—then this is the place for you. Lots of displays and video presentations. By TTC take the 511 streetcar from Bathurst subway station to Exhibition Place. Open Tues to Sun 10 A.M. to 4:30 P.M. Admission: adults $3, students and seniors $1, children under 4 free.

Canadian Baseball Hall of Fame Ontario Place 597-0014

Though Canadians don't claim to have originated the game, it's a documented fact that a baseball game was played in Beechville, Ont., on 4 June 1838—one full year before the game was "invented" in Cooperstown, NY. Since the inception of the professional leagues there have always been Canadians in the majors, and this is the place to learn about them. Among other facts, you'll discover that Babe Ruth hit his first and only minor league home run at Hanlan's Point in Toronto. Test your skills at the hands-on hitting and pitching displays— see if you can beat Nolan Ryan's fastball of 100.4 m.p.h.

Open daily 10 A.M. to 9 P.M. during Ontario Place season (mid-May to early Sept). Free with admission to Ontario Place. Open Sat only during off-season, 10 A.M. to 5 P.M. Admission: adults $2, children under 12 with an adult are free.

The famous Stanley Cup is on display at the Hockey Hall of Fame.

By TTC take the 511 streetcar from Bathurst subway station to Exhibition Place. Then walk 10 min. southwest to the entrance of Ontario Place. (You'll be able to see the Cinesphere dome.) Once inside Ontario Place follow the signs to the Hall of Fame.

OTHER MUSEUMS

Osborne Collection of Early Children's Books
Toronto Public Library
40 St. George St. near College
393-7753

This world-renowned collection is unique in Canada and holds many literary treasures. Begun in 1949 with a gift from Edgar Osborne, the collection now numbers more than 15,000 volumes and includes such rarities as Eleanor Mure's earliest extant version of *The Three Bears* (1831) and a 14th-century manuscript of *Aesop's Fables*. From Queen's Park subway station walk

An early children's alphabet book entitled A New Lottery Book of Birds and Beasts, *1771. (Osborne collection, T.P.L.)*

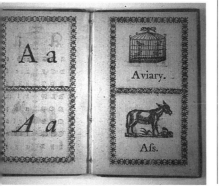

or take the 506 streetcar west to St. George St. The library is a short walk north. Parking is available behind the building; enter from College St. Open Mon to Fri 10 A.M. to 6 P.M., Sat 9 A.M. to 5 P.M. Free admission.

Post Office Museum
260 Adelaide St. E. near Jarvis
865-1833

Toronto's first post office has been given second life in its original building. Authentic right down to the quill pens, sealing wax and postmaster's period costume. You can even have your mail cancelled with an original postmark dated 1834. From King subway station walk or take the 504 streetcar east to Jarvis St. Then walk 1 block north to Adelaide St. Open daily 10 A.M. to 4 P.M. Free admission.

The Puppet Centre
171 Avondale Ave.
near Yonge and Sheppard
222-9029

The only puppet collection in Canada open to the public. The Puppet Centre has over 400 puppets on display including beautifully carved marionettes, early Punch and Judy puppets and Shadow figures from Indonesia and China. Plays are frequently presented; phone for the performance schedule. Reservations are required. The $4 admission fee to performances includes the museum fee. The gift shop sells a wide variety of handcrafted puppets. From Sheppard subway station take any non-express Sheppard East bus to Willowdale Ave. and walk south to Avondale Ave. The Puppet Centre is in the Glen Avon school. Open Mon to Fri 9 A.M. to 4 P.M. Admission $2.

Marine Museum of Upper Canada
Exhibition Place
392-6827

Exhibits trace the history of shipping and settlement on the Great Lakes. The museum is housed in the last remaining building of Stanley Barracks, officers' quarters for Fort York, built in 1841. You'll see relics from shipwrecks, working steam whistles, the fully restored tug *Ned Hanlan,* a fur-trading post and a wireless room. By TTC take the 511 streetcar from Bathurst subway station to Exhibition Place. Open Mon to Sat 9:30 A.M. to 5 P.M., Sun noon to 5 P.M. Admission: adults $2.50, children under 12 and seniors $1.50, family $7.

Canadian Warplane Heritage
Foundation
Hamilton Civic Airport
1-679-4183

Aviation memorabilia abounds. If Hurricanes, Avengers and Mustangs are your interest, this collection is sure to please. Over 40 aircraft on display. Drive south on Hwy. 403 and take the Fiddlers Green Rd. exit. The route from there is well marked with Airport signs. Open daily 10 A.M. to 4 P.M. Admission: adults $3, seniors and students $2.50, children $1.50.

The Beth Tzedec Museum
1700 Bathurst St. near Eglinton
781-3511

Located in the Beth Tzedec Synagogue, the museum displays rare Jewish artifacts, both religious and secular. It is the best collection of its kind outside Israel and Manhattan, and includes a spectacular Majolica Passover Plate c.1673.

Toronto Historical Board

By TTC take the 7C bus from Bathurst subway station to the Avenal Dr. stop, just steps away from the synagogue. Phone for hours. Free admission.

Museum of the History of Medicine
288 Bloor St. W. at St. George
922-0564

The theme here is 5000 years of health care. Don't miss the Nakht of Thebes exhibit, which deals with the autopsy of a 3200-year-old mummy. From St. George subway station walk 1 block west to the Academy of Medicine building at the corner of Bloor St. and Huron St. Open Mon to Fri 9:30 A.M. to 4 P.M. Free admission.

Courtesy Redpath Sugar

Redpath Sugar Museum
95 Queen's Quay E.
366-3561

The oldest sugar company in Canada has put together a collection of memorabilia and exhibits about the history of the sugar industry in Canada. Public parking lot west of the refinery. Open Mon to Fri 10 A.M. to noon, 1 P.M. to 3:30 P.M. Free admission.

Halton County Radial
Railway Museum
R.R. #2, Rockwood
(519) 856-9802

The museum features more than 40 authentic antique electric rail vehicles; some of these run on the site's 1.6-km (1-mi.) loop of track. Gift shop and snack bar. Take Hwy. 401 west to Exit 312 and drive north 14.5 km (9 mi.) to the museum. Open May through Oct. Phone for hours. Admission: adults $3.50, students $2.25, seniors and children $1.75.

William Ashley Crystal Museum
50 Bloor St. W. near Yonge
964-2900

A private collection of exceptionally beautiful Czechoslovakian glassware on display on the second floor of the William Ashley store. Open Mon to Wed 10 A.M. to 6 P.M., Thurs and Fri 10 A.M. to 7:30 P.M., Sat 9:30 A.M. to 5:30 P.M. Free admission.

Market Gallery
South St. Lawrence Market,
2nd floor
95 Front St. E.
392-7604

Rotating exhibits of artifacts, maps, paintings, documents and photographs from the extensive City of Toronto collection. Open Wed to Fri 10 A.M. to 4 P.M., Sat 9 A.M. to 4 P.M., Sun noon to 4 P.M. Free.

Ontario Agricultural Museum
Milton
1-878-8151

A great place to spend a day. Ontario's rural past and the history of agriculture in the province are portrayed on this 32-ha (80-acre) site with the help of 30 transplanted historic buildings, barns full of antique farm machinery and herds of livestock. An 1830s and an 1860s farmstead have both been recreated. You can also visit a 1928 Ford dealership, a blacksmith shop, a shingle mill and a carriage works. Costumed staff demonstrate weaving, spinning and blacksmithing. Take Hwy. 401 west to Exit 320B. Go north to Regional Rd. 9, then west to Tremaine Rd. and south to the museum. Open daily mid-May to mid-Sept, from 10 A.M. to 5 P.M. Admission: adults $3, students and seniors $1.50, children under 6 free.

Henry Moore (British 1898–1986). Large Two Forms, 1966 and 1969. Bronze L. 610 cm. (Courtesy of the Art Gallery of Ontario)

PUBLIC ART GALLERIES

Art Gallery of Ontario
317 Dundas St. W. at McCaul
977-0414

Canada's largest, and boasting the highest per capita membership of any art gallery in North America, the AGO is famous for its permanent collection and its Henry Moore Sculpture Centre. The AGO is home to more than 11,000 works including many fine Canadian pieces. Emily Carr, Cornelius Kreighoff, Homer Watson and the Group of Seven are displayed along with Picasso, Renoir, Degas, Rembrandt, Rubens and Van Dyck. The Henry Moore Sculpture Centre displays the world's largest public collection of Moore's works and should be on everyone's must-see list.

The gallery is constantly offering special exhibitions and major international shows. Phone to find out what's in town.

The AGO houses a fine restaurant, coffee shop, gift shop and an art rental and sales gallery.

By TTC exit at St. Patrick subway station and walk or take the 505 streetcar 3 blocks west on Dundas St. You'll know you're there when you see Moore's huge *Two Forms* sculpture on the corner. Open daily 11 A.M. to 5:30

ART GALLERY OF ONTARIO

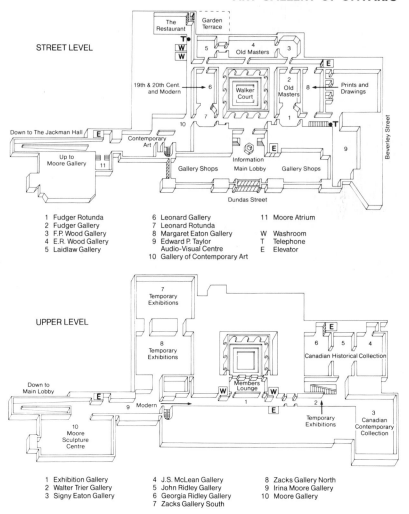

STREET LEVEL

1 Fudger Rotunda
2 Fudger Gallery
3 F.P. Wood Gallery
4 E.R. Wood Gallery
5 Laidlaw Gallery

6 Leonard Gallery
7 Leonard Rotunda
8 Margaret Eaton Gallery
9 Edward P. Taylor
   Audio-Visual Centre
10 Gallery of Contemporary Art

11 Moore Atrium

W Washroom
T Telephone
E Elevator

UPPER LEVEL

1 Exhibition Gallery
2 Walter Trier Gallery
3 Signy Eaton Gallery

4 J.S. McLean Gallery
5 John Ridley Gallery
6 Georgia Ridley Gallery
7 Zacks Gallery South

8 Zacks Gallery North
9 Irina Moore Gallery
10 Moore Gallery

P.M., Wed until 9 P.M. Closed Mon from early Sept until mid-May. Wheelchair accessible. Admission: family $7, adults $3.50, students and seniors $1.50, accompanied children under 12 free. Everyone free Wed evening; seniors free Fri.

Admission to the AGO allows you to enter one of Toronto's finest historic homes, The Grange, located directly south of the gallery. See Sightseeing/Historic Sites.

The staircase in The Grange. (Courtesy of the Art Gallery of Ontario)

10 AGO BESTS
Dr. Roald Nasgaard
Chief Curator, Art Gallery of Ontario

1. **Frans Hals,** *Isaak Abrahamsz Massa,* 1626
2. **Claude Lorrain,** *Carlo and Ubaldo Embarking in Pursuit of Renaldo,* 1667
3. **Thomas Gainsborough,** *The Harvest Wagon,* c.1784
4. **Camille Pissarro,** *Le Pont Boieldieu à Rouen Temps Mouille,* 1896
5. **Pablo Picasso,** *Nude with Clasped Hands,* 1905–6
6. **Augustus John,** *The Marchesa Casati,* 1918–19
7. **Lawren Harris,** *Above Lake Superior,* c.1922
8. **Paul-Emile Borduas,** *Black and White Composition,* 1956
9. **The Henry Moore Collection**
10. **Claes Oldenburg,** *Giant Hamburger,* 1962

Henry Moore (British 1898–1986). The Henry Moore Sculpture Centre. Original plasters. (Courtesy of the Art Gallery of Ontario)

This gallery at the McMichael houses the "Raven's Work"—an exhibition of historical Northwest Coast Indian art. (Photo by John Reeves)

The McMichael Canadian Collection
Islington Ave., Kleinburg
893-2787

Truly one of Canada's national treasures, the building and the grounds alone are worth the visit. The cathedral-like squared-log and fieldstone structure contains 7400 m² (80,000 sq.ft.) of exhibition space. The exclusively Canadian collection emphasizes the works of the famous Group of Seven, but other artists are also represented. The second-floor exhibits of Canadian Indian and Inuit art should not be overlooked.

The 40-ha (100-acre) grounds along the banks of the Humber River are a perfect place for contemplative walks. Along the entrance drive on a little knoll is the burying ground of most members of the Group of Seven. There is a very good gift shop, and stop in at the restaurant for fabulous scones with jam and cream. And if you have the time, you should stroll down the main street of historic Kleinburg.

10 CURATOR'S FAVOURITES
Ian Thom
Curator, The McMichael
Canadian Collection

1. **Lawren Harris,** *Mount Lefroy*
2. **David Milne,** *Black*
3. **A. Y. Jackson,** *First Snow, Algoma*
4. **Arthur Lismer,** *In My Studio*
5. **artist unknown,** *Tlingit Dying Warrior Maskette*
6. **Emily Carr,** *Shoreline*
7. **Franklin Carmichael,** *Winter Hillside*
8. **J. E. H. MacDonald,** *Leaves in the Brook*
9. **Tom Thomson,** *Byng Inlet, Georgian Bay*
10. **Joe Talirunilli,** *Migration*

McMichael

CANADIAN ART COLLECTION D'ART CANADIEN

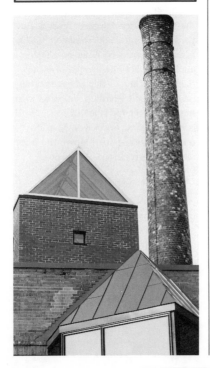

By car take Hwy. 400 north to Major Mackenzie Dr. and turn west to the village of Kleinburg. By TTC exit at Islington subway station and take the 37 bus north to Steeles Ave. Vaughan Transit buses run from there into Kleinburg. Phone 832-2281 for connecting bus times.

From 1 May through 31 Oct, open daily 10 A.M. to 5 P.M., Sun until 6:30 P.M. From 1 Nov through 30 April, open Tues to Sun 11:30 A.M. to 4:30 P.M., closed Mon. Admission: adults $3, students and seniors $1.50, children under 5 free; seniors free Wed.

The Power Plant
Harbourfront
231 Queen's Quay W.
973-4949
Toronto's newest public art gallery. Its mandate is to exhibit contemporary Canadian art with a particular interest in showing innovative and experimental work. Open Tues to Sat noon to 8 P.M., Sun noon to 6 P.M. Free admission.

The Toronto Sculpture Garden
115 King St. E. at Church
485-9658
This outdoor sculpture garden showcases contemporary works designed for the site. Situated directly across from historic St. James' Cathedral, just 3 short blocks east of King St. subway station. The terrace of the neighbouring La Maquette restaurant is a pleasant spot if you want to enjoy the garden over a meal or a drink. Open daily until dusk. Free admission.

Contemporary Canadian art is showcased at the Power Plant. (Harbourfront Corporation)

MAJOR PRIVATE ART GALLERIES

Toronto's art community is vibrant and vigorous. Private art galleries, many owner-operated, exhibit a wide variety of artworks. Contemporary Canadian artists are especially well represented. Whatever your taste, you will be able to find a gallery to suit you.

Galleries are located all across town. However, many are concentrated in two places, each with its own "feel": chic Upper Yorkville and 80 Spadina Ave., amidst the wholesalers and fabric jobbers. The "At the Galleries" advertisement in the arts section of the *Globe and Mail* (Tues to Sat) is a good place to discover which gallery is showing whom. As well, *NOW* and *Toronto Life* magazines carry weekly gallery listings. Most galleries are closed Sun and Mon and usually open at 10 A.M. other days.

Gallery Moos
136 Yorkville Ave.
near Avenue Rd.
2nd floor
922-0627
Contemporary Canadian, American and European painting, sculpture and graphics. New shows every three weeks are usually solo exhibitions. Gallery artists have included Danby, Etrog, Chagall, Moore, Miro and Picasso.

Galerie Dresdnere
12 Hazelton Ave. near Yorkville
923-4662
Contemporary and historical Canadian art as well as international master graphics. Artists have included Riopelle, Borduas, the Group of Seven, Christo and Bacon.

Mira Godard Gallery
22 Hazelton Ave. near Scollard
964-8197
Contemporary Canadian painting, sculpture and original prints. Artists have included Colville, Tanabe and Lemieux.

Waddington and Shiell Galleries
33 Hazelton Ave. at Scollard
925-2461
Specializes in Canadian and American contemporary art, including Inuit carvings.

The Sable-Castelli Gallery
33 Hazelton Ave. at Scollard
(lower level)
961-0011
Contemporary Canadian and international art. Artists have included Fischl and Craven.

Ballenford Architectural Books
98 Scollard St. near Bay
960-0055
This bookstore often exhibits original architectural drawings and models.

Gallery One
121 Scollard St. near Bay
929-3103
Contemporary Canadian and international painting and sculpture including extensive Inuit and African art departments. Artists have included Frankenthaler, Poons, Drapell and Bush.

The Innuit Gallery of Eskimo Art
9 Prince Arthur Ave.
near Avenue Rd.
921-9985
This gallery was the first to devote itself solely to exhibiting work by Arctic artists and is now generally believed to be the finest gallery of Inuit art in North

The Innuit Gallery of Eskimo Art, Toronto

America. Sculpture, limited edition prints, drawings and wall-hangings are always in stock. Monthly exhibitions feature different artists or Inuit themes.

Kaspar Gallery
27 Prince Arthur Ave.
near Avenue Rd.
968-2536
Contemporary Canadian art as well as 19th-century historical oils and watercolours.

The Isaacs Gallery
179 John St. near Queen W.
595-0770
Primarily concerned with contemporary Canadian painting, sculpture and works on paper with a particular interest in early North American Indian art. Artists have included Kurelek, Snow and Wieland.

Jane Corkin Gallery
179 John St. near Queen W.
3rd floor
979-1980
Contemporary and historical fine art photography with some ceramic and sculpture work.

Klonaridis
179 John St. near Queen W.
2nd floor
979-1090
Contemporary Canadian and international abstract painting and sculpture.

Olga Korper Gallery
80 Spadina Ave. near King W.
4th floor
363-5268
Contemporary Canadian sculpture, painting and works on paper. Artists have included Comtois, Averbuch and Thurlbeck.

Wynick/Tuck Gallery
80 Spadina Ave. near King W.
4th floor
364-8716
Contemporary Canadian painting, sculpture and works on paper.

Bau-Xi Gallery
340 Dundas St. W.
near University
977-0600
Directly across from the Art Gallery of Ontario, this gallery specializes in contemporary Canadian painting, original prints and drawings. Work by Shadbolt and Plaskett, among others, is available here.

Roberts Gallery
641 Yonge St. near Bloor
924-8731
Founded in 1842, this is the oldest commercial art gallery in Canada. It deals exclusively in contemporary Canadian art and has represented, among others, Group of Seven member A.J. Casson throughout his career.

Carmen Lamanna Gallery
788 King St. W. near Bathurst
363-8787
Contemporary Canadian painting and sculpture. Artists have included Ewen and Collyer.

S. L. Simpson Gallery
515 Queen St. W. near Spadina
362-3738
Contemporary Canadian experimental works of art. Multimedia painting, sculpture and works on paper. Artists have included Van Halm, Spero and Charlesworth.

Odon Wagner Gallery
194 Davenport Rd.
near Avenue Rd.
962-0438
Traditional works of art featuring European painting of the 18th, 19th, and 20th centuries. Prices range from $5,000 to over $150,000.

Interference Hologram Gallery
1179A King St. W. near Dufferin
Suite 008
535-2323
This nonprofit organization is one of the very few galleries in North America that exhibits holographic art exclusively. You can watch a twenty-minute educational video that describes the art of holography or simply view the current exhibition. The gallery features Canadian and international artists. Open Wed to Sat noon to 6 P.M.

The Animation Gallery
1977 Queen St. E. near Woodbine
2nd floor
691-4105
The first gallery of its kind in Canada devoted exclusively to the exhibition and promotion of original animation art. If you've been looking for original hand-painted production artwork of your favourite animated character, such as Casper the Friendly Ghost, Fred Flintstone, George Jetson or Mickey Mouse, this is the place to visit.

PRINT SHOPS

Marci Lipman Graphics
231 Avenue Rd. near Dupont
922-7061
Fine art posters, custom framing, limited edition prints and unique handmade gifts.

The Allery
322½ Queen St. W. near Spadina
593-0853
Mainly 18th- and 19th-century original prints.

AUCTION HOUSES

D&J Ritchie
429 Richmond St. E.
near Parliament
364-1864
Catalogue sales are held every five to six weeks and usually run over several consecutive nights. Items are generally of high quality and most times include jewellery, antiques, Oriental rugs and paintings. Walk-around sales occur usually one Sat a month and feature 20th-century items of lesser value.

Gallery Sixty-Eight Auctions
3 Southvale Dr. near Bayview
421-7614
Specializing in 19th- and early 20th-century artworks, this auction house has a particular interest in the art deco period. Catalogue sales are held usually every six weeks.

Robert Deveau Galleries
297–299 Queen St. E.
near Sherbourne
364-6271
This gallery deals primarily in fine art and antiques. Once a month a Persian and Oriental carpet sale is held, and once every two months an estate auction takes place. By appointment only.

Waddington-McLean and Co.
189 Queen St. E. near Jarvis
362-1678
Canada's oldest auction house, founded in 1850, holds sales every week on Wed and Sat at 9:30 A.M. Items run the gamut from household goods to Victoriana. Catalogue sales are held twice a year, when higher-quality paintings, antiques, Oriental rugs and collectibles go on the block.

Sotheby's of Canada
9 Hazelton Ave. near Yorkville
926-1774
World-renowned for fine art and estate auctions, Sotheby's 1987 Canadian sales set price records for works by Krieghoff, Harris and Riopelle, to name a few. Auctions are held twice a year at the Four Seasons Hotel at Bloor and Avenue Rd. Phone for auction dates.

ENTERTAINMENT/CULTURE 9

HOW TO BUY TICKETS

Each year, 5 million people attend dance, music and theatre performances in Toronto. There are several options for purchasing tickets. You can go directly to the theatre box offices, which generally open at 10 A.M., and choose from the remaining tickets right up until the start of each show.

Or you can buy your tickets over the phone (with VISA or MasterCard) from the following ticketing services, used by most of the larger productions. The tickets will be mailed to you or else held for pick-up, at one of their many outlets scattered across the city.

Ticket Master Teletix (formerly BASS) 872-1111
Mon to Fri 9:30 A.M. to 9 P.M., Sat 9:30 A.M. to 6 P.M., Sun noon to 6 P.M.

Ticketron Teletron 872-1212
Mon to Fri 9 A.M. to 8 P.M., Sat 9 A.M. to 6 P.M.

For a real entertainment bargain, make your way to the **Five Star Tickets** booth outside the Eaton Centre at the corner of Yonge St. and Dundas or the one in the lobby of the Royal Ontario Museum. They sell half-price tickets to theatre, dance, opera, symphony and popular music concerts on the day of performance. Half-price tickets are available the day *before* the performance for out-of-town theatres such as The Shaw Festival and The Stratford Shakespearean Theatre. All sales are first-come, first-served, cash only, without refunds or exchanges.

Many smaller theatres offer early-week discounts and Sunday PWYC (pay-what-you-can) matinees.

AT THE MOVIES

The Festival of Festivals
Since its inception in 1975, Toronto's annual Festival of Festivals has been recognized by audiences, film makers and critics as quite simply one of the best film festivals in the world. The festival premieres, with stunning success, over 250 of the world's most original and engaging films.

The festival runs for slightly over a week, beginning the first Thurs after Labour Day (early Sept). Tickets are available for single performances, gala evenings, film series, and in sets of 10. You can even have fun—for free—watching the passing parade of stars outside the gala premieres. For information call the Festival Box Office at 968-FILM (open July to the end of the festival).

FIRST-RUN

Toronto is clearly a movie-lover's town—just look at the line-ups at the abundance of movie theatres. Complete movie listings are provided every day in the *Globe and Mail* and Toronto *Star* entertainment sections.

The best movie buy of the week is Cineplex Odeon's $3.50 Tuesdays.

RERUN AND REPERTORY

Toronto is fortunate to have five downtown independent theatres, which show movies ranging from recent runs to nostalgics at prices below the major chains. Many shows are one-night-only, and sometimes a theme week is featured, such as all sci-fi, Japanese-directed films, or Bogart movies.

You'll find listings daily in the "Independent Movie Guide" in the *Globe and Mail*, weekly in *NOW* magazine and by the month in the *Festival* newspaper available at the repertory theatres.

**The Bloor Cinema
506 Bloor St. W. near Bathurst
532-6677**

**The Fox Beaches
2236 Queen St. E. near Woodbine
691-7330**

The Kingsway Theatre
and **The Nostalgic
3030 Bloor St. W.
near Royal York Rd.
236-1411**

**Revue Cinema
400 Roncesvalles Ave.
near Dundas W.
531-9959**

SPOKEN WORDS

Readings at Harbourfront

This reading series affords a rare glimpse into the literary work of a vast number of Canadian and international authors, who often read from their newly published or in-progress work. Readings take place every Tues night throughout the year (except over Christmas and during the International Festival of Authors in Oct), at Harbourfront. Phone 973-4000 to confirm program and location. A yearly membership means great discounts on Special Events tickets and free admission to regular readings. Otherwise each reading costs about $5.

The International Festival of Authors

Solidly established as North America's premiere gathering of authors, this festival celebrates a wealth of literary talent with more than a week of readings at Harbourfront. Such bright lights as John Irving, Joyce Carol Oates, Nadine Gordimer, Robertson Davies and Alice Munro have read at past festivals along with the finest European and Latin American authors.

You can buy single tickets or a "Collected Works" pass for all readings. Phone 973-4000 for information.

Chapters Bookstore Café
**2360 Yonge St. near Eglinton
481-2474**
Most Mon evenings Chapters serves dinner followed by a reading or talk by a selected author, for about $15. Admission to just the reading is about $5. It's a good idea to make reservations.

THEATRE

Toronto is North America's third largest producer of live theatre after New York and Chicago. The variety is endless, from crowd-pleasing Broadway musicals and Neil Simon comedies to the noncommercial, often exotic and controversial small theatre productions.

Of special note is the **World Stage** theatre festival, which takes place every other year at Harbourfront. The 1988 festival included presentations from Japan, Russia, Czechoslovakia and Yugoslavia as well as North American and European plays. Phone 973-3000 for information.

Royal Alexandra Theatre
260 King St. W. near Simcoe
593-4211
In 1906 Cawthra Mullock, a 21-year-old Toronto millionaire, hired architect John Lyle (of Union Station fame) to design the finest theatre on the continent. The result was a sumptuous 1500-seat beaux-arts masterpiece featuring North America's first cantilevered balconies and an interior finished with European silks and velvets, rose and cherry woods and marble.

Mullock further distinguished his theatre by obtaining from King Edward VII a patent naming his consort, the Princess Alexandra of Denmark, as patron, thereby permitting Mullock to display the royal coat of arms and call his theatre "Royal."

The Royal Alex brought the finest British and American stage stars to Toronto while encouraging home-grown Canadian talent. The fortunes of the theatre declined after World War II

Royal Alexandra Theatre. (Drawing by Chris Darling)

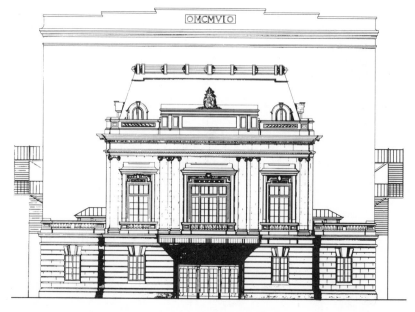

SEATING ARRANGEMENT

THE 🏛 NEW

ROYAL ALEXANDRA THEATRE

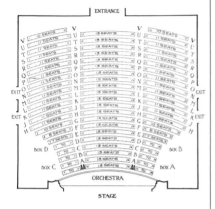

until, in 1963, "Honest Ed" Mirvish intervened and restored it to its former splendour. It has been a success ever since, and audiences can once again enjoy the best live theatre performances.

By subway exit at St. Andrew and walk 1 block west.

O'Keefe Centre
1 Front St. E. at Yonge
393-7469

The O'Keefe had an auspicious beginning in October 1960 when it premiered *Camelot* starring Richard Burton, Robert Goulet and Julie Andrews. With 3200 seats, this is one of the largest proscenium theatres in North America and one of the few theatres in Toronto that can stage full-scale Broadway shows and musicals. It is the home of the National Ballet of Canada and the Canadian Opera Company.

By subway exit at Union Station and walk 1 block east.

St. Lawrence Centre
27 Front St. E. near Yonge
366-7723

The St. Lawrence Centre houses the 890-seat Bluma Appel Theatre and the 498-seat Jane Mallett Theatre. Film, music, dance and theatre occur in this versatile performance space throughout the year. The Canadian Stage Company, Theatre Plus and Music Toronto regularly present their artistry here.

By subway exit at Union Station and walk 2 blocks east.

BLUMA APPEL THEATRE

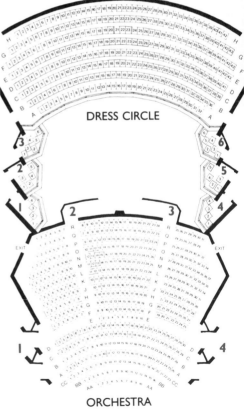

ORCHESTRA

St. Lawrence Centre for the Arts

ROY THOMSON HALL

Balcony Level

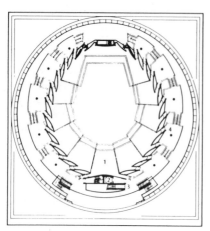

1 Seating section
2 Elevator
3 Escalators
4 Access galleries

Mezzanine Level

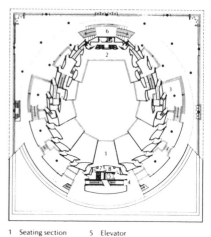

1 Seating section
2 Choir seating area
3 Access galleries
4 Escalators
5 Elevator
6 Open staircases
7 Lighting booth
8 Sound booth

Main Floor

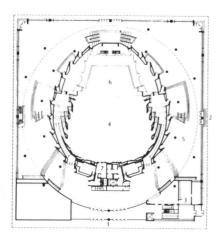

1 Simcoe Street entrance
2 King Street entrance
3 Box office
4 Seating section
5 Lobby
6 Stage
7 Projection booth

Musicians' Level

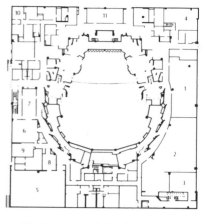

1 RTH offices
2 Symphony offices
3 TMC offices
4 TS library
5 Rehearsal hall
6 Board room
7 Green room
8 Recording
9 Catering
10 Artists' rooms
11 Lounge

Roy Thomson Hall
60 Simcoe St. at King
593-4828

Canadian Arthur Erickson's design features a distinctive swooping curtain wall of reflective glass. Since its inaugural performance in 1982, Roy Thomson Hall has been acclaimed for its acoustic acuity and its elegant interior spaces. All 2812 seats enjoy unobstructed views. As well as performances by the resident Toronto Symphony Orchestra and Toronto Mendelssohn Choir, popular music concerts are often held here.

By subway exit at St. Andrew and walk 1 block west. Underground parking for 400 cars.

Roy Thomson Hall

Massey Hall
178 Victoria St. at Shuter
363-7301

Toronto's venerable Massey Music Hall opened its doors in 1894, a gift from one of Toronto's most philanthropic families, who had amassed a fortune from their farm equipment company, Massey-Ferguson.

Massey Hall is filled with history. For nearly a century people have gathered here to discuss politics, watch boxing matches, enjoy the high arts or take religion. Sir Winston Churchill and David Lloyd George spoke here, Isadora Duncan danced here, Charles Laughton read here, and Robert Perry and Captain Amundsen described their explorations of the North and South poles to spellbound audiences here. Enrico Caruso once sang from the fire escape to the crowds who couldn't fit into the sold-out concert hall.

Courtesy of David Crighton © 1989

MASSEY HALL

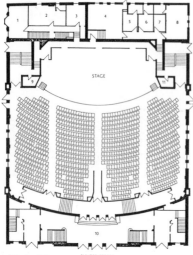

Main Floor

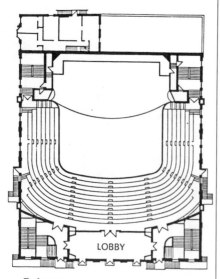

Balcony

It's now showing its age, but Massey Hall is still known for its excellent acoustics. Although the once resident Toronto Mendelssohn Choir and Toronto Symphony Orchestra have moved to Roy Thomson Hall, a wide range of music and entertainment is still available in Toronto's original concert hall. In 1985 Massey Hall was designated a National Historic Site, ensuring that this significant part of Toronto's—indeed Canada's—heritage will not be lost.

By subway exit at the north end of the Queen St. stop and walk a short distance east on Shuter to Victoria.

**Elgin and Winter Garden Theatres
189–191 Yonge St. near Queen**
Situated on different levels of the same building, both theatres were built in 1913 to showcase vaudeville acts. Designated a National Historic Site, the theatres are now undergoing extensive renovation and restoration. Great

lengths are being taken to recreate the unique Eden-like atmosphere of the original Winter Garden, the only remaining theatre of its kind in the world. The ceiling will be covered, as it once was, with 15,000 real beech boughs, and the gardenesque wall murals will be brought back to their original splendour. When they reopen in fall 1989, the 1600-seat Elgin and the 1000-seat Winter Garden theatres will feature Canadian theatre as well as popular touring shows.

Pantages Theatre
244 Victoria St. near Shuter

Built in 1920, in an age when movie houses were designed in the grand theatre tradition, the Pantages is being restored to its former opulence and will reopen in fall 1989 as a 2100-seat live theatre venue. The inaugural production will be *The Phantom of the Opera*.

The 1600-seat Elgin Theatre has recently been restored to its former grandeur. (Photo by Panda Associates)

Pantages' inaugural performance—The Phantom of the Opera. (Photo by Clive Barda/Bob Marshak)

An early 1920s photograph of the interior of the Pantages Theatre. (Courtesy: Cineplex Odeon)

SMALLER THEATRES

Actor's Lab Theatre
155A George St. near Jarvis
363-2853
Highly experimental and often out-
rageous theatre performances from a
Toronto-based company that has
toured throughout the U.S. and Europe.

Alumnae Theatre
70 Berkeley St. at Adelaide E.
364-4170
Founded in 1918 by women graduates
at University College, this company still
looks for scripts with strong women's
roles for their annual seven-play season.
There are two small performance
spaces in this renovated 1900s fire hall,
with somewhat more experimental
work performed in the upstairs studio.

Bathurst St. Theatre
736 Bathurst St. near Bloor
588-6800
Innovative dance troupes, concerts
featuring international recording artists,
and a range of theatre companies perform in this 600-seat refurbished church
throughout the year.

Bayview Playhouse
1605 Bayview Ave. near Eglinton
481-6191
Popular comedies and musicals play
year-round in this 500-seat theatre.

Skylight Theatre
Earl Bales Park
4169 Bathurst St.
630-4868
This Greek-style outdoor amphitheatre
seats 1500 and presents performances
under the stars throughout the summer.

Ryerson Theatre
43 Gerrard St. near Yonge
977-1055
Dance, theatre, music and film have all
been presented at this 1250-seat
theatre.

Berkeley St. Theatre
26 Berkeley St. near Front E.
368-2856

The home of the Canadian Stage Company. The upstairs performance space seats 180, and downstairs seats 260.

The Canadian Stage Company
26 Berkeley St.
362-7041

This acclaimed theatre company annually presents a free "Dream in High Park" play to outdoor audiences in the park just east of the Grenadier Restaurant (arrive at least an hour before the show and take a picnic), as well as a wide range of theatrical performances at the St. Lawrence Centre and the Berkeley St. Theatre.

Crowds at The Canadian Stage Company's annual theatrical production of The Dream in High Park. (Photo by Michael Cooper)

Du Maurier Theatre Centre
Harbourfront
231 Queen's Quay W.
973-3000

A multipurpose performance space designed to accommodate various art forms. It features wonderful acoustics, a moveable stage, wraparound balconies and a 300-seat house. Several performing arts series are presented throughout the year.

Factory Theatre
125 Bathurst St. at Adelaide
864-9971

Contemporary Canadian plays staged in a 1910 concert hall. An excellent showcase for up-and-coming talent.

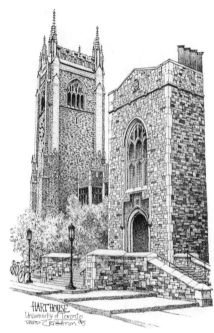

Courtesy of David Crighton © 1989

Hart House Theatre
7 Hart House Circle
(U of T campus)
978-8668

Apart from the Royal Alexandra, Hart House is the oldest operating theatre in Toronto: it opened in 1919 in one of the U of T's most beautiful buildings. A variety of theatre companies perform here year-round.

Leah Posluns Theatre
4588 Bathurst St. near Sheppard
630-6752

This ultramodern 500-seat facility offers a popular five-play series from Oct through May. Internationally known artists are often featured.

Poor Alex Theatre
296 Brunswick Ave. near Bloor W.
927-8998

A small, intimate space with three resident companies: Theatre Columbus, Crow's Theatre and Theatre Smith-Gilmour. All are known for staging original Canadian works.

Studio Theatre
Harbourfront
235 Queen's Quay W.
973-4000

An intimate performance space, seating 200.

Tarragon Theatre
30 Bridgman Ave. near Bathurst
531-1827

The home of vital new works by Canadian playwrights. David French, Michel Tremblay and Mavis Gallant have premiered their plays here. A nine-play series is offered each year to audiences who have come to expect exciting, high-quality performances.

Theatre Français
534-6604

Appearing primarily at the Du Maurier Theatre Centre at Harbourfront, this French-language company performs everything from contemporary Michel Tremblay to classic Molière.

Theatre Passe Muraille
16 Ryerson Ave. near Queen W.
363-2416

One of the best smaller theatres in the country. For over 20 years Passe Muraille has consistently contributed to the repertoire of outstanding original Canadian plays. Its small, intimate theatre bar is one of the best in town.

Young People's Theatre (YPT)
See With the Kids/Entertainment

OUT-OF-TOWN THEATRE

**The Stratford Shakespearean
Festival
Stratford
(519) 271-1600
363-4471 toll free from Toronto**
An international reputation is enjoyed
by the largest and most celebrated classical repertory theatre in North America. Though best-known for its Shake-
speare productions, the festival company does present the works of other
dramatists as well. The festival annually
attracts over half a million visitors, and
to many Canadians a trip to Stratford
has become a yearly ritual. Leave yourself enough time for a walk beside the
picturesque River Avon.

*David Schurmann, Christopher Newton and Al
Kozlik in the Shaw Festival production of* Peter
Pan. *(Photo by David Cooper)*

**The Shaw Festival
Niagara-on-the-Lake
(416) 468-2172
361-1544 toll free from Toronto**
From April to mid-Oct every year the
world-renowned Shaw Festival presents
stunning performances of the works of
Bernard Shaw and other playwrights at
three venues in Canada's
"Williamsburg." An integral part of the
Shaw Festival experience is a leisurely
stroll down the main street of this historic lakeside town.

The Guelph Spring Festival
See Sightseeing/Calendar of Events

The Canadian Opera company's Joey and Toby Tanenbaum Centre.

CLASSICAL MUSIC

The Canadian Opera Company
363-6671

The fifth largest producer of opera in North America, the COC has performed over 90 operas in Toronto alone since its inception in 1950. Under the artistic direction of Lotfi Mansouri (1976–88), audiences have been presented with many Canadian and North American premieres, and the company's touring has brought it further international recognition. In 1983 the COC pioneered the use of surtitles, projecting libretto translations onto a screen above the stage. This, while perhaps upsetting purists, has certainly helped to broaden the base of the opera audience.

The company presents their season of seven operas at the O'Keefe Centre from Oct to June. Chamber productions and rehearsals take place at the Joey and Toby Tanenbaum Centre, at the corner of Berkeley St. and Front St. E.

The Toronto Symphony
Orchestra
593-7769

Prospering under the musical direction of Andrew Davis from 1975 to 1988, the TSO has toured Europe, the Far East, the U.S. and Canada. At home it has built a following that now supports ambitious performance seasons and extensive touring schedules. In his new role as conductor laureate, Davis continues to oversee the development of classical and pop series, offered each year from Sept to June in Roy Thomson Hall. Subscription tickets are available through the Toronto Symphony Ticket Centre at 598-3375.

The Toronto Mendelssohn Choir
598-0422

The Mendelssohn Choir, directed by El-
mer Iseler, is perhaps the finest choral
ensemble of its kind in North America.
Since its first concert, in 1895 in Massey
Hall, the 190-voice choir has gathered
accolades from around the world. Touring in Canada, the States and Europe has
brought international fame, and its recordings of Handel's *Messiah* and Bach's
St. Matthew Passion are choral classics.

Torontonians are fortunate in being
able to hear the choir regularly perform
at Roy Thomson Hall. The ensemble's
annual *Messiah* is one of the city's favourite Christmas traditions.

The Elmer Iseler Singers
971-9723

The 20-voice Iseler Singers are noted
for their extensive choral repertoire,
which spans five centuries. They present
concerts throughout Canada, the U.S.
and Europe and, as the professional core
of the Toronto Mendelssohn Choir,
perform regularly at world festivals.

The Canadian Brass
967-1421

Concerts presented by this quintet tend
to be quite accessible, partly because
the members mix their considerable
musical talents with a zany sense of hu-
mour and partly because the musical
programs are eclectic, moving easily
from Bach and Mozart to Gershwin and
dixieland. Performing on 24-carat gold-
plated instruments, the ensemble has
recorded some 20 disks and has toured

The Canadian Brass
*The Toronto Symphony—Gunther Herbig, Mu-
sic Director Designate*

Tafelmusik Baroque Orchestra—Jean Lamon, Music Director

Opera Atelier

widely, attracting a large international following that demands over 100 concert dates a year.

The Orford String Quartet
861-8600

Since its founding in 1965 at Quebec's Orford Arts Centre, this internationally acclaimed group has given more than 2000 concerts in over 300 cities. It has recorded over 40 disks, including an outstanding complete cycle of the Beethoven string quartets. Every spring the quartet presents a series at Harbourfront.

U of T Faculty of Music
80 Queen's Park Cres.
978-3744

Recitals and concerts performed by music students and faculty feature symphony orchestras, choral and operatic groups, guitar ensembles and jazz bands among others. Prices are very low. A free noon-hour series is held most Thurs, featuring film, lectures and chamber music. At the Edward Johnson Building, 80 Queen's Park.

Tafelmusik Baroque Orchestra
964-6337

This orchestra performs and records Baroque music on original instruments. They have toured internationally and present a series of 10 concerts from Sept to May at Trinity-St. Paul's Church, 427 Bloor St. W.

Opera Atelier
234-9366

A Baroque opera/ballet company that receives great reviews wherever they play. The group strives for authenticity —the operas are performed by candle-light, original instruments are used whenever possible, and costumes and set designs are lavish. They stage an opera each spring and fall at the MacMillan theatre in the Edward Johnson Building, 80 Queen's Park.

The Chamber Players of Toronto
862-8311

This is Toronto's longest-standing professional string orchestra. They play classical music from many periods and usually feature a guest soloist at each concert. A series of six concerts is presented at the St. Lawrence Centre's Jane Mallett Theatre.

Nexus
971-9723

This world-renowned percussion group performs classical and contemporary music. They tour widely as a chamber music group and with major symphony orchestras.

CHURCH RECITALS

The following downtown churches offer free lunch-time recitals—a great escape in the middle of a busy day.

St. Paul's Anglican Church
227 Bloor St. E. at Jarvis
961-8116
Thurs 12:10 to 12:35 P.M., Oct to May

St. James' Cathedral
65 Church St. at King
364-7865
Tues 1 to 1:30 P.M., Sept to June

Metropolitan United Church
Queen St. E. at Church
363-0331
Thurs 12:30 to 1:30 P.M., July and Aug

OUT-OF-TOWN CLASSICAL MUSIC

Music at Sharon
(416) 478-2389

A classical music series is presented each July at the historic Sharon Temple in Sharon (near Newmarket). The acoustics are superb in this beautiful temple. Take a picnic and make it a day trip. Also see Sightseeing/Out-of-Town Attractions.

The Guelph Spring Festival
See Sightseeing/Calendar of Events

DANCE

Premiere Dance Theatre (PDT)
Harbourfront
Queen's Quay Terminal
973-4000

The Premiere Dance Theatre is the only theatre in Canada designed specifically for dance. A fabulous 16-week dance series is presented between Sept and May. The programming usually includes American and European artists as well as superb Canadian talent. The PDT often takes risks in providing a forum for new and innovative work.

The National Ballet of Canada
362-1041

Recognized as one of the world's best classical ballet companies, the National has also been garnering critical acclaim of late for its contemporary dance repertoire. As artistic director from 1983 until his death in 1986, Erik Bruhn encouraged the creation of new works for the company by young and inventive choreographers such as Robert Desrosiers, Danny Grossman and David Earle.

The National Ballet of Canada: Gizella Wit-kowsky in Swan Lake *(left) and Owen Montague in* Don Quixote *(right). (Courtesy David Street/The National Ballet of Canada)*

The National's season runs from Nov to May at the O'Keefe Centre and usually features seven to nine full-length ballets. Attending their Christmas presentation of *The Nutcracker* has become for many a family tradition.

CONTEMPORARY DANCE

The dance scene in Toronto is one of creative ferment, with exciting works by bold new choreographers being produced at an amazing rate. You can count on the performances of the companies listed here to be athletic, theatrical, sometimes jarring but always breathtaking. In particular, the work of award-winning choreographers Robert Desrosiers, Danny Grossman, Randy Glynn and Paula Moreno should not be missed.

The Randy Glynn Dance Project *performing* Kyrie. *(Photo by Cylla Von Tiedemann)*

Danny Grossman Dance Company performing
La Valse (Photo by Cylla Von Tiedemann)

The Paula Moreno Spanish Dance Company

Denise Fujiwara of Toronto Independent Dance Enterprise. (Photo by Stephen Katz)

Desrosiers Dance Theatre
362-0756

Danny Grossman Dance Theatre
531-8350

The Randy Glynn Dance Project
920-7463

The Paula Moreno Spanish Dance Company
924-6991

Toronto Independent Dance Enterprise (T.I.D.E.)
365-1039

Toronto Dance Theatre
967-1365

Dancemakers
535-8880

Danceworks
534-1523

Canadian Children's Dance Theatre
924-5657

Members of the Canadian Children's Dance Theatre performing Figure Painting. (Photo by Cylla Von Tiedemann)

NIGHTLIFE 10

Complete entertainment listings are in *NOW* magazine, *Metropolis* and Friday's Toronto *Star.*

JAZZ

Albert's Hall
481 Bloor St. W. near Bathurst
964-2242
The hall is directly above the Brunswick Tavern. Without a doubt, the place to go for the best blues in the city.

Café des Copains
48 Wellington St. E. near Yonge
869-0148
Live jazz downstairs Thurs to Sat.

Chick 'n' Deli
744 Mt. Pleasant Rd.
near Eglinton
489-3363
Uptown jazz live on Sat. Patio in summer. Usually crowded.

George's Spaghetti House
290 Dundas St. E.
near Sherbourne
923-9887
A Toronto jazz institution made famous by celebrity jazz musicians the likes of Moe Koffman, Don Thompson and Ed Bickert. Mon to Sat.

Meyers Deli
69 Yorkville Ave. near Bay
960-4780
185 King St. W. near University
593-4190
Live late-night jazz Tues to Sat. Full deli menu to boot. Line-ups most nights. Dancing.

New York Hotel
1150 Queen St. W.
near Dovercourt
533-0046
Live jazz Mon to Wed.

Trader's Lounge
The Sheraton Centre
123 Queen St. W. at Bay
361-1000
Sat afternoon jazz.

Also
Beaton's, see Night Clubs/Lounges
Clinton Tavern, see Pubs and Bars

NIGHT CLUBS/LOUNGES

Beaton's, The Westbury Hotel
475 Yonge St. near Carlton
924-0611
Live high-gloss pop and polished local acts. A popular retreat after Maple Leaf Gardens. Also live jazz with Sun brunch.

Notes Piano Lounge
The Brownstone Hotel
15 Charles St. E. at Yonge
924-7381
The Yorkville crowd. Casual atmosphere. Piano stylings.

PWD
88 Yorkville Ave. near Bay
923-9689
Yorkville night club. Latin rhythms, soca and dancing.

A NICE QUIET BAR

Bosun's Bar, The Hotel Admiral
249 Queen's Quay W.
near Spadina
364-5444
Nautical motif in this bar with a beautiful view of the waterfront. Nightly piano music.

The Bottom Line
17 Yorkville Ave. at Yonge
968-2911
In the heart of Yorkville. Friendly atmosphere and good food.

Club 22, Windsor Arms Hotel
22 St. Thomas St. near Bloor W.
979-2341
Piano stylings at night. An elegant bar in one of Toronto's oldest and most distinguished hotels. Just next to the Courtyard Café, Club 22 is frequented by members of Toronto's entertainment scene.

Consort Bar, King Edward Hotel
37 King St. E. near Yonge
863-9700
Elegant and quiet, with piano at night.

The Library Bar
Royal York Hotel
100 Front St. W. at York
368-6175
Quiet and relaxed, with the large, comfortable chairs you'd expect in a private library and, of course, lots of books.

The Lion Dog
The Long Bar
The Sheraton Centre
123 Queen St. W. at Bay
361-1000
The Lion Dog is a comfortable cross between a British pub and a library bar. The Long Bar houses the longest stand-up bar in Metro and has excellent views over the Nathan Phillips Square nightscape.

The Skylight Lounge, L'Hotel
225 Front St. W.
near University
597-1400
Beautiful atrium surroundings with lots of large benjamina fig trees.

Also see Restaurants—Centro Grill and Wine Bar (Italian)

PUBS AND BARS

PUBS

Toronto's British heritage exhibits itself in the number of British-style pubs, great places for the company, the conversation and a Guinness. Most are busy with the regulars. The food is better than what you'd get in the U.K., but if it's good food you're after, see Restaurants/British.

Artful Dodger
12 Isabella Ave. near Yonge
964-9511

Duke of Gloucester
649 Yonge St. near Isabella
961-9704
There are others in the "Dukes" chain downtown—check the Yellow Pages.

Photo by Brian Pel

The Guvnor
1240 Yonge St.
near Summerhill subway
922-9310

The Idler
255 Davenport Rd.
near Avenue Rd.
962-0195

The Jack Russell Pub
27 Wellesley St. E. near Yonge
967-9442

Jersey Giant
71 Front St. E. near Church
368-4095

Madison Avenue
14 Madison Ave. near Bloor W.
927-1722
The Madison has three floors and a variety of rooms, bars, nooks and crannies. Close to U of T, it's a favourite spot for students in search of excellent English beers and pub grub. Great nachos.

Pauper's
539 Bloor St. W. near Bathurst
530-1331

Red Lion
449 Jarvis St. near Carlton
924-8106

The Spotted Dick
81 Bloor St. E. near Yonge
927-0843

The Toad in the Hole
525 King St. W. near Spadina
593-8623

The Unicorn
An Irish Rovers Free House
175 Eglinton Ave. E. near Yonge
482-0115

SINGLES BARS

Most singles bars tend towards the brassy and the flashy with canned music, but they are *very* busy.

Brandy's
58 The Esplanade at Church
364-6671
Yonge-Eglinton Centre
2300 Yonge St. near Eglinton
489-5303
Usually filled to the brim with the Bay St. finance/legal crowd.

Charley's
44 Eglinton Ave. W. near Yonge
486-6665
There are so many singles bars in the Yonge/Eglinton vicinity that locals call the area "Yonge and Singleton." This is just one of them.

Earl's Tin Palace
150 Eglinton Ave. E. near Yonge
487-9281
Another crowded singles bar.

Hector's
49 Eglinton Ave. E.
483-1048
Yet another Yonge and Eglinton singles bar.

Peter's Backyard
214 King St. W. near John
593-1707
Eatery-drinkery.

Scotland Yard
56 The Esplanade at Church
364-6572
Just along from Brandy's. Brokers and lawyers.

Spinnakers
207 Queen's Quay W. at York
362-3406
Located in the renovated Queen's Quay Terminal among the boutiques and shops, Spinnakers overlooks Toronto harbour and the islands.

Also see Restaurants—The Amsterdam Brasserie, The Rotterdam Brewing Company (Brew Pubs), Rhodes (Fast Food/Burgers)

LIVELY BARS

Allen's
143 Danforth Ave.
near Broadview
463-3086
Very popular bar with a comfortable atmosphere, good food and an extensive beer menu.

Black Bull
298 Queen St. W. near Beverley
593-2766
Most of the patrons are nighthawks. Cramped and steamy, the Bull's rough-and-tumble atmosphere, pool table and tiny stage are well loved by the torn-jeans-and-T-shirt crowd.

The Black Swan
154 Danforth Ave.
near Broadview
469-0537
East-side version of the Black Bull. Popular with the baseball crowd.

Courtesy of David Crighton © 1989

The Brunswick Tavern
481 Bloor St. W. near Bathurst
964-2242

Populated by the university crowd, particularly the engineers. Wet T-shirt and beer drinking contests. Albert's Hall upstairs is the best blues room in the city.

Clinton Tavern
693 Bloor St. W. near Christie
535-9541

Off the beaten track with lots of character and lots of great live entertainment. Good Sun afternoon jazz jams.

The Epicure
512 Queen St. W. near Spadina
363-8942

Used to be home base for some of TO's best-known groups such as Parachute Club. Now regularly graced by a liberal sprinkling of theatre types. Good bar to sit and watch the ball game in. Patio in summer.

Free Times Café
320 College St. near Spadina
967-1078

This place is primarily a folk club with character, and they provide the *New York Times* on Sun.

The Gem
1159 Davenport Rd.
near Ossington
654-1182

Just like a U.S. bar. The Gem is one of Toronto's best-kept secrets. (We've spoiled that now!) Eclectic decor, great patio, watering hole for city musicians.

The Hard Rock Café
283 Yonge St. near Dundas
362-3636

A lot of big talent played here in the good old days. While those glories have passed, it remains a popular place.

Hemingways
142 Cumberland St.
near Avenue Rd.
968-2828

In the heart of trendy Yorkville, it has developed a cult following among the advertising set. Is it the famous Leopard Lager or the renowned waitresses? Also Toronto's ANZAC (Australian/New Zealand Activity Club) hangout.

Tijuana Donna's Willow
193 Danforth Ave.
near Broadview
469-5315

Friendly neighbourhood pub in the front and two dining rooms serving primarily Mexican food. A large willow tree in the middle of their patio gives the establishment its name and a lovely setting for summer night drinks.

Also see Restaurants—Bellair Café (Continental), Studebaker's (North American), Don Quijote (Spanish), Bemelmans (Late Night), The Squeeze Club (Pool Halls)

TAP ROOMS

In the Canadian tradition, don't expect many creature comforts in your tap room, and mind the regulars. The following are Toronto classics.

Cameron Public House
408 Queen St. W. near Bathurst
364-0811
The Cameron is historic yet very cool. Those who know that "scuzzy" is a compliment will appreciate the fact that this place is scuzzy. Great decor and real grassroots music at the back.

The Morrissey
817 Yonge St. near Church
923-6191
Always busy. Who hasn't had a draft (or two) at the Morrissey?

The Pilot Tavern
22 Cumberland St. near Bay
923-5716
A shade more stylish than the Morrissey, this venerable and worthy institution has established itself as *the* neighbourhood tap room in town. And they serve Dow ale. Tasty hamburgers too.

The Wheat Sheaf
667 King St. W. near Bathurst
364-3996
The oldest continuously operating tavern in Toronto. Ball teams and regulars.

The Bamboo—an integral part of the Queen St. W. scene. (Photo by Brian Thompson)

ROCK CLUBS

The Bamboo
312 Queen St. W. near Spadina
593-5771
Great Caribbean food and a lot of good local reggae and Latin talent. The best outdoor bar in the city with a burgerteria on the roof. Still the place to hear bands like the Hopping Penguins. Used to be a Parachute Club venue. Also home to some great "Martian Awareness" parties on St. Patrick's Days gone by.

The Cabana Room
460 King St. W. near Spadina
368-0729

Tends towards hardcore rock and underground music. A former Ontario College of Art hangout. Upstairs at the "quaint" Spadina Hotel.

The Diamond
410 Sherbourne St. near Gerrard
927-9010

Dance to the DJ or watch great live bands. The best small concert venue in the city books mainstream acts.

El Mocambo
464 Spadina Ave. at College
961-2558

Many a Torontonian has fond memories of walking under those neon palms at

Courtesy of David Crighton © 1989

the El Mo. Though its glories may have faded, this place is part of Toronto's history. Even the Rolling Stones played here. Be nice to the bouncers; their reputation is somewhat more infamous.

Grossman's
379 Spadina Ave. near College
977-7000

One of Toronto's original tap rooms now provides underground music to the university crowd. Also features dixieland jazz every Sat afternoon.

Horseshoe Tavern
370 Queen St. W. near Spadina
598-4753

The best sound system in the city. The Horseshoe books a mixture of mainstream rock, blues and C&W including plenty of southern U.S. acts. Many big names have played here over the years. During its "punk" period the Stranglers played here in 1978. Now it's a regular stop for bands like the Northern Pikes, Blue Rodeo and Prairie Oyster.

Lee's Palace
529 Bloor St. W. near Bathurst
532-7383

New and underground music. A lot of Toronto's great talent surfaced here. Lee's has the city's best sight lines for viewing a band. The Dance Cave upstairs is the best hardcore rock dance club in TO.

The Rivoli
334 Queen St. W. near Spadina
596-1908

A great place with a nice boulevard patio. A mixed bag of new and underground music and comedy entertainment. The original home to some of

The Berlin—one of Toronto's well-known upscale discos. (Photo by Brian Thompson)

Toronto's best new bands including Shadowy Men on a Shadowy Planet, Cowboy Junkies and Blue Rodeo.

Siboney Club
169 Augusta Ave.
in Kensington Market
977-4277
Mixed bag of hardcore rock and mainstream. The new hot night spot in town, with a large bar and a good view of the stage.

The Silver Dollar
484 Spadina Ave. at College
925-8832
Features sunny sounds—calypso, reggae, soca, ska and world beat music.

Sneaky Dee's
562 Bloor St. W. near Bathurst
532-2052
This place serves up good Mexican food from its 24-hour kitchen, and if you're lucky the bands will continue to play into the wee, wee hours.

Stilife
217 Richmond St. W. near Jarvis
593-6116
Upscale and posh. Selective entry. This is the sort of place where record companies like to have record release parties. It's rumoured Springsteen went here after a gig.

DISCOS

Berlin
2335 Yonge St. near Eglinton
489-7777
A popular Yonge and Eglinton entry. It's been described as a postmodern disco.

Toronto's street musicians can often provide some very good impromptu entertainment. (Photo by Brian Pel)

The Big Bop
651 Queen St. W. near Bathurst
366-6699

A multilevel danceteria for the youthful, suburban crowd. Usually has good music.

The Copa
21 Scollard St. near Bay
922-6500

Huge disco playing up-to-date music.

The Gilson Place Hotel
556 Sherbourne St.
near Wellesley
921-4167

Formerly The Isabella, this place has been around for a long time. Huge patio, entertaining DJs.

RPM
132 Queen's Quay E. at Jarvis
869-1462

This huge disco brings in name acts. Has a large unlicensed area for the underaged.

DINNER THEATRES

Harper's Restaurant and Dinner Theatre
38 Lombard St. near Yonge
863-6223

Their highly recommended two-hour show *A Little Night Magic,* complete with sorcerers and prestidigitators, has proven a favourite with Torontonians and visitors.

His Majesty's Feast
1926 Lakeshore Blvd. W.
769-1165

For over a decade saucy wenches have served up a king's feast while King Henry VIII and his courtiers keep you laughing in this wild comedy cabaret. Lots of fun.

Limelight Dinner Theatre
2026 Yonge St. near Eglinton
482-5200
Local productions of Broadway musicals and comedies.

The New York Hotel Dinner Theatre
1150 Queen St. W. near Dufferin
533-0046
Since 1980, this theatre has been presenting the popular musical comedy *Let My People Come*.

Second City
110 Lombard St. near Jarvis
863-1111
Who can forget the Mackenzie Brothers? This is where the popular television series *SCTV* got its start. The satirical troupe offers up great improvisational comedy.

Stage West Dinner Theatre
5400 Dixie Rd.
Mississauga
238-0042
Known for bringing in celebrity performers to play name-brand theatre. A very good buffet is offered.

Yuk Yuk's Komedy Kabaret
2335 Yonge St. near Eglinton
489-7817
1280 Bay St. near Bloor
967-6425
Showcases a steady stream of stand-up comics. Over the years they have brought in many of North America's best comedians. In fact Howey Mandel polished up a lot of his routines here.

Martin Short, Catherine O'Hara and Robin Duke perform on stage at Second City. (Photo by Rich Alexander)

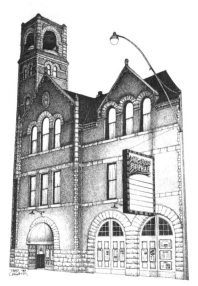

Courtesy of David Crighton © 1989

COUNTRY AND WESTERN

Birchmount Tavern
462 Birchmount Rd. at Danforth
698-4115
Popular C&W bar with live entertainment every night but Mon. Southern U.S. bands are often booked as well as strong local talent such as The Razorbacks and The Good Brothers.

Graceland
1199 Kennedy Rd. near Lawrence
755-3311
The sign at the entrance says "No toe caps and no colours"—a reference to motorcycle gang jacket colours. Live entertainment Thurs, Fri and Sat showcasing mostly well-known Canadian groups. Usually once a month, in conjunction with CFGM radio, they bring in big-name acts such as U.S. recording artists Sweethearts of the Rodeo and Jerry Reed. Free country dance lessons every Wed.

El Condor
30 Carrier Dr.
off Hwy. 27
675-1014
A west-end C&W club with live entertainment Tues and Thurs through Sat nights, mostly local bands. The restaurant serves full-course meals. No cover charge.

Also, The Horseshoe Tavern and The Diamond (see Rock Clubs) often book some very good C&W bands. Two recent concerts at The Diamond featured Kris Kristofferson and Emmylou Harris.

GAY CLUBS

Downtown Toronto is home to more than 15 gay pubs and clubs. For a complete and up-to-date listing, pick up a free copy of *Xtra!* magazine.

SPORTS/RECREATION

SPORTS/RECREATION

Whether you're a spectator or a participant, the Toronto region offers you a wider variety of sports and recreation possibilities than any other city in Canada. Being right on Lake Ontario and so close to cottage country means there's a wide array of water-related pursuits readily at hand. And the snowbelts north of the city are ideal for downhill and cross-country skiing. As well, Toronto is fortunate to have professional sports teams in baseball, hockey and football—and if you ask a Torontonian, they're all contenders. Depending on the time of year, you can watch the Canadian Open golf tournament at nearby Oakville, the Player's tennis championship at York University or the Molson Indy at Exhibition Place. And when it comes to track and field, Toronto is home to the world-record sprinter, Ben Johnson. As well, Metro is dotted with courts, playing fields, diamonds, arenas, and stadiums of every shape and kind.

The Ontario Sports Centre (495-4000) can give you the phone numbers of any amateur sports association in the province and has information on every amateur sport including tournaments, where to play, where to get equipment and how to participate. Each Metro Toronto municipal recreation department publishes listings of the activities and programs they offer throughout the year. The White Pages also list sports associations.

BICYCLING

Toronto's City Cycling Committee, an official body of Toronto City Council, claims that Toronto is the leading cycling city in Canada today.

The Toronto Bicycling Network (the TBN) maintains a hotline at 766-1985. This service (updated every week) provides information 24 hours a day on cycling in the city and in the surrounding countryside and also informs you of upcoming TBN day and weekend trips. Rides are offered from beginner to expert levels. You may join any of the planned tours for $5, which provides insurance coverage and which is refunded if you buy a year's membership ($30). The group's somewhat tongue-in-cheek motto "Ride to eat, eat to ride" is taken more seriously during their tea shop tours or their ice cream shop tours. They also offer bed and breakfast, bike and sketch, fall colours and sportif tours.

Toronto's cycle path system extends over 60 km (37 mi.) of trails. It is the city's fortune to be blessed with a multitude of ravines in which development has not been permitted. Many of the cycle paths lead you through these ravines, away from cars and smog.

The City of Toronto distributes a recreational bicycle route guide showing both on-street and off-street routes, location of bike sales and rental shops and places of interest. This route guide—as well as the cycling newsletter "The City Cyclist"—is available free of charge in bike shops, libraries, community centres and the City Hall Resource Centre. There are also several guides to city bicycle routes, available at bookstores.

Some words to the wise about bicycling in Toronto. First and foremost, please wear a helmet. Heavy traffic can be hazardous. In Toronto bicycles are considered vehicles of the road. That means they have a legal right to be on the road—except major highways—

with all other vehicles, but it also means that they must obey traffic laws. Riding on sidewalks is illegal, and traffic violations will result in tickets and fines. The TTC allows bicycles on the subway at all times except rush hours —6:30 A.M. to 9:30 A.M. and 3:30 P.M. to 6:30 P.M. Bicycles can also be taken on all Toronto Islands ferries during the week, but are not allowed on the Centre Island ferry on weekends.

ROUTES

THE MARTIN GOODMAN TRAIL

This trail was a gift from the Toronto *Star* to the city in 1984 in honour of former *Star* president Martin Goodman. It's 20 km (12 mi.) of great cycling along the city's waterfront from Etienne Brûlé Park on the lower Humber River in the west to the end of the Beaches Boardwalk in the east. It's very flat terrain and you can get off the trail at many junctures en route if you've a mind to visit something downtown. The route passes Sunnyside Pool Complex, Exhibition Place, Ontario Place, Harbourfront, Greenwood Race Track and the Beaches.

TORONTO ISLANDS

Start by taking the ferry from behind the Harbour Castle Westin Hotel to the Toronto Islands. Ferries land at Wards Island, Centre Island and Hanlan's Point. Ferry service information is available at 392-8193. By landing at Wards Island and bicycling the wooden boardwalk that runs the length of the islands to Hanlan's Point and back, you will have travelled more than 10 km (6 mi.). For a shorter trip, simply cycle one-way to Hanlan's Point and return by ferry to the city.

HIGH PARK

This 160-ha (400-acre) park in the central southwest of the city is woven with interconnecting park roads and paths. Once in the park, you can pick your own route. Popular High Park is usually a beehive of activity and offers a large number of attractions, plus refreshments for the thirsty cyclist. See also Parks/Gardens.

DON VALLEY TRAILS

Much of the Don River Valley and the valleys of its tributaries inside the city is public parkland. The entire length of this parkland is traversed by a paved asphalt path for walkers, joggers and cyclists. Two favoured cycle routes are the 5-km (3-mi.) Edwards Gardens– E. T. Seton Park route and the 2-km (1.2-mi.) Taylor's Creek route. Both are quiet and scenic. Start the first from the Edwards Gardens parking lot off Leslie St. south of Lawrence Ave. E. Follow the path south as it runs along the banks of the beautiful West Don River. The second route is reached off Don Mills Rd. N. in Taylor's Bush Park. The trail starts just beyond the parking lot and follows Taylor's Creek.

HUMBER VALLEY TRAILS

This route is a favourite of city cyclists. It starts at the beautiful formal James Gardens, located off Scarlett Rd. south of Eglinton Ave. W., and proceeds south beside the Humber River for 6 km (3½ mi.) to the Old Mill on Bloor St. W. In between, it curves through scenic Lambton Woods and Etienne Brûlé Park.

LESLIE ST. SPIT

Great cycling any time, but this is a perfect route for a hot day, since you benefit from the cooling breeze off the lake. Start at the foot of Leslie St. and cycle out the spit headland to the lighthouse at the south tip. It's a 10-km (6.2-mi.) return ride, and you will be treated to some of the best views of Toronto's skyline and an opportunity for some exceptional birdwatching. See also Parks/Gardens.

RENTALS

From the beginning of May to the end of summer, bicycles can be rented by the hour at McBride's, 180 Queen's Quay W. (367-5651), or on the Toronto Islands at either Centre Island or Hanlan's Point. Phone 365-7901.

CYCLING STORES

Bikenergy
19 Yorkville Ave. near Yonge
968-9368

Pedlar Cycle
169 Avenue Rd. at Davenport
968-7100

Spinning Wheels
521 Parliament St. near Carlton
923-4626

Local Motion
5252 Yonge St. near Sheppard
733-3663

Veneto Cycle
1193 Bloor St. W. near Dufferin
532-8734

Bloor Cycle
1169 Bloor St. W. near Dufferin
536-9718

BICYCLING OUTSIDE TORONTO

The Ontario Cycling Association provides touring maps of southern Ontario and can put you in touch with bicycle clubs and commercial bicycle tour operators. Call 495-4141 Mon to Fri 8:30 A.M. to 4:30 P.M. They also operate a hotline (497-6837): a recorded message gives you the tour calendar for the week and other up-to-date information on upcoming tours, mountain bike touring and road racing.

BOWLING

There are a number of 5 and 10 pin bowling lanes in the city that stay open 24 hours a day. These include:

Newtonbrook Bowlerama
5837 Yonge St. near Finch
222-4657

Plantation Bowlerama
5429 Dundas St. W. near Kipling
239-3536

Thorncliffe Bowlerama
45 Overlea Blvd. near Don Mills
421-2211

CAMPING

Provincial Parks Information, Whitney Block, Queen's Park, Toronto M7A 1W3 will provide you with a list of provincial parks and recreation and conservation areas. Serious campers should consider Algonquin Park or one of the national or provincial parks. See Sightseeing/Out-of-Town Attractions.

EQUIPMENT RENTAL

The following sporting goods stores rent out camping equipment. Deposits are the rule and you should book in advance.

**Blacks Camping International
2196 Queen St. E. at Balsam
690-4800**

**Trail Head
40 Wellington St. E. near Church
862-0881**

To rent a camper van or motor home, look under "Recreational Vehicles" in the Yellow Pages. Also see Transportation.

CRICKET

Though not a widely played game in Canada, cricket does have its die-hard adherents. Cricket pitches are located at:

Sunnybrook Park, off Bayview Ave. between Lawrence Ave. and Eglinton Ave. E.; **Eglinton Flats,** at the corner of Jane St. and Eglinton Ave. W.; and **G. Ross Lord Park,** off Dufferin St. between Steeles Ave. W. and Finch Ave. W.

CRUISING

Ontario is boating country. It has a shoreline on four of the five Great Lakes and contains over a quarter of a million inland lakes. With that choice available, Ontario is literally a boater's mecca. All boaters new to Ontario waters should obtain the "Canadian Aids to Navigation System" booklet from the Canadian Coast Guard at 1 Yonge St., 20th floor, Toronto M5E 1E5; 973-3078. If you plan to cruise one of the canal systems, you'll need a permit. For brochures on fees, hours of operation and locking procedures, contact Environment Canada Enquiry Centre, Place Vincent Massey, 6th Floor, Hull, PQ K1A 0H3; (819) 997-2800.

Marina listings are available from:

**Fisheries and Oceans Canada
Small Craft Harbours Branch
P.O. Box 5050
867 Lakeshore Rd.
Burlington, ON
L7R 4A6
(416) 336-6020**

Navigation charts are available at local marinas and marine supply stores or by contacting:

**The Canadian Hydrographic Service
Department of Fisheries and Oceans
P.O. Box 8080
1675 Russell Rd.
Ottawa, ON
K1G 3H6
(613) 998-4931**

Search and Rescue emergency services are co-ordinated through RCC Trenton (1-800-267-7270). The Ontario Provincial Police patrols inland lakes and can be contacted in emergencies by dialling "0" and asking the operator for Zenith 50000; then ask to be connected to the nearest OPP detachment.

It is illegal in Ontario to discharge waste from pleasure craft. Sewage *must* be pumped out on shore. The Ministry of the Environment (424-3000) can tell you where to obtain a listing of pump-out stations.

Pleasure boat operators should find out when during the day weather information is broadcast in their area. Besides local stations, Weather Radio Canada broadcasts 24 hours a day, 7 days a week, from the CN Tower on 162.475 MHz over VHF-FM.

The Canadian Power Squadron (293-2438) offers powerboat information and navigation and safety training.

PUBLIC BOAT LAUNCHES

Etobicoke Creek Mouth
(on the west side,
south of Lakeshore Blvd. W.)

Mimico Creek Mouth
(on the west side,
south of Lakeshore Blvd. W.)

Ashbridge's Bay
(in Ashbridge's Bay Park, south of Lakeshore Blvd. E. near Greenwood Race Track)

Bluffers Park
(bottom of Brimley Rd.
in Scarborough)

ROUTES

If you have a larger craft you might consider the following voyages in addition to touring the Great Lakes:

RIDEAU WATERWAY

This historic canal, built between 1826 and 1832, is peaceful and picturesque as it passes through numerous locks from Kingston to Ottawa. For information contact:

Rideau Canal
12 Maple Ave. N.
Smiths Falls, ON
(613) 283-5170

GEORGIAN BAY ISLANDS NATIONAL PARK

Canada's only all-island national park. Lots of opportunities to moor and swim. Located in southern Georgian Bay. For information contact:

Superintendent
Georgian Bay Islands National Park
Box 28
Honey Harbour, ON
P0E 1E0
(705) 756-2415

TRENT-SEVERN WATERWAY

You enter the waterway at Trenton on Lake Ontario (approximately

160 km/100 mi. east of Toronto) and proceed north to Georgian Bay and Georgian Bay Islands National Park through 38 conventional locks, two hydraulic lift locks and a marine railway. The cruise passes several rural Ontario villages. For information contact:

Superintendent
Trent-Severn Waterway
P.O. Box 567
Peterborough, ON
K9J 6Z6
(705) 742-9267

FISHING

Ten years ago, no one would have seriously thought of Toronto as a fishing destination. Thanks, however, to vigorous stocking programs of salmon and trout by both Ontario and New York State, the entire Ontario shore of Lake Ontario, particularly near Toronto, is now one of the best salmon and trout fishing grounds in the world. Huge specimens of coho and chinook salmon, and lake, rainbow and brown trout are regularly taken, and catching your limit is no longer a rare feat. Though most of these salmonoids do not breed in Lake Ontario, continued stocking and the abundance of bait fish in the Toronto region ensures the continuance of this excellent fishery. And the extent of this fishery has produced a flourishing charter business along the Toronto lakefront.

Other Ontario species such as northern pike, small mouth bass, large mouth bass, perch and walleye are readily taken in Ontario's lakes and rivers. Advice on where to fish outside the Toronto region is available from the Wildlife Branch, Ministry of Natural Resources, Queen's Park, Toronto M7A 1W3; 965-4251. Or phone the sports fishing line at 965-7883.

Fishing in the Humber River near the Old Mill by Bloor St. (Ministry of Natural Resources)

FISHING REGULATIONS

The Ontario Ministry of the Environment annually publishes *Fishing Regulations in Ontario,* free of charge from any office of the Ministry of Natural Resources and from most fishing stores, bait shops and marinas and often the Brewers' Retail beer stores. The *Regulations* include daily limits, information on licences, fish sanctuaries, and the fishing season for each species. Residents aged 18 to 65 and all nonresidents require a licence to fish in Ontario. You are only allowed one line per angler, except when ice-fishing, when two lines are usually permitted.

The Ontario Travel Information offices at 900 Bay St. (965-4008) and on the lower level of the Eaton Centre can also provide fishing regulation brochures.

CONTAMINANTS

The results of the Ontario government's fish contaminant monitoring program are published annually in the *Guide to Eating Ontario Sport Fish.* Anglers should obtain a copy of the guide at bait shops, sports stores or the Brewers'

Retail, or contact the local office of the Ministry of Natural Resources before consuming any fish. As a general rule, the larger the fish, the greater its build-up of contaminants. Therefore, the fish least likely to be a trophy may be the safest to eat.

CHARTERED TRIPS

The Ontario Charter Boat Association contains approximately 150 members. Of these, about 100 are in or near Toronto. The Yellow Pages and the sports sections of the local newspapers list many charter boat operators who are only too eager to take you on what may be the fishing experience of a lifetime. Ontario Charter Boat Association members must comply with strict regulations. Look for their logo. The largest charter service is:

Adams Charter Service
P.O. Box 7001
Oakville, ON
L6J 6L5
845-0490 or 844-1377
Fishing charters on Lake Ontario for both salmon and trout. All equipment and tackle is supplied. Charters are from

THE TORONTO STAR GREAT SALMON HUNT

The biggest fishing tournament in the world, held from early July to early Sept, attracts over 20,000 entrants from across Canada, the U.S., Europe and Japan. The grand prize of over $120,000 is awarded to the individual who catches the largest salmon over the contest period. There are additional prizes for the heaviest brown trout and the heaviest

rainbow trout. Molson's Breweries offers a prize of $50,000 to the first angler to catch a 50-lb. (22.5-kg) salmon. Anyone who enters the tournament is eligible for a grand prize draw worth $75,000. There are also weekly prizes for those who enter any eligible fish in the contest. Phone 897-1620.

The Toronto *Sun*/Budweiser annually sponsor a fishing derby with $300,000 in prizes. Phone 890-6959.

THE CATCH

Trout
Rainbow: In Lake Ontario, 1 to 7 kg (2 to 15 lbs.)

Brown: In Lake Ontario, 1 to 5.5 kg (2 to 12 lbs.)

Lake: 1 to 4.5 kg (2 to 10 lbs.)

Salmon
Chinook, the largest and most prized of the salmonoids. Average weight: 9 kg (20 lbs.)

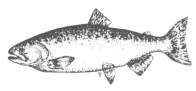

Coho: 2 to 4.5 kg (5 to 10 lbs.)

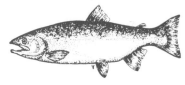

Other Lake Ontario residents
Walleye: 1 to 4.5 kg (2 to 10 lbs.)
Perch: 0.25 to 0.5 kg (½ to 1 lb.)
Northern Pike 1 to 7 kg (2 to 15 lbs.)

Department of Fisheries and Oceans

7 A.M. to 1 P.M. or from 2 P.M. to 8 P.M. Rates are $50–$75 per hour (depending on size of boat) for a 6-hour trip, divided by the number of passengers (8 maximum).

TACKLE SHOPS

Tackle shops are not only the place to purchase equipment and bait but they are also a great source of fishing information. As well as the many specialty stores in and around Toronto that supply tackle, equipment and bait, all Canadian Tire stores and some department stores sell a wide selection of fishing equipment.

Skinner's Sports
50 King St. E. near Yonge
863-9701
One of two fishing shops in downtown Toronto. An institution with the Bay St. crowd.

Pollack Sporting Goods
337 Queen St. E. near Parliament
363-1095
A large selection of fishing tackle and live bait.

LeBaron's Sporting Goods
5863 Yonge St. near Finch
225-3322

Prize salmon from Lake Ontario. (Photo David Towers, courtesy of Adams Charters)

Soles Sporting Goods
235½ Yonge St. near Dundas
364-0175

WHERE TO FISH IN TORONTO

Other than in Lake Ontario itself, the following are fishing areas to consider in the City of Toronto:

GRENADIER POND, HIGH PARK

Panfish, northern pike and large mouth bass.

TROUT POND, HANLAN'S POINT

A well-stocked trout pond. A limit of two fish per person.

THE ROUGE RIVER ESTUARY

Not only salmon and trout in season but northern pike, perch, panfish and both large mouth and small mouth bass. (By car take Hwy. 401 east to Port Union Rd., then south to Island Dr., east to Rouge Hills Dr. and south 1.6 km (1 mi.) to the fishing grounds.)

THE DUFFIN CREEK ESTUARY

Salmon and trout plus many other species. (By car exit Hwy. 401 east at Liverpool Rd., go west on Bayly St. to Squires Beach Rd., south to MacKay Rd., west to Jordelle, south then west to Montgomery Park and south on Frisco Rd.)

FITNESS
(Aerobics/Weights/Jogging)

CLASSES/FACILITIES

YMCA
Three locations:

Metro Central
20 Grosvenor St. near Yonge
921-5171

North York
567 Sheppard Ave. E. at Bayview
225-7773

West End
931 College St. at Dovercourt
536-1166

PARCOURS TRAILS

Vita Parcours trails are exercise trails with well-placed exercise stations along the way. Two are at:

Taylor's Creek Park
Enter park from Don Mills Rd., from

Halden Ave. just north of Cosburn Ave., or from Dawes Rd.

Serena Gundy Park
Access from Wilket Creek Park off Leslie St., either just south of Lawrence Ave. E. or just north of Eglinton Ave. E.

At the YMCA, you can pay by the day ($5 for youths and children, $10 for adults). For this price you can use all the facilities including pool, saunas, whirlpools, tracks, weight rooms, squash courts, racquetball courts and fitness classes. Baby-sitting services are also available.

YWCA Fitness Centre
2532 Yonge St. near Eglinton
487-7151
Pay per class. Fitness and aerobics only. Babysitting available at $2.50 per hour during the morning classes.

Body Alive
70 Yorkville Ave. near Bay
964-1274
Pay per class. Phone for the daily schedule. Aerobics only, with various levels and types of classes.

Gold's Gym
675 Yonge St. near Bloor
962-9001
You can use, for a daily fee, all the facilities including aerobics classes, sunbeds, free weights, Nautilus equipment and saunas. Open 24 hours a day.

Downtown Tennis Club
21 Eastern Ave. near Parliament
362-2439
Per-class fee for fitness classes or for using the Nautilus equipment for the day. Phone for class times. You can also book a tennis court.

Variety Village Sport Training and
Fitness Centre for the
Disabled
3701 Danforth Ave.
near Birchmount
699-7167
Fitness facilities for the disabled.

A number of private health and fitness clubs in Toronto are open to members who pay an initiation fee and annual dues. Some hotels have private health clubs for their guests, while others have affiliations with independent health clubs.

EXERCISE GEAR

Collegiate Sportsworld
Eaton Centre (lower level)
598-1626

Runner's Choice
College Park (lower level)
777 Bay St. near College
597-0023

Women's Sports
561 Mt. Pleasant Rd. near Manor
481-2531

Feet First Footcare
First Canadian Place
368-3338
2600 Yonge St. near Eglinton
481-3338

Sporting Life
2665 Yonge St. near Eglinton
485-1611

JOGGING ROUTES

Metro Parks (392-8186) or Parks and Recreation (392-7251) will advise you which nearest park is suitable for jogging.

As well, Toronto's extensive ravine system contains miles of jogging routes. The ones given below are just a few of the most popular.

THE MARTIN GOODMAN TRAIL

See Bicycling, this chapter

THE BEACHES BOARDWALK

Offers 3 km (2 mi.) of boardwalk or beach jogging from Donald Summerville Pool Complex in the west to the Scarborough city limits in the east. Passes beautiful Kew Gardens and, in the summer, myriads of sun worshippers and windsurfers.

THE BELTLINE

A midtown jog, 4.4 km (2.7 mi.) long. The Beltline Railroad has long since passed into memory, but its cinder trackbed remains. The old thoroughfare starts just south of where Roselawn Ave. crosses over the Allen Expressway (at Elmridge Dr.). It then runs southeast over Bathurst St. and Avenue Rd. to just south and west of Davisville subway station. Much of the trail passes behind the Forest Hill mansions and is heavily treed.

HIGH PARK

High Park offers miles of trails, both paved and grassed. You can pick your own route as you go. With Grenadier Pond, Colborne Lodge, formal gardens and hundreds of acres of well-treed parkland, this is among the most scenic jogs in the city.

HUMBER RAVINE

Like most of the city ravines, the Humber River watershed is protected as parkland. An 11-km (7-mi.) asphalt pathway extends from Raymore Park (near Royal York Rd. and Lawrence Ave. W.) to the Humber Marshes at Lake Ontario. In between, it passes through beautiful James Gardens and Lambton Woods as well as five other city parks.

GOLF

There are approximately 160 golf courses within a 60-km (40-mi.) radius of Toronto. Here's a sampling of the finest in various categories, as recommended by Toronto golf course architect Douglas Carrick.

MUNICIPAL COURSES
(In Metro)

Don Valley Golf Course
4200 Yonge St. at Hwy. 401
North York
392-2465
18 holes, Par 71, 6400 yards
Green fees: Under $15
Starting times: No
Power carts: No
Opening time: Weekends 6 A.M., weekdays 7 A.M.
Comments: The course winds through a mature wooded valley with the Don River coming into play on 7 holes. Several elevated tees and greens call for different shots.

Humber Valley Golf Course
40 Beattie Ave.
Rexdale
392-2488
18 holes, Par 70, 5600 yards
Green fees: Under $15
Starting times: No
Power carts: No
Opening time: Weekends 6 A.M., weekdays 7 A.M.
Comments: Mature tree-lined fairways, well conditioned, fairly flat and easy to walk. The Humber River comes into play on a few holes.

Lakeview Golf Course
(west side of Dixie Rd. between
QEW and Lakeshore Blvd. W.)
Mississauga
278-4411
18 holes, Par 70, 6023 yards
Green fees: $15–$20
Starting times: No

Power carts: No
Opening time: Weekends 6 A.M., weekdays 7 A.M.
Comments: Gently rolling, mature tree-lined fairways, picturesque layout.

PAY-AS-YOU-PLAY COURSES
(In Toronto area)

Glen Abbey Golf Club
Dorval Dr., north off QEW
Oakville
844-1800
18 holes championship length, Par 73, 7102 yards
Green fees: $70–$80
Starting times: Yes
Power carts: Mandatory
Opening time: Weekends 7 A.M., weekdays 7:30 A.M.
Comments: Excellent Jack Nicklaus–designed layout, long and challenging with bunkers, water hazards and five spectacular valley holes. Home of the Canadian Open.

Westview Golf Club
Leslie St. and Vandorf Rd.
Gormley
773-0446
27 holes championship length, Par 72, 6732 yards, 6775 yards, 6873 yards
Green fees: $20–$25
Starting times: No
Power carts: 37
Opening time: Weekends 6 A.M., weekdays 7 A.M.
Comments: Rolling terrain with several mature tree-lined fairways, elevated greens and tees. Water comes into play on 5 holes, making this a very challenging layout with a lot of variety.

Nobleton Lakes Golf and Country Club
Hwy. 27, 3.2 km (2 mi.) north of King Sideroad
Nobleton
859-4070
18 holes championship length, Par 72, 7024 yards
Green fees: $20–$30
Starting times: Yes
Power carts: 90
Opening time: Weekends 6 A.M., weekdays 7 A.M.
Comments: Very challenging layout over rolling terrain with several mature tree-lined fairways, numerous bunkers and several well-placed water hazards. The 16th hole features an island green Par 3.

Glen Eagle Golf Club
5 km (3 mi.) north of Toronto on Hwy. 50
Bolton
964-8890
18 holes championship length, Par 72, 6900 yards
Green fees: $20–$25
Starting times: Yes
Power carts: Mandatory
Opening time: Weekends 6 A.M., weekdays 7 A.M.
Comments: Long, challenging layout over rolling terrain, with several well-placed bunkers.

PRIVATE COUNTRY CLUBS

Some private clubs offer reciprocal playing privileges for members of other private clubs visiting the Toronto area. Arrangements should be made ahead of time, and a letter of introduction from your home club manager is often advisable.

St. George's Golf & Country Club
1668 Islington Ave.
231-3393
18 holes championship length, Par 71, 6477 yards
Comments: Consistently ranked one of Canada's top courses. Outstanding championship layout designed by renowned architect Stanley Thompson and remodelled by C. E. Robinson. Course is routed over rolling terrain with several fairways winding through magnificent oak woods. Masterfully shaped bunkers and greens.

The National Golf Club
Hwy. 7 East to Pine Valley Dr.
Woodbridge
746-3111
18 holes championship length, Par 72, 6965 yards
Comments: Probably Canada's most difficult and challenging course. Designed by U.S. golf architect George Fazio. Course features narrow, contoured fairways with spectacular bunkering and extremely fast and undulating greens. Water comes into play on several holes. Long and accurate tee shots and properly placed approach shots are a must to score well at the National.

Summit Golf & Country Club
Yonge St., south of Stouffville Rd.
Richmond Hill
884-8189
18 holes championship length, Par 71,
6560 yards
Comments: Championship layout over
dramatically rolling terrain with several
outstanding elevated tees. Every hole is
cut through mature forest. Summit is
blessed with possibly the finest natural
character of any course in southern
Ontario.

Credit Valley Golf Course
On Hwy. 5, 1 km (½ mi.) west of
Hwy. 10
Mississauga
275-2512
18 holes championship length, Par 71,
6610 yards
Comments: Immaculately groomed, picturesque championship layout. The final
14 holes are routed through the
secluded Credit River Valley, with
water coming into play on 8 holes.
Designed by one of Canada's finest golf
course architects, C. E. Robinson, the
course is highlighted by beautifully contoured greens and bunkers and mature
trees lining every fairway. The 11th hole
is one of Canada's most spectacular Par
3's, playing directly down the throat of
the Credit River with a carry of over
190 yards across water from the back
tee.

HIKING

In Metro you can hike along nature trails
in the ravine system (see Bicycling and
Jogging) and in conservation areas. The
Metropolitan Toronto and Region Conservation Authority (661-6600) pro-

vides information and brochures. An excellent guide to nature walks is *Toronto's
Backyard: A Guide to Selected Nature
Walks* by Gregory and MacKenzie, available at local bookstores.

Outside Metro you can hike the
famous Bruce Trail, a continuous
718-km (445-mi.) footpath from
Niagara to Tobermory at the tip of the
Bruce Peninsula. You can pick up or
leave the trail at many points near
Toronto. The best guide (it includes extensive maps) is *The Bruce Trail
Guidebook,* sold in most bookstores and
camping supply stores.

HORSEBACK RIDING

A helpful booklet containing information on Ontario's many riding stables is
available from Ontario Travel, 900 Bay
St. (965-4008), or from the Ontario
Travel Information Office, lower level,
Eaton Centre. The following stables are
in or very near Toronto.

Central Don Riding Academy
In Sunnybrook Park,
south of Eglinton Ave. E.
near Leslie
444-1479 or 444-4044
This huge stable offers an indoor arena,
dressage, hunter-jumper and cross-
country facilities, as well as English in-
struction and horse rentals. The
mounted contingent of the Toronto
police force has stables next door.
Open year-round.

**Rocking Horse Ranch
On Hwy. 11, Richmond Hill
884-3292**

Scenic, one-hour western trail rides are offered here. No children under 8 or people over 90 kg (200 lbs.). It is best to book ahead. Open most of the year, but only on weekends in winter. Closed Mon unless it's a holiday. By public transit exit at Finch subway station and take the Newmarket GO bus. Tell the driver that you would like to be let off at the Rocking Horse Ranch.

**The Circle M Ranch
Hwy. 27, 1.5 km (1 mi.) north of
Hwy. 7
851-0503**

A licensed operator, Circle M offers western trail rides through about 60 ha (150 acres) of scenic landscape. Open daily in the summer. Phone for reservations.

**The Rouge Hill Stables
Hwy. 2, 0.5 km (¼ mi.) east of
Sheppard Ave. E.
284-6176**

This licensed operator offers supervised one-hour-long western trail rides through the picturesque Rouge Valley. Children under 9 are not accepted, and there is a 90 kg (200 lb.) weight limit. Reservations are required. Phone and ask about special longer rides.

HORSE RACING

**Woodbine Race Track
Hwy. 27 at Rexdale Blvd.
675-6110**

One of North America's great thoroughbred race tracks, Woodbine is the home of Canada's most important thoroughbred horse races—the Queen's Plate (July) and the Rothman's International (Oct). The Queen's Plate, for 3-year-olds, is the oldest-running stakes race in North America and your best chance to see royalty in Toronto. At the Rothman's International, Canada's richest horse race, contending thoroughbreds from the world over compete for a $700,000 purse.

Woodbine has a 1-mi. dirt oval and two turf courses. Races from May through late Oct. Intertrack racing in late March, April and Nov. Local newspapers carry race information. The clubhouse features six bars, a dining room and a cafeteria. The Grandstand has two lounges and several beverage rooms. On race nights, a special bus service runs from Islington subway station.

**Greenwood Race Track
1669 Queen St. E. near Woodbine
698-3131**

Thoroughbred and standardbred harness racing. The racing season is spread over three annual meetings: the spring meet runs from 1 Jan to the middle of March; the summer meet runs from the end of May to 1 Sept; and there is a brief gathering from mid-Dec to 31 Dec.

**Mohawk Raceway
Off Hwy. 401, 48 km (30 mi.) west
of Toronto
416-854-2255**

Standardbred harness racing in the spring and in the fall.

POLO

For most of us polo is strictly a spectator sport. If you're in the mood for spectating, the Toronto Polo Club's Gormley Polo Centre, off Leslie St. north of Hwy. 7 (489-7100), offers three tournaments a year. The annual Heart and Stroke Foundation International Polo Tournament takes place there over the first two weekends in July. There are also tournaments on the fourth weekend of July and the second weekend in Aug.

PROFESSIONAL SPORTS

HOCKEY

The Toronto Maple Leafs and their home, the venerable Maple Leaf Gardens (60 College St.) are nothing short of institutions in Toronto. They say that every game is still sold out, which is all the more amazing when you remember they haven't won a Stanley Cup—and haven't been serious contenders—since 1967. Team owner Harold Ballard is himself a Toronto institution. Never shy of making his views known, whether on his own team, women's lib or Muscovites, he is the man Torontonians either love or hate. The Maple Leafs have won no less than 11 Stanley Cups since their first in 1932. Many a Torontonian longs for the glory days of the '60s, when the Leafs and the Montreal Canadiens were the dominant hockey teams in the NHL. Right now, they've got nowhere to go but up. For information on the Toronto Maple Leafs call 977-1641.

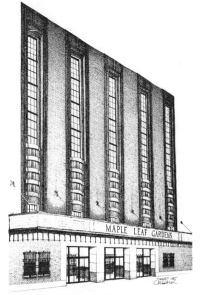

Courtesy of David Crighton © 1989

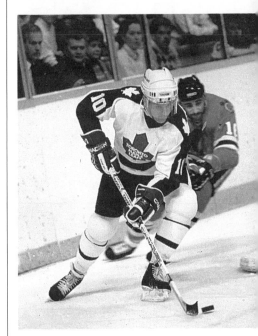

Photo by Graig Abel

Toronto's powerful Fred McGriff. (Toronto Blue Jays)

FOOTBALL

The Toronto Argonauts play in the Canadian Football League. In the past, their record was anything but impressive. Things have turned around considerably in the 1980s, though, with the Argonauts winning the Grey Cup in 1983 and being a contender since. The Argos play all their games in the SkyDome. For information call 595-1131, 10 A.M. to 6 P.M. daily, or go to the downtown ticket office in the Sheraton Centre, main lobby, Mon to Fri 10 A.M. to 5 P.M.

BASEBALL

Canada's only American League franchise, the Toronto Blue Jays have played here since 1976. If you didn't know better, you might think baseball was Canada's national sport. In the summer in Toronto, *everyone* becomes a baseball nut, and next to the weather, the ball game is the favourite topic of conversation. The Blue Jays were the American League East Division champions in 1985 and were contenders in 1986 and 1987, when George Bell was nominated the American League's most valuable player. The Blue Jays play their home games in the new SkyDome. For information on games and tickets, phone 595-0077. The Jays also have a downtown ticket office in the bottom of the Commerce Court tower at King and Bay.

Toronto's new SkyDome, complete with retractable roof, is located adjacent to the CN Tower.

SKYDOME

Toronto's high-tech stadium, SkyDome will be the world's first multipurpose stadium with a retractable roof (which opens or closes in 20 minutes). Rising south of Front St. and just west of the Metro Toronto Convention Centre,

SkyDome seats 52,000 fans for baseball and 54,000 fans for football. SkyDome includes SkyVision, the world's largest scoreboard/replay screen. In case you're wondering, the annual rental tag for the private boxes ranges from $100,000 to $225,000—and as of Jan 1989 they're almost sold out.

TENNIS

Many of the world's top seeds compete at the Player's tennis championships, held every summer at the National Tennis Centre on the York University campus, off Steeles Ave. W. near Jane St. Reservations are a must. Call 665-9777.

AUTO RACING

Fans can attend a slate of races throughout the season at Mosport Park. Mosport is on the Can-Am circuit and is one hour from Toronto. Take Hwy. 401 eastbound to the Bowmanville exit (Exit 431) north, then proceed on Waverly Rd. and follow the signs. Call 665-6665.

Every July, Toronto plays host to the Molson Indy, the last race of the season in the CART/PPG Indy Car World Series. (The first race in this series is the famous one at Indianapolis.)

Carling Bassett-Seguso competing at the Player's Canadian championship tournament in Toronto. (Photo by Michael Burns)

MOLSON INDY

In mid-July every year the whine of high-performance Indy cars can be heard along the Toronto waterfront. The Molson Indy track consists of 103 laps of a 2.86-km (1.8 mi.) course that twists

through the streets of Exhibition Place and along Lakeshore Blvd. Speeds topping 305 km/h (190 mph)—faster than a 747 at takeoff—are hit in the straightaway. Stars such as Andretti, Fittipaldi and Rahal have burned rubber here.

Speed and thrills at the annual Molson Indy.

SAILBOARDING/SAILING

The Ontario Sailing Association (495-4240) gives information on rentals and lessons for windsurfing and sailboarding as well as sailing. There's always enough wind on Lake Ontario for excellent surfing, and windsurfers are seen everywhere along the Toronto waterfront. Two particularly popular spots are the Beaches Boardwalk and the Scarborough Bluffs. In the Beaches area, behind the Donald Summerville Pool Complex at the western end of the boardwalk, you can rent sailboards by the hour or by the day from Wind Promotions (694-6881). Several stores in the city specialize in windsurfing equipment:

Old Fire Hall Sports
Harbourfront
249 Queen's Quay W. (Pier 4)
477-4604 or 364-2331

Silent Sports Marine
113 Doncaster Ave. near Yonge
Thornhill
889-3772
Also offers lessons.

Wind Sports
2088 Yonge St. near Eglinton
322-3717
Also offers lessons.

A walk along the Toronto waterfront at any time between early spring and late fall will give ample proof that Toronto is

Summer sails in the sunset in Toronto's harbour.
(Photo by Ottmar Bierwagen)

Windsurfing on Lake Ontario.

a sailing city. There are thousands of slips along the Toronto waterfront for boats and crafts of all shapes and sizes. The Ontario Sailing Association (495-4240) provides information on sailing lessons and rentals.

Many of the numerous yacht clubs in the area offer guest slips and sailing courses. Try:

Royal Canadian Yacht Club
869-1967

Port Credit Yacht Club
278-5578

Queen City Yacht Club
368-6418

Harbourfront has slips to rent—phone the Marine Manager at 973-4097.

Pier 4 Sailing Schools offers lessons and public rentals on the central waterfront. Call 366-0390.

SCUBA DIVING

Although there is no worthwhile recreational diving to be done in Lake Ontario, Toronto is only 2 hours away from Fathom Five National Underwater Park, the only such park in Canada. Fathom Five offers spectacular diving among a multitude of shipwrecks in remarkably clear water, with lots of islands to provide protection from winds. Charter boats are readily available in Tobermory for day trips. Many divers camp in nearby campsites. In Lake Huron near Tobermory on the Bruce

Each winter the huge reflecting pool at Nathan Phillips Square becomes one of the city's favourite skating rinks. (Photo by Ottmar Bierwagen)

Peninsula. By car take Hwy. 400 north to Hwy. 89, follow this to Hwy. 10, then go north to Tobermory.

In Toronto there are numerous dive shops. Several offer excursions and courses in addition to equipment and air. Two of the best-known are:

TAM Dive
246 King St. E. near Sherbourne
861-1664

Water Sports
540 Mt. Pleasant Rd.
near Davisville
488-1105

SKATING

During winter, ice rinks all over Metro are maintained by the local municipalities. For information on the rink closest to you, call 392-7251. During the cold months there is free outdoor skating downtown at Nathan Phillips Square (in front of the new City Hall), the Ryerson rink (at the corner of Gould St. and Victoria St.), where you can skate among large Canadian granite boulders, and the rink behind College Park (at College St. and Yonge). All are open Mon to Sat 9 A.M. to 10 P.M., Sun 10 A.M. to 6 P.M. The Scarborough Civic Centre rink is open every day till 11 P.M. And Canada's biggest outdoor rink at Harbourfront is open from 10 A.M. to 10 P.M. daily.

SKIING

DOWNHILL

Ontario Travel provides information on where to downhill ski. They will also send out winter packages including descriptions of ski resorts. Call 965-4008 or, from out-of-town, 1-800-268-3735 (English) or 1-800-268-3736 (French). For a 24-hour recorded ski conditions report, call 963-2992.

In the city, Centennial Park Ski Hill at Rathburn Rd. and Renforth Dr. in Etobicoke (394-8750) has some short runs, two T-bars and rentals. Earl Bales Park on the southeast corner of Bathurst St. and Sheppard Ave. W. in North York (392-8186) has four short downhill slopes, rentals and lessons.

Most of the ski hills north of the city, in and around the Collingwood-Barrie snowbelt, have snowmaking equipment and modern lifts.

BLUE MOUNTAIN

Collingwood
(705) 445-0231
Distance from Toronto: 1½–2 hours
Vertical drop: 220 m (720 ft.)
Lifts: 3 triple chairlifts, 6 double, 1 beginner, 3 poma lifts, 1 rope tow
Runs: 26, longest is 1200 m (3940 ft.)
Terrain: 27% novice, 61% intermediate, 12% advanced
Average snowfall: 280 cm (110 in.)
Facilities: rental and repair shop; ski shops; ski school; daycare; snowmaking; night skiing until 10 P.M.; Blue Mountain Inn
Open 7 days a week.

TALISMAN

Kimberly
1-800-265-3754 toll free
Distance from Toronto: 1½ hours
Vertical drop: 195 m (640 ft.)
Lifts: 3 T-bars, 1 rope tow, 3 double chairlifts
Runs: 20
Terrain: 15% novice, 45% intermediate, 40% advanced
Average snowfall: 213 cm (84 in.)
Facilities: Talisman Mountain Resort Hotel (73 rooms); daycare; day lodge with cafeteria and bar; full rentals; ski school; snowmaking; Fri night skiing until 10 P.M.
Open 7 days a week.

HORSESHOE VALLEY

Between Barrie and Orillia
(705) 835-2790
Distance from Toronto: 1½–2 hours
Vertical drop: 115 m (377 ft.)
Lifts: 5 double chairlifts, 3 triple, 3 T-bars
Runs: 36, longest is 1500 m (4920 ft.)
Terrain: 30% novice, 39% intermediate, 31% advanced
Average snowfall: 330 cm (130 in.)
Facilities: ski school; rental and repair shops; three cafeterias and a snack bar; dining lounge; piano lounge and dining room; retail and gift shop; snowmaking; on-site inn; night skiing every night until 10 P.M.
Open 7 days a week.

HIDDEN VALLEY

Huntsville
(705) 789-5942
Distance from Toronto: 2½ hours
Vertical drop: 100 m (330 ft.)
Lifts: 1 quad-chairlift, 2 double, 1 rope tow
Runs: 11 slopes and trails, longest run is 432 m (1415 ft.)
Terrain: 30% novice, 50% intermediate, 20% advanced
Average snowfall: 318 cm (125 in.)
Facilities: ski chalet with cafeteria; Hidden Valley Resort Hotel (100 rooms); rentals; ski school; snowmaking
Open 7 days a week.

CROSS-COUNTRY

The City of Toronto Parks (392-7259) and Metro Parks (392-8186) offer advice on the best parks to ski in. For a 24-hour recorded ski conditions report, call 963-2911.

City parks that have cross-country trails and facilities are: Earl Bales Park, G. Ross Lord Park, Sunnybrook Park, Taylor's Creek Park, E. T. Seton Park, Etienne Brûlé Park and Lambton Woods. Most of these have heated washrooms and ample parking. A unique place to ski is on the famous Zooski Trails at the Metro Zoo (which has rentals).

GEAR

Some of the excellent ski equipment stores in Toronto are:

Oscar's Ski and Sports
1201 Bloor St. W.
near Lansdowne
532-4267

Sporting Life
2665 Yonge St. near Eglinton
485-1611

Sign of the Skier
2794 Yonge St. near Lawrence
488-2118

The Summit Ski and Bike Shop
1211 Hurontario St. near QEW
278-4446

Buyers should also check out the Ski Show at the CNE, particularly its Ski Patrol Ski Swap. Held every Thanksgiving weekend (early Oct).

RENTALS

High Park Cycle and Sports
1168 Bloor St. W. near Dufferin
532-7300
Downhill and cross-country ski equipment.

Blacks Camping International
2196 Queen St. E. at Balsam
690-4800
Cross-country ski equipment only.

Trail Head
40 Wellington St. E. near Church
862-0881
Cross-country ski equipment only.

SWIMMING

POOLS

Plenty. Toronto has 12 outdoor pools, 19 indoor pools at community centres and 19 indoor pools at schools. City pools are free, and lockers and keys are provided. For information on schedules and program times, call 392-7259 or 392-7286, Mon to Fri 8 A.M. to 4:30 P.M. On especially hot days some outdoor pools stay open till 1 A.M. Call 392-7838 after 3 P.M. to find out which ones they are.

The cities of Scarborough, Etobicoke, North York, York and the Borough of East York maintain their own pools. For details, call their Parks and Recreation departments, in the Blue Pages.

BEACHES

The Toronto waterfront is dotted with beaches. Some of the most popular are the beaches on Centre Island, Wards Island, the Beaches Boardwalk area and Cherry Beach near the Leslie St. Spit. In recent years there have been pollution problems all along Lake Ontario, and beaches have sometimes been closed for short periods. Call Metro Parks (392-8186) to find out which beaches are suitable for swimming.

If you're looking for more than just a swim, head to Canada's largest water park, Sunshine Beach Water Park. See With the Kids/Day Trips.

TENNIS/SQUASH/ RACQUETBALL

Squash and racquetball courts are available to nonmembers for a daily fee at the three YMCA locations in the city (see Fitness, this chapter). Phone ahead for reservations.

PUBLIC TENNIS COURTS

Toronto's more than 165 courts are available at different times to the public, groups with permits and community tennis clubs. Check with each court to find out when the courts are available. Call the city Parks and Recreation department at 392-7291.

Most public courts are available on a first-come, first-served basis, and the general rule is, you can have the court for no more than half an hour if someone is waiting.

The southeast quadrant of Eglinton Flats (at Eglinton Ave. W. and Jane St.) is the site of a major public pay-as-you-play tennis facility including 12 surfaced and lighted courts. Phone 392-2486.

The least-used public courts are on the Toronto Islands near Hanlan's Point. Other less well used courts are on Lakeshore Blvd. W. between the Argo Rowing Club and the Legion Hall.

The other Metro municipalities also have lots of public tennis courts. Contact their Parks and Recreation departments, in the Blue Pages.

PRIVATE TENNIS CLUBS

Some private tennis clubs, including several downtown, offer visitors pay-as-you-play courts. Look in the Yellow Pages, or try:

**Downtown Tennis and Nautilus
21 Eastern Ave. near Parliament
362-2439**

EQUIPMENT

These stores specialize in tennis, squash, racquetball and badminton equipment, stringing services and court clothing.

**Straub Sports
1268 Yonge St. near Summerhill
923-5128**

**Forum Racquet Clinic
40 Madison Ave. near Bloor W.
962-5619**

SHOPPING

SHOPPING AREAS

Toronto has virtually unlimited shopping possibilities, from some of Canada's most exclusive boutiques to some of the best bargains going. Our recommendations are based on quality, selection, uniqueness and sometimes low price, but by no means are these the only stores in the city worth visiting. We have concentrated on downtown, and any stores listed outside the core are included because of some special feature.

Most shops are open Mon to Sat, with later hours (usually to 9 P.M.) on Thurs and Fri. Stores are closed Sun unless they provide essential services, such as gas stations and pharmacies, or are in designated tourist areas. An 8% retail sales tax applies to most purchases.

BLOOR W./YORKVILLE

Toronto's most exclusive shopping area. In fact, Bloor St. between Avenue Rd. and Yonge St. is ranked as one of the 10 most expensive shopping streets in the world. Yorkville, the area immediately north of Bloor St., has firmly established itself as the centre of haute couture in Toronto. Lots of trendy restaurants and outdoor cafés where you can sip a spritzer and recover from your shopping splurges.

YONGE ST. STRIP

"The Strip" extends from Bloor St. south to Queen St. Shopping runs the gamut from quality to just plain weird, but the real attraction is the colourful and sometimes eccentric throngs of people who crowd onto the Strip seven days a week.

UPPER YONGE VILLAGE

The shopping area of Yonge St. that runs between Eglinton Ave. and Lawrence Ave. caters to the upwardly mobile who live in the adjoining neighbourhoods. Fresh pasta shops, bakeries, specialty butcher shops, bookstores, some quality women's and men's clothing stores plus a number of very good restaurants.

THE BEACHES

Well-loved for its small-town atmosphere, low-rise streetscape and shore-hugging boardwalk. Just the place for a casual stroll by the lake or some leisurely browsing in the many eclectic, funky shops that line Queen St. E. Lots of ice cream parlours and outdoor cafés.

CHINATOWN

Ever-increasing in size, Chinatown now stretches along Dundas St. from Bay St. to Spadina Ave. and north along Spadina to College St. Authentic Chinese restaurants, markets, specialty shops and

DOWNTOWN SHOPPING

1 Hazelton Lanes
2 Hudson's Bay Centre
3 The Colonnade
4 College Park
5 Atrium on Bay
6 First Canadian Place
7 St. Lawrence Market
8 Queen's Quay Terminal
● CN Tower
■ SkyDome
← Traffic Direction
Not all one-way streets are shown

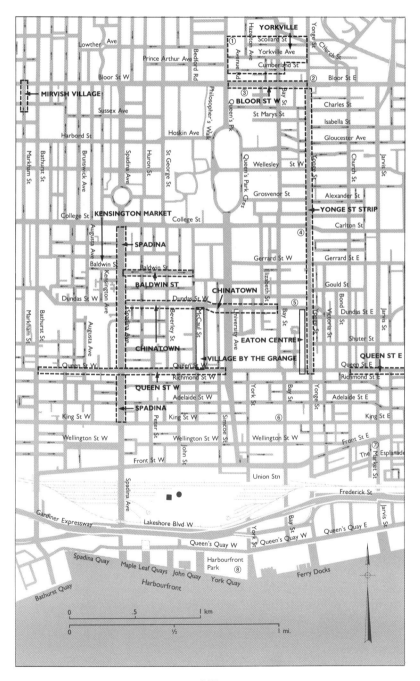

Courtesy of David Crighton © 1989

movie theatres. Thanks to its tourist area designation, it is business as usual on Sundays.

BLOOR WEST VILLAGE

A village atmosphere typifies this tree-lined section of Bloor St. W. just north and west of High Park. Many specialty food shops in the European tradition as well as some quality clothing stores.

QUEEN ST. W.

Queen St. between University Ave. and Bathurst St. abounds with used book-stores, craft shops, bohemian and new-wave clothing stores and some of the best restaurants and bars in Toronto.

QUEEN ST. E.

Queen St. between Church St. and Parliament St. is an area in transition. You'll find antique shops and interior design galleries side by side with junk shops and greasy spoons.

BALDWIN ST.

Two blocks north of the Art Gallery of Ontario, Baldwin St. has always catered to the university crowd. Shopping consists of an interesting mix of used record and vintage clothing stores, health food shops and some excellent eateries.

SPADINA

Spadina Ave. between King St. and College St. is Toronto's "Fashion District"—so say the street signs in this area. Clearances and bargains galore.

MARKHAM (or MIRVISH) VILLAGE

On Markham St. just west of Bathurst St. and south of Bloor St., grand Victorian homes have been converted into bookstores, galleries, antique shops and restaurants. Open on Sundays.

MT. PLEASANT/EGLINTON

Known for its high concentration of antique shops.

THE DANFORTH

Danforth Ave. between Broadview Ave. and Pape Ave. is still very much thought of as Toronto's "Greektown," though it's changing to reflect the lifestyles of the young professionals buying and renovating houses on the neighbouring streets. Greek markets, gift stores and a lot of authentic Greek restaurants thrive here.

ST. CLAIR W./DUFFERIN

Little Italy is known for its vibrant streetlife with lots of outdoor cafés, markets and street vendors. A good selection of Italian designer clothing and shoe stores, pasta shops and restaurants.

GERRARD ST.

In the last 10 years Gerrard St. west of Coxwell has taken on a bazaar-like quality and become the place for East Indian shopping and dining in Toronto.

RONCESVALLES AVE.

Historically the heart of the Polish district, here you'll find plenty of opportunities to sample Eastern European foods and wares.

THE UNDERGROUND

Toronto's underground shopping concourse is the largest in the world, with over 7 km (4 mi.) of shopping malls. The concourse runs uninterrupted from under Union Station and the Royal York Hotel in the south to the Eaton Centre in the north (except for a short stretch at the Bay/Queen intersection) and affords a dazzling variety of shops and services. And of course it's climate-controlled, so whether it's a cold winter day or a blistering heat wave, you can always shop in comfort. **Shopping Hint:** It's a great place for Sat shopping, since the business crowd is gone for the weekend and you have the place almost to yourself.

SHOPPING MALLS

Eaton Centre
Yonge St. at Dundas
598-2322
Each week, over a million visitors make the Eaton Centre Toronto's No. 1 tourist attraction. The three-level galleria with its 300 stores, combined with Eaton's 1-million sq.ft. (90 000 m^2) flagship store, provides the shop-till-you-drop crowd with literally acres of retail offerings. Simpsons department store, connected to the megacomplex by a pedestrian crossover at Queen St., adds almost another 1 million sq.ft. No matter how often you go, you'll still be overwhelmed. Note the centre's renowned sculpture, Flight Stop, created by Canada's own Michael Snow; the 60 life-size Canada geese appear to be coming in for a landing. While in Eaton's, rub the bronze foot of the Timothy Eaton statue—for good luck.

Toronto's No. 1 tourist attraction—the Eaton Centre. (Photo by Ottmar Bierwagen)

Fairview Mall
1800 Sheppard Ave. E.
near Don Mills
491-0151

Hudson's Bay Centre
Bloor St. E. at Yonge
928-5031

The Promenade
1 Promenade Circle
(south of Hwy. 7,
north of Steeles)
Thornhill
764-0020

Scarborough Town Centre
Hwy. 401 and McCowan
296-5490

Sherway Gardens
The Queensway at Hwy. 427
621-1070

Woodbine Centre
Hwy. 27 and Rexdale Blvd.
674-5200

Yorkdale
Hwy. 401 and Dufferin
789-3261

BOUTIQUE COMPLEXES

The Atrium on Bay
20 Dundas St. W. at Yonge
593-1796

This bronze statue of Timothy Eaton sits just inside the store near the Dundas St. entrance. Rub the toe for good luck. (Photo by Brian Thompson)

College Park
Yonge St. at College
597-1221

The Colonnade
131 Bloor St. W. near Avenue Rd.
925-5157

I First Canadian Place
King St. at Bay
862-6175

Hazelton Lanes
55 Avenue Rd. near Bloor
968-8600

Queen's Quay Terminal
207 Queen's Quay W. at York
363-5017

The Sheppard Centre
Yonge St. and Sheppard
226-5151

Village by the Grange
49 McCaul St. near Dundas
598-1414

WOMEN'S CLOTHING

The designer boutiques in some of the large downtown department stores such as Eaton's, Simpsons and The Bay offer a large selection of women's wear ranging from moderately priced garments to the very exclusive.

Brigitte
75 Yorkville Ave. near Bay
921-7337
European swimwear.

Yorkville—a glittery mix of haute couture, trendy fashion and specialty boutiques.

Alan Cherry
711 Yonge St. near Bloor
967-1115
High-fashion European-designed clothing for women and men from such well-known names as Giorgio Armani, Mario Valentino and Gian Marco Venturi. Haute couture furs and a bridal salon as well. Just up the street, at 719 Yonge, is **23 Steps,** the Alan Cherry Designer Clearance Centre (923-9785). Prices start at 50% off.

Club Monaco
403 Queen St. W. near Spadina
979-5633
(other locations)
Classic, casual, preppy styles of
women's, men's and children's clothing
designed by Alfred Sung and made from
all-natural fabrics. The signature full-
length terry bathrobes are wonderful. A
small café at the back of the store lets
you quench your thirst while you shop.

Creeds
45 Bloor St. W. near Yonge
923-1000
Très exclusive, très expensive. Designer
boutiques in the store carry Sonia
Rykiel, Emanuel Ungaro, Chanel (the
only one in Canada) and Christian
Lacroix to name a few. A full line of
high-fashion shoes and accessories as
well.

Ms. Emma Designs
275 Queen St. W. near McCaul
598-2471
Original handcrafted women's wear
made from natural fabrics. Soft lines,
feminine styling. Seamstresses work
from the designs right in the shop.
Comfortable, friendly atmosphere with
always a cat or two wandering about.

Frida Craft Store
39 Front St. E. near Yonge
366-3169
More than a craft store. Clothing for
women, men and children in all-natural
fabrics. You'll find (among other things)
romantic old-fashioned stylings for
women, colourful hand-loomed men's
shirts from Guatemala, one of Toronto's
best selections of scarves (silk, cotton,
batik), an array of hand-loomed or
block-printed bedspreads and cushions,
and crafts from over 50 countries. Open
7 days a week. A great Sunday browse.

*Frida Craft Store is one of many unique shops
near the St. Lawrence Market.*

Heritage House
Toronto-Dominion Centre
King St. at Bay
947-0408
(other locations)
Classic and elegant suitings and co-ordinates for business and casual wear.

Holt Renfrew
50 Bloor St. W. near Yonge
922-2333
(other locations)
A classy, upscale department store. Shop from boutique to boutique of designer clothes and accessories for women and men. All arranged in an elegant and refined setting, complete with doorman.

Ira-Berg
1510 Yonge St. near St. Clair
922-9100
Mostly imports with designer lines such as Celine, Byblos and Genny. Everything from sportswear to coats and suits to evening gowns. Classic, conservative and expensive.

Irish Shop
110 Bloor St. W. near Avenue Rd.
922-9400
A variety of styles for women and men by mostly Irish designers in wools, cottons, tweeds, linens and lace. The emphasis is on fine fabrics and tailoring. A wide selection of sweaters.

Justin's
24 St. Clair Ave. W. near Yonge
960-5457
A designer discount store offering end of line and samples (with labels cut out) at 20% off retail, and 50 to 60% savings during their sales.

Kettle Creek Canvas Co.
828 Yonge St. near Bloor
968-1232
(other locations)
Canadian-designed women's and men's recreational and casual clothing made from 100% cotton, canvas, oxford cloth and twills. Sturdy, well-made apparel for the outdoorsy set.

Le Chateau
85 Bloor St. W. near Bay
968-0576
Eaton Centre
979-3122
(other locations)
A lot of trendy fun fashion clothing for the teens and twenties crowd (women and men). Prices tend to be in the low to moderate range.

Liptons
50 Bloor St. W. near Yonge
922-1330
(other locations)
Mostly Canadian-designed women's clothing with a focus on casual wear, business wear and evening dresses. Lots of velvet and taffeta at Christmas.

Ada MacKenzie
94 Cumberland St. near Bay
922-2222
Since 1930, importers of European apparel in sizes 8 to 20. Classic investment clothing with a good selection of coats (including Aquascutum) and casual wear. Moderately expensive.

Paul Magder Furs
202 Spadina Ave. near Queen W.
363-6077
New and used fur coats and accessories for women, men and children. Off the rack, and therefore better prices than the exclusive styles for sale on Bloor St.

Marks and Spencer
Eaton Centre
979-1907
(other locations)
The venerable British chain carries conservative, good-quality apparel for women, men and children at reasonable prices, as well as a large selection of sweets and frozen foods imported from the U.K. One of the best places we know to buy underwear and shortbread.

Morning Star Trading
31 Baldwin St. near McCaul
977-3976
(other locations)
Mostly cotton garments for women and men, with a lot of comfortable East Indian styles. Walking into this store with its wooden floors, silver jewellery, beaded bracelets and wicker bags is like a flashback to the 60s.

Norma
116 Cumberland St. near Bay
923-5514
The Canadian designer Norma mixes current fashion trends with interesting textures such as hand-knits, leathers, fur and feathers to create her distinctive line of women's clothing. Prices range from $500 to $3,000. She also specializes in designing unique children's jackets.

Sellers-Gough Furs
174 Spadina Ave. near Queen W.
368-7643
Made-to-measure and a large selection of off-the-rack furs for women and men. Opened in 1880, this is Toronto's oldest furrier.

Sportables
55 Bloor St. W. near Yonge
967-4122
Queen's Quay Terminal
366-7410
Classic casual wear for women and men from such designers as Ralph Lauren, Perry Ellis and Anne Klein. This is where you buy your cashmere crewneck, cuffed wool pants, paisley scarf and trench coat, with Vivaldi's "Four Seasons" as background music. One of the city's largest coat departments.

Alfred Sung
Hazelton Lanes
922-9226
Distinctively styled suits, separates and sportswear primarily for the business woman. Much of the collection features all-wool and pure silk fabrics.

Winners
57 Spadina Ave. near King
585-2052
(other locations)
Designer clothing and accessories (sans labels) at 25 to 50% off. No substandards, and often some unbelievable bargains. Also lots of brand-name children's clothing.

ACCESSORIES

Hermes
Hazelton Lanes
968-8626
The only Hermes boutique in Canada carries many of the famous French line of accessories for women and men including silk scarves and ties, purses, briefcases, watches and jewellery.

La Vie en Rose
Eaton Centre
595-0898
Specialists in designer lingerie. Printed silks, stretch lace teddies, bustières and other undergarments. You'll find all the newest styles here.

Margo's Custom Hats
7 Pleasant Blvd. at Yonge
924-9878
Pre-made and custom-made hats of every description for every occasion, guaranteed to fit. Bridal headpieces designed as well.

MEN'S CLOTHING

Abercrombie and Fitch
2 First Canadian Place
Exchange Tower
Adelaide St. W. at York
860-0770
High-quality casual wear from the famous U.S. chain.

Walter Beauchamp Tailors
145 Wellington St. W. at Simcoe
595-5454
A King and Bay tradition now somewhat removed from King and Bay. Good suit selection including Cambridge, Samuelsohn and Hardy Amies, and excellent custom-mades.

George Bouridis Custom Made Shirts
193 Church St. near Dundas
363-4868
Impeccable custom-made shirts.

Bill Brady
104 Yorkville Ave. near Bay
922-6600
Full range of men's clothing. Suits from $600 to $900 made by the likes of Hardy Amies and Paragi.

The Brick Shirt House
601 Yonge St. near Wellesley
964-7021
They're best known for their large selection of in-house and imported-label shirts, though their suits and casual clothing are well worth a look.

Brown's
545 Queen St. W. near Spadina
368-5937
1975 Avenue Rd. near Wilson
489-1975
For over 60 years Brown's has been offering fashionable clothing exclusively for men 5'1" to 5'7".

Bulloch Tailors
65 Front St. E. at Church
367-1084
Custom-made suits and alterations. Popular with Bay St. lawyers, bankers and brokers.

Thomas K. T. Chui
754 Broadview Ave.
near Danforth
465-8538
The tailor for many of Canada's rich and powerful. Superb quality.

Classica Uomo
150 Bloor St. W. near Avenue Rd.
961-0683
Very expensive European designer clothing. Suits by Venturi, Gautier, Ferre and Uomo.

The Coop
3287 Yonge St. near Lawrence
486-9944
Contemporary casual clothing with an especially fine collection of imported sweaters. They carry suits from Hugo Boss and Alfred Sung.

Alan Goouch
89 Bloor St. W. near Bay
964-8395
(other locations)
Everything from jeans to pricey businesswear. Suits range from the designs of Hugo Boss to more Establishment fashions. They pride themselves on the popularity of their shirts and ties.

Halpern Esq. Shirt Shop
Eaton Centre
591-9390
(other locations)
A well-stocked shirt and tie boutique focussing on classic styles.

Hobberlin's
Atrium on Bay
599-5017
Custom tailors in Toronto for more than 100 years. Traditional styles. Off-the-rack suits include the expensive Warren K. Cook line and the moderately priced Progress and Cambridge.

Irish Shop for Men
110 Bloor St. W. near Avenue Rd.
922-9400
High-quality tweeds, sweaters, hats and more from the Emerald Isle. Both traditional and contemporary styles.

Cy Mann Clothiers
1170 Bay St. near Bloor
977-5442
(other locations)
Well-known custom tailors. They'll make you anything from the ultra-conservative to the ultramodern.

Marek The Best of Europe
110 Bloor St. W. near Bay
923-5100
(other locations)
Expensive, eye-catching imported designer neckware, belts, wallets and other accessories.

Mark's Work Wearhouse
773 Yonge St. near Bloor
964-6604
(other locations)
Reasonably priced clothes for working and for weekends, including footwear and outerwear. Always a good stock of jeans.

Lou Myles Disegnatore
88 Avenue Rd. near Bloor
975-9333
They make their own suits, both custom-made and ready-to-wear, from a large selection of fabrics. Prices start about $850. They tell us that Sugar Ray Leonard, Lee Iacocca and Vic Damone are some of their best customers.

Numero Uno Uomo
1997 Yonge St. near Davisville
488-0020
Specializes in Italian high fashion designer wear. Expensive shirts, ties, suits and more. Suits include Armani and Valentino designs.

George Richards Kingsize Clothes
36 King St. E. near Yonge
868-1360
2454 Yonge St. near Eglinton
487-2131
The name says it all. Casual and businesswear for the taller or larger man.

Harry Rosen
117 Richmond St. W. near York
586-7739
82 Bloor St. W. near Bay
972-0556
(other locations)
This large chain carries an extensive selection and full lines of ties, shirts, casual wear and accessories. Suits range from $700 to $1,400. Popular lines include Samuelsohn and Zegna. Frequented by the Establishment business crowd.

Stollery's
1 Bloor St. at Yonge
922-6173
A Toronto institution at one of the city's busiest intersections. Three full floors of men's and ladies' apparel, often at discounted prices. Famous for its classic British woollen wear and its large selections of traditional suits, shirts and ties.

Studio 267
267 Yonge St. near Dundas
366-4452
(other locations)
Their selection of suits includes Italian labels such as Zegna, Valentino, Boss, Armani, Hardy Amies, plus their own styles. Full lines of accessories, designer sweaters and casual wear.

Tilley Endurables
Queen's Quay Terminal
865-9910
(other locations)
The company started with their now famous multipurpose hat and expanded into shirts, pants, shorts, skirts and bomber jackets. Hardy, functional and stylish clothing for men and women.

The Yorkviller
75 Yorkville Ave. near Bay
921-9229
Expensive men's imported underwear and swimsuits.

VINTAGE AND USED CLOTHING

Courage My Love
14 Kensington Ave.
near Dundas W.
979-1992
Vintage clothes, new clothes, imported clothes, lamps, lots of jewellery. Prices range all over the map, with some bargains.

The Yonge St. Arcade opposite Temperance St., as it appeared at the turn of the century. (Metropolitan Toronto Library, T 12415)

Divine Decadence
7 Charles St. W. near Yonge
922-2105

Victorian lace and linen, boater hats, long black gloves, or that perfect Edwardian evening gown can all be found here. Period clothing in excellent condition for men, women and children.

L'Elegante
122 Yorkville Ave.
near Avenue Rd.
923-3220

Designer resale fashions. Chic women's clothing—sizes 6 to 16—with such labels as YSL, Oscar de la Renta and Chloé. Slightly used handbags, jewellery and accessories are also sold.

Extoggery
115 Merton St. near Yonge
488-5393
3250 Yonge St. near Lawrence
482-2811
2267 Bloor St. W.
769-5161

Large inventories of second-hand clothing for men and women. The quality varies from store to store. Company policy for holding goods only for a limited period ensures turnover.

Fashion Mine
80 Scollard St. near Bay
923-3332

A very good upscale fashion resale store for women with a large selection of day wear, evening wear and shoes.

The Shoppe D'Or
18 Cumberland St. near Yonge
923-2384
They were in the business long before second-hand wardrobes were trendy. Recent styles, mostly European-designed day dresses and suits, evening gowns and accessories.

SHOES, MEN'S AND WOMEN'S

Bally
50 Bloor St. W. near Yonge
924-4772
1 First Canadian Place
(concourse level)
363-9853
High-quality and classic styles of expensive men's and women's shoes.

Brown's Shoe Shops
Hazelton Lanes
968-1806
Eaton Centre
979-9270
High-fashion and classic shoes, boots and bags for men and women in the moderate to high price range. The Eaton Centre store carries the women's line only.

Calderone
Eaton Centre
979-9718
Toronto-Dominion Centre
King St. at Bay
368-2163
Shoes, boots and matching bags handmade in Italy, Spain and Brazil for men and women. Moderately priced contemporary styles.

Capezio
70 Bloor St. W. near Bay
920-1006
Italian-designed shoes for women. Stylish and moderately priced.

Corbò
110 Bloor St. W. near Avenue Rd.
928-0954
Exotic, avant-garde designer shoes from Italy and France for men and women. Expensive.

David's
66 Bloor St. W. at Bay
920-1000
Unarguably the most expensive and perhaps the best men's and women's shoe store in Toronto. Only imports, with the finest quality shoes and bags from such designers as Bruno Magli, Maud Frizon, Yves St. Laurent, Valentino, Enrico Covieri and Roger Vivier.

Hobbit
14 Wellesley St. W. near Yonge
967-7115
Birkenstock shoes and sandals.

Pino Carina Shoes
92 Bloor St. W. near Bay
968-2298
Eaton Centre
979-1641
(other locations)
Definitely leaning towards the avant-garde. Shoes and boots for men and women at moderate to high prices.

Roots Natural Footwear
195 Avenue Rd. near Davenport
927-8585
Eaton Centre
977-0041
(other locations)
Well-made Canadian shoes, boots, bags and belts for men and women. Known for comfortable fit and classic casual styling.

Town Shoes
25 Bloor St. W. near Yonge
922-1731
Eaton Centre
979-9914
Moderately priced fashionable women's shoes and boots. Popular designers carried here include Alberta Ferretti, Perry Ellis and Evan-Picone.

Harry Young Shoes
67 Front St. E. near Church
363-2015
1499 Yonge St. near St. Clair
924-4431
Elegant, conservative shoes for men and women. Both stores carry Amalfi, Evan-Picone, Sebago and Florsheim.

JEWELLERY

Beni Sung Fine Jewellery
45 Bloor St. W. near Yonge
(in the Creeds store)
923-1000
Distinctive fine jewellery designed by the award-winning Beni Sung. Prices range from $75 to $60,000. If you're looking for something unusual in pearls or semiprecious stones, this is a good place to start.

Birks
Eaton Centre
979-9311
(other locations)
Probably the best-known jewellery and fine silver establishment in the city. For generations Birks has catered to those who appreciate quality.

Richard Booth Fine Jewellery
138 Cumberland St. near Bay
Unit 9
960-3207
Custom designers and manufacturers. Many one-of-a-kind pieces and a good selection of gold and silver jewellery. Prices from $75 to the high thousands.

European Jewellery
111 Bloor St. W. near Bay
967-7201
Original jewellery designed and created on-site. You can choose from their portfolio or have them create something totally new. Complete with on-duty policeman.

Gold Shoppe
25 Bloor St. W. near Yonge
(entrance on Balmuto)
923-5565
Best known as an estate jewellery and fine silver shop, it has been a fixture on Bloor St. for years and years.

KSP Jewellery
Hazelton Lanes
922-4100
Eaton Centre
598-4100
Stylish costume jewellery at prices that range from $20 to $500.

Silverbridges
162 Cumberland St.
near Avenue Rd.
923-2591
Designer Peter Wong works with sterling silver to create distinctive jewellery designs. Right beside the Four Seasons Hotel.

ANTIQUES

Not only are there more antiques available in Toronto than in quaint rural Ontario but there are more *good* antiques and oftentimes at more competitive prices. Antique shops tend to cluster in Toronto, so if you just want to browse try: Mt. Pleasant south of Eglinton; Markham St.; and Yorkville and Davenport.

Harbourfront Antique Market
390 Queen's Quay W. at Spadina
340-8377
Whether you're looking for a teaspoon like grandma's or a clock like grandpa's, they probably have it here. About 100 dealers during the week and over 200 on Sun. Closed Mon.

Antique Aid
187-A Queen St. E. near Jarvis
368-9565
A little of everything. Glass, furniture, silver, china, jewellery and paintings.

Antiques by Telfer/Troy/Howard
581 Mt. Pleasant Rd. near Manor
485-2283
Excellent selection of quilts, samplers, folk art, spatterware, country furniture and more.

Atelier Art and Antiques
588 Markham St. near Bloor
532-9244
If you have a passion for folk art you can indulge it here. Lots of decoys, paintings and carved figures.

Edward E. Denby
20 Birch Ave. near Yonge
921-2493
All sorts of militaria.

The Door Store
43 Britain St. near Sherbourne
863-1590
Antique doors, windows, fireplace mantles and more. Thank goodness someone is recycling these works of art.

Guildhall Antiques
577 Mt. Pleasant Rd. near Manor
487-7697
A definite concentration on pine and Canadiana. Many large pieces.

Journey's End Antiques
612 Markham St. near Bloor
536-2226
Large displays of silver, china, glass and memorabilia. Also postcards, fine furniture, primitives.

Labell's Toy Soldiers
100 Front St. W.
(in the Royal York Hotel)
362-8697
The store for toy soldier collectors. A wide variety of old and new models from finely painted antique lead Britains to their own lines of Canadian historical figures. They also carry Dinky and Matchbox toys.

Jack Morris Antiques
1212 Yonge St. near Birch
925-5541
Jewellery, silver, china, glass, and 18th-
and 19th-century European furniture.

Mt. Pleasant Galleries
563 Mt. Pleasant Rd. near Manor
487-9030
Fine antique furniture gallery. Specializes in mahogany dining room suites.

Nitty Gritty Antiques and
Collectibles
111 Jarvis St. at Richmond
364-1393
Canadian antiques and a large number of
milk-paint reproductions.

O'Neil Antiques
100 Avenue Rd. near Davenport
968-2806
Excellent selection of refinished pine
pieces and Canadiana. They always have
a good stock of pine frame mirrors,
decoys and harvest tables on hand.

The Paisley Shop
889 Yonge St. near Davenport
923-5830
A well established antique store specializing in fine pieces of 18th-century
English furniture.

The Port Dalhousie Trading
Company
104 Avenue Rd. near Davenport
920-0323
Known for the quality of their refinished
oak and pine furniture as well as their
large variety of folk art items.

Upper Canada Antiques
588 Markham St. near Bloor
536-8667
Canadiana, militaria, old toys, old tools,
housewares and lots of framed mirrors.

Stanley Wagman & Son Antiques
33 Avenue Rd. at Yorkville
964-1047
Their specialty is 18th- and 19th-
century French provincial and formal
furniture.

Whimsy Antiques
597 Mt. Pleasant Rd. near Manor
488-0770
The focus here is on pine and Canadiana.
Finished pieces include flat-to-wall cup-
boards and armoires.

ART SUPPLIES

Curry's Art Store
756 Yonge St. near Bloor
967-6666
Since 1911 Curry's has been supplying
equipment and materials to the fine art
and graphic art communities. With their
large inventory, you can generally always find what you need. Student discounts.

Grafix
344 Queen St. W. near Spadina
593-5888
Discount art supplies. Well stocked, and
with helpful staff.

**Gwartzman's Canvas and
Art Supplies
448 Spadina Ave. near College
922-5429**

A tiny, chaotic store that sells graphic
and fine art supplies in Spadina style
(that is, discount prices). This is the
place to have your linen canvas primed
and stretched.

**Loomis and Toles
214 Adelaide St. W.
near University
977-8877
963 Eglinton Ave. E. near Leslie
423-9300**

Wide selection of artists' materials and
drafting supplies.

BOOKS AND MAGAZINES

It would not be an exaggeration to say
that one of the reasons many people
come to Toronto is for the superb quality and rich diversity of its bookstores.

NATIONAL CHAIN STORES

**Classic Bookshops
Cumberland Terrace
2 Bloor St. W. at Yonge
922-2461
The Royal Bank Plaza
Front St. at Bay
865-0090
(other locations)**

A quality chain. Fairly good photography
and educational sections in addition to
best sellers. The Royal Bank Plaza store,
in the heart of Toronto's financial district, stocks a large business section.

Courtesy of David Crighton © 1989

**Coles The Book People
726 Yonge St. near Bloor
924-1707
Eaton Centre
979-9348
(other locations)**

One of the world's largest bookstore
chains. Shelf after shelf of best sellers
and usually a large section of discounted
remainders. Not much ambience, but a
great place to run in and buy a paper-
back at lunchtime.

W. H. Smith
Eaton Centre
979-9376
I First Canadian Place
862-7933
Toronto-Dominion Centre
(concourse level)
King St. at Bay
362-5967
(other locations)
Good all-round selection—a little of everything. They sell some stationery and art supplies as well.

UNIQUE TO TORONTO

Bakka Science Fiction Book Shoppe
282 Queen St. W. near Spadina
596-8161
Sci-fi addicts come from great distances to stock up on the new and used books and magazines found in Canada's largest science fiction bookstore.

Ballenford Architectural Books
98 Scollard St. near Bay
960-0055
The country's largest collection of books on architecture, urban design and landscape architecture.

The Book Cellar
1560 Yonge St. near St. Clair
967-5577
General and international books and magazines, plus jazz, classical and New Age records and tapes.

The Book Cellar—Yorkville
142 Yorkville Ave. at Avenue Rd.
925-9955
General selection with some emphasis on literature, travel and art. Large domestic and international magazine and newspaper section. Open Sun, and in the summer until midnight on Fri and Sat.

Book City
501 Bloor St. W. near Spadina
961-4496
621 Yonge St. near Wellesley
962-8661
348 Danforth Ave. near Chester
469-9997
All three stores are open late seven nights a week. Good all-round selection, with strong literature, sci-fi and mystery sections. The Danforth store sells a lot of home renovation and children's books.

The Albert Britnell Book Shop
765 Yonge St. near Bloor
924-3321
A true gem. Albert Britnell opened his bookshop in 1893, and some of the staff have been serving customers here for over 30 years. It has the feel of an old English bookstore, and they actually encourage browsing. You can buy the weekly *New York Times Book Review* here. Special-order service.

Can-Do Bookstore
311 Queen St. W. near University
977-2351
The only store in Canada that stocks over 15,000 books solely for the driven do-it-yourselfer. Books that will teach you all you need to know to tackle just about any kind of repair or hobby.

The Cookbook Store
850 Yonge St. at Yorkville
920-COOK
They have every cookbook you've heard of and then some. You'll also find a large selection of wine and food magazines, and cooking videos that you can rent or buy. Celebrity chefs have been known to drop by for book signings.

Edwards Books and Art
356 Queen St. W. at Spadina
593-0126
387 Bloor St. E. at Sherbourne
961-2428
2200 Yonge St. at Eglinton
487-5431
2179 Queen St. E. at Lee
698-1442
The Queen St. store has a great feel—old, with lots of wood. All specialize in art books, but carry good-quality books in other categories. They advertise spectacular bargains in the Sat *Globe and Mail*. Open daily.

Glad Day Book Shop
598-A Yonge St. near Wellesley
961-4161
Gay and lesbian books, magazines and cards.

Librairie Champlain
107 Church St. at Richmond
364-4345
With over 125,000 books, this is one of the best French-language bookstores outside Quebec. Newspapers, magazines, records, computer software, posters and greeting cards are also sold.

Lichtman's News and Books
595 Bay St. at Dundas
591-1617
144 Yonge St. near Richmond
368-7390
842 Yonge St. near Bloor
924-4186
(other locations)
Newspapers, journals and magazines from around the world. This is the place to go to find out what's been happening at home, wherever home may be. Also a wide selection of books.

Longhouse Books
497 Bloor St. W. near Brunswick
921-9995
Strictly Canadian and Native American books. The store founders share a passionate commitment to Canadian writing talent. Among the 25,000 titles in stock is the largest collection of Native books in North America.

The Bob Miller Book Room
180 Bloor St. W. near Avenue Rd.
922-3557
A serious books lover's store, well known for its literature, philosophy and theology offerings. Hidden away in the basement of an office building.

David Mirvish Books on Art
596 Markham St. near Bloor
531-9975
Beautiful art books, art gallery catalogues, classic fiction and nonfiction, often drastically reduced during weekend sales. Check their advertisement in the Sat *Globe and Mail* for a list of discounted books. Open daily noon to 6 P.M.

Nautical Mind
249 Queen's Quay W. near York
869-3431
Books on sailing, seamanship, model
making, oceanography, naval and
maritime history, and boat construction
and maintenance. The store acts as chart
agents for the Canadian and American
governments.

Open Air Books and Maps
25 Toronto St. at Adelaide E.
363-0719
Tucked away in the bottom floor
(watch the steps), this is a special store
for those who love to travel. Atlases,
guidebooks, nature books and travel literature. It's a great place to browse on
a grey Toronto day.

Pages Books and Magazines
256 Queen St. W. near University
598-1447
Concentrates on philosophy, cultural
theory and contemporary fiction as well
as fine art, photography and design. Lots
of small-press books. Open daily.

SCM Bookroom
333 Bloor St. W. near St. George
979-9624
A progressive academic bookstore well
known for its theology department.
You'll also find well-stocked shelves of
philosophy, feminism, politics,
psychotherapy and Third World literature. Special-order service.

Sleuth of Baker Street
1543 Bayview Ave. near Eglinton
483-3111
Over 25,000 new and out-of-print
detective fiction and spy novels cram
the floor-to-ceiling shelves. The only
store of its kind in Canada.

Theatrebooks
25 Bloor St. W. near Yonge
(entrance on Balmuto)
922-7175
The theme is the performing arts.
Books on musicals, opera, film, dance,
and a vast collection of plays.

This Ain't the Rosedale Library
483 Church St. near Wellesley
929-9912
A wonderfully eclectic selection, including more baseball titles than you've ever
seen under one roof. Books on boxing,
photography, rock and jazz, political
treatises, poetry and lots of contemporary fiction. Magazines too.

Toronto Women's Bookstore
73 Harbord St. near Spadina
922-8744
Feminist focus.

University of Toronto Bookstore
214 College St. at St. George
978-7907
Much more than university course
books. Magazines, best sellers and com-
puters. In a beautifully restored former
library.

World's Biggest Bookstore
20 Edward St. at Yonge
977-7009
This store has to be seen to be believed. A former bowling alley, it contains 27 km (17 mi.) of shelving on two floors and over 1 million books. Lots of remainders and sale prices. Open daily; 1 block north of the Eaton Centre.

Writers & Co.
2005 Yonge St. near Davisville
481-8432
No mass-market here. Stocked with nothing but quality literature, poetry and literary criticism—and a large baseball section. Browsing is encouraged.

BOOKS (USED AND RARE)

Many of the more notable used/rare book dealers are located on a stretch of Queen St. W. between McCaul St. and Spadina Ave.

Abelard Books
519 Queen St. W. near Spadina
366-0021
A good selection of used books on philosophy, history, mediaeval studies and theology.

About Books
280 Queen St. W. near Spadina
593-0792
Used books on everything from philosophy to plumbing. The literature section is usually well stocked.

Atticus Books
84 Harbord St. near Spadina
922-6045
Within the past 10 years, this store has built a reputation for its consistently fine collection of used scholarly books. Antiquarian manuscript leaves are also available from time to time.

Old Favourites Book Shop
250 Adelaide St. W.
near University
977-2944
Probably the biggest used and antiquarian bookstore in Toronto. Over 350,000 titles at any one time, with a particular strength in Canadiana and equestrian books. Book-search service—they'll keep you on file for as long as it takes to find your book.

Village Book Store
239 Queen St. W. near University
598-4097
Specializes in out-of-print and rare books on Canadian art, antiques and book collecting. They also sell new books on antiques and collectibles.

CHINA

William Ashley
50 Bloor St. W. near Yonge
964-2900
An amazing selection of fine china, crystal and silver at excellent prices. More brides register here than anywhere else in the city. Always crowded.

The Bronze Dolphin
1365 Yonge St. at Rosehill
929-0218
Known as *the* place for Rosenthal crystal. Lots of china as well.

CRAFTS

The One-of-a-Kind Canadian Craft Show, held every November in the Automotive Building at Exhibition Place, features a vast selection of distinctive handmade gift items. See Sightseeing/Calendar of Events.

Algonquians
670 Queen St. W. near Bathurst
368-1336
A good selection of native Canadian Indian soapstone carvings, paintings, masks, porcupine quill jewellery and beadwork.

Clay Design Studio/Gallery
170 Brunswick Ave. at Harbord
964-3330
The retail showroom of a talented group of ceramicists. Raku pottery, earthenware plates and platters, and ceramic jewellery.

Dexterity
173 King St. E. near Jarvis
367-4775
Exquisite hand-blown glass, stained glass, ceramics, wooden furniture and garments.

Five Potters' Studio
131A Pears Ave.
near Avenue Rd.
924-6992
The same five women potters have produced work in this studio for 30 years. You'll find their distinctive styles in

sculptural and functional pieces of stoneware or porcelain.

The Glass Art Gallery
21 Hazelton Ave. near Yorkville
968-1823
Beautiful glass work by artists with international reputations.

The Guild Shop
140 Cumberland St. near Bay
921-1721
The nonprofit retail outlet for the Ontario Crafts Council. Works in glass, ceramics, wood, metal and fibre. Also an excellent selection of contemporary Inuit art.

The Pottery Shop
140 Yorkville Ave.
near Avenue Rd.
923-1803
Ongoing exhibits of works in clay.

Prime Canadian Crafts
229 Queen St. W. near University
593-5750
An excellent cross-section of traditional and contemporary Canadian craftwork. Displays feature pottery, hand-blown glass, wooden items, jewellery and fibreworks. Artists represented by this gallery will often undertake private commissions.

FABRICS

Elegance Paris Fabrics
91A Scollard St. near Bay
966-3446
A wonderful selection of fine European silks, woollens and cottons. Garment-length remnants are available at reduced prices.

Maryan's Fabric
3213 Yonge St. near Lawrence
488-6111
Imported European fabrics with a particularly large assortment of bridal and evening wear material. A good source for Viyella.

The Original Stitsky's
754 Bathurst St. near Bloor
537-2633
A fabric supermarket. Three large floors with everything from upholstery material to bridal and haute couture fabrics. They claim to have Toronto's largest notions floor.

HOME FURNISHINGS

Art Shoppe
2131 Yonge St. near Eglinton
487-3211
A rather eclectic mix of fine traditional and contemporary furniture. The store takes up an entire city block.

DeBoer's
College Park
596-1433
5051 Yonge St. near Sheppard
226-3730
A wide variety of contemporary high-quality furniture. They carry Canada's largest collection of fine leather-upholstered pieces.

Downright
17 Church St. at Front
868-1350
Duvets in all sizes and descriptions, filled with down, feather or synthetic materials. They offer a large selection of co-ordinated fabrics for duvet covers, pillow shams, bedskirts and draperies.

IKEA
15 Provost Dr.
near Sheppard and Leslie
222-4532
Gigantic store offering reasonably priced Scandinavian-designed furniture and furnishings. Lots of wood, plain or lacquered in bright colours. Everything from kitchen cabinets to corkscrews.

Industrial Revolution
345 Danforth Ave. near Chester
463-6235
Hi-tech, mostly Canadian-made furniture. A lot of tubular metal painted white and black. Well-known for their storage and shelving systems. Some furniture is sold unassembled. Moderately priced.

Ridpaths
906 Yonge St. near Davenport
920-4441
Housed in a heritage building built by Mr. Ridpath after World War I, this fine furniture gallery offers mostly traditional styles and a full interior design service.

KITCHENWARE

The Compleat Kitchen
87 Yorkville Ave. near Bay
920-6333
A cozy little store that carries professional cooking equipment for the home and up-to-date serving accessories. They will ship anywhere in Canada.

Dinetz Restaurant Equipment
231 King St. E. near Sherbourne
368-8657
A restaurant supply store. Items such as glassware and dishes sold in quantity only—by the dozens. Good buys on Paderno pots and Henckels knives.

Embros
1170 Yonge St.
near Summerhill subway
923-1808
One of the best kitchenware stores in the city, stocking only items that meet professional standards. This is where you can buy your ice cream maker, cappuccino and espresso machine, or any one of 25 different kettles.

Fortune Housewares
388 Spadina Ave. near College
593-6999
For over 30 years Fortune has been stocking quality European cookware, knives, enamel cookware and other essentials for modern kitchens.

Junors
Eaton Centre
598-2720
(other locations)
Located in many of the city's major malls. Kitchen gift items, gadgets, sets of pretty glasses, salad bowls, and more.

MARINE SUPPLIES

Genco Sails
544 King St. W. near Spadina
364-2891
In addition to manufacturing sails for all types of boats, this store sells good foul-weather gear and sportswear.

Lackie's Marina Dock Shoppe
Pier 4
249 Queen's Quay W. near York
366-6538
Marine accessories including nautical clothing, footwear and gifts.

Mason's Chandlery Store
1 Port St. E.
Port Credit
278-7005
A hardware store for all types of boats. Everything that's needed to keep boats looking good and running smoothly.

PHOTO SUPPLIES/FILM PROCESSING

Benjamin Film Laboratories
287 Richmond St. E.
near Sherbourne
863-1131
Film developing, enlargements, duplicating and video transfers. Same-day service for regular-size prints.

Black's Cameras
The Arcade
137 Yonge St. near Richmond
947-9278
Eaton Centre
598-1596
Commerce Court North
King St. at Bay
869-0341
(other locations)
Fast film processing, plus photographic equipment and supplies.

Toronto's famous Yonge St. Strip is a magnet for crowds 24 hours a day. (Photo by Ottmar Bierwagen)

Japan Camera Centre 1 Hour Photo
333 Yonge St. near Dundas
977-7171
College Park
598-1133
First Canadian Place
366-1207
Eaton Centre
598-1474
Fast, reliable film developing.

Henry's
119 Church St. near Queen E.
868-0872
Photographic equipment, repairs and trade-ins. Quality products and an informed staff.

Queen St. Camera Exchange
85 Queen St. E. near Church
862-0300
One of the best stores in town for new and used cameras and accessories. The knowledgeable staff takes time with customers.

RECORDS

A & A Records
351 Yonge St. near Dundas
unlisted number
Only one store separates this Yonge St. icon from Sam the Record Man, and the two have been in friendly competition for years. Their storefront signs can't be missed and add to the overall Yonge St. glitz. You'll find a large selection of records and tapes here, with the emphasis on pop.

Around Again
18 Baldwin St. near Beverley
979-2822
Mostly used LPs, cassettes and CDs, with most types of music available. The classical section is especially good. A store for serious record collectors and those who like to listen before they buy.

The Classical Record Shop
Hazelton Lanes
961-8999
In addition to classical, you'll find jazz, Broadway soundtracks and some pop recordings. The staff is knowledgeable, and they provide a special-order service.

Peter Dunn's Vinyl Museum
355 Yonge St. near Dundas
977-1176
402 Bloor St. W. near Brunswick
964-0065
2491 Lakeshore Blvd. W.
near Royal York Rd.
259-1991
Ask about their membership card, which gives you 20% off non-catalogue items. Lots of second-hand records, tapes and CDs. Most kinds of music (but classical only at the Bloor store).

Jazz and Blues Record Centre
66 Dundas St. E. at Bond
593-0269
The place for jazz and blues. Imports are their specialty, and they do a large mail-order business in the U.S. and Canada. You can often uncover some real finds in the used album section.

Sam the Record Man
347 Yonge St. near Dundas
unlisted number
A Toronto institution. Huge inventory of records and tapes, and a growing CD section. Jazz, blues, rock, classical—it's all here, including the hard-to-find.

Vortex Records
427 Queen St. W. near Spadina
591-8728
139 Dundas St. E. near Church
366-2046
Used records, specializing in rare and British.

SOUVENIRS

The shops listed here have above-average selections. And keep an eye out for interesting souvenirs from street vendors.

Impulse Shop
Art Gallery of Ontario
317 Dundas St. W. at McCaul
977-0414

The Centre Souvenirs
Eaton Centre
598-1962

CN Tower Gift Shop
301 Front St. W. at John
366-0876

Royal Ontario Museum Gift Shop
100 Queen's Park at Bloor
586-5783

SPORTS EQUIPMENT

Also see Sports/Recreation

Eddie Bauer
50 Bloor St. W. near Yonge
961-2525
High-quality clothing for hikers, campers, fishermen and cross-country skiers.

Blacks Camping International
16 Carlton St. near Yonge
597-0488
2196 Queen St. E. near Balsam
690-4800
A well-known name in the outfitting business. Excellent lines of equipment and clothing for climbing, canoeing and backpacking. Rental equipment is available.

Collegiate Sportsworld
Eaton Centre (lower level)
598-1626
(other locations)
A chain found in many of the city's shopping malls. Sports equipment and clothing.

Mountain Equipment Co-op
35 Front St. E. near Church
363-0122
Buy a membership and you can take advantage of lower co-op prices. Quality camping, hiking, mountain climbing and cross-country skiing equipment and clothing. Also carries books for the outdoor enthusiast.

Physical Assets—The Fitness Store
124 Davenport Rd.
near Avenue Rd.
925-2021
Every kind of exercise and fitness equipment. Top-of-the-line exercise bikes, rowing machines, treadmills, mini-trampolines, etc. Staff will help you design a home fitness program.

Runners' Choice
College Park
597-0023
Excellent selection of top-quality training, aerobics and court shoes.

Sporting Life
2665 Yonge St. near Eglinton
485-1611
Known by their full-page *Globe and Mail* ads. Specialize in skiing, tennis and other racquet sports gear and clothing. Large selection of Ralph Lauren clothing.

Trail Head
40 Wellington St. E. near Church
862-0881
Good-quality clothing and equipment for various outdoor activities. Top-name canoes, kayaks, tents, sleeping bags and cross-country skis. Some equipment can be rented.

STAMPS AND COINS

Toronto is one of the world's leading stamp centres, rivalling New York and London. If philatelics or numismatics are your interest, visit the following:

**Charlton's International
15 Birch Ave. near Yonge
964-7580**
One of Canada's leading coin dealers.

**R. Maresch & Son
330 Bay St. at Adelaide W.
Suite 703
363-7777**
Well-established stamp dealer and auction house.

**George S. Wegg
36 Victoria St. at King E.
363-1596**
A storefront location with everything from start-up kits for kids to rare and unusual stamp-related items.

FOOD STORES

MARKETS

**St. Lawrence Market
95 Front St. E. at Jarvis**
Fresh everything, all under one roof. Stop in for breakfast or lunch. The peameal bacon or hot sausage on a bun are both out of this world. Open Tues to Thurs 8 A.M. to 6 P.M., Fri 8 A.M. to 7 P.M., Sat 5 A.M. to 5 P.M. Closed Sun and Mon.

**Kensington Market
Kensington Ave. and Baldwin
(College/Spadina area)**
A sprawling multi-ethnic street market with the babel of a dozen languages haggling over the prices of live chickens, tropical fruits, fresh vegetables and even vintage clothing. The most colourful and vibrant of the city markets, bar none.

**Chinatown
Dundas W./Spadina area**
Honest to goodness Chinese outdoor market. An experience unto itself.

MEAT

In addition to the shops mentioned here, you can't find a greater concentration of specialty butcher shops than in St. Lawrence Market.

**The Big Carrot Natural Food Market
348 Danforth Ave. near Logan
466-2129**
Toronto's first natural-food supermarket. Their meat counter offers poultry, beef, venison, lamb and buffalo. You can even get ground buffalo to make burgers for the barbeque. They also carry fresh and frozen fish.

**Simon De Groot Meat Products
481 Church St. near Wellesley
923-5600**
This Dutch butcher's shop is a carriage trade favourite. Fine cuts of meat and frozen food. They also carry a variety of Indonesian foods and spices.

**European Quality Meats and Sausages
176 Baldwin St. near Spadina
(Kensington Market)
596-8691**
Always busy, but the line-ups move quickly. Very good prices, courteous service. Some of the best home-made sausages in town.

FISH/SHELLFISH

St. Lawrence Market, of course.

Michael's Mussels, Oysters and Clams
172 Harbord St. near Bathurst
960-0536

Rodney's Oyster House
209 Adelaide St. E. near Jarvis
(downstairs)
363-8105

BAKERIES

Dr. Cheese and the Cake Lady
119 Harbord St. near Spadina
962-2253
Cakes, cookies, brownies, plus teapots, teacups and cookie jars. Holiday items are a specialty.

Colourful Kensington Market has the feel of an old European street market. (Photo by Ottmar Bierwagen)

Dufflet Pastries
787 Queen St. W. near Bathurst
368-1812
This famous Toronto bakery supplies excellent cakes and pies to many of the city's better restaurants—but if you can't wait, drop into their store for innovative dessert creations.

Harbord Bakery and Callandria
115 Harbord St. near Spadina
922-5767
Great egg bread and bagels. Sticky buns on Sat morning are the best in the city— Sat's long line-ups move quickly.

Haymishe Bagel Shop
3031 Bathurst St. near Lawrence
781-4212
Great bagels and a wide variety of breads.

Kensington Natural Bakery
287 Augusta Ave. near College
960-2359
Very good whole-grain-crunchy-granola kind of healthy bakery.

Kensington Patty Palace
172 Baldwin St. near Spadina
596-6667
The best spicy Jamaican meat pies in town.

Mary Macleod's Shortbread
2494 Yonge St. near Castlefield
482-3096
367 Eglinton Ave. W.
near Avenue Rd.
482-0683
One of our favourites. Who could believe there were so many variations on the shortbread theme?

Oliver's
2433 Yonge St. near Eglinton
485-1051
Bakery/restaurant popular with the upwardly mobile. Lots of great desserts.

Pallas Bakery
629 Danforth Ave. near Pape
461-1248
Delicious baklava and other honey-dipped pastries in the heart of Greektown.

Patachou Patisserie
875 Eglinton Ave. W. at Bathurst
782-1322
1095 Yonge St.
near Summerhill subway
927-1105
Tantalizing French pastries. Perfect for Sat morning croissants and cappuccino.

Yung Sing Pastry Shop
22 Baldwin St. near McCaul
979-2832
A true Chinese bakery. Try the lotus buns or almond cookies.

CANDY STORES/CHOCOLATES

Holt Renfrew
50 Bloor St. W. near Yonge
922-3200
Weekly shipments from Belgium.

Laura Secord
Eaton Centre
977-8445
(other locations)
A Canadian institution. They've produced delicious, high-quality chocolates and candies for over 75 years.

Sweet Temptations
Queen's Quay Terminal
(main level)
861-0557
Hand-made Belgian chocolates are their specialty including the famous Manon and Gudrun brands.

Teuscher of Switzerland
Hazelton Lanes
961-1303
First Canadian Place
King St. at York
947-9892
Finest quality chocolates shipped in
every week from Zurich. All of their
chocolates are preservative- and
additive-free—some are also sugar-free.
Famous for their champagne (Dom
Perignon) truffles.

GOURMET FOOD SHOPS AND TAKE-OUTS

Daniel et Daniel
248 Carlton St. at Parliament
968-9275
All kinds of gourmet food. Everything
from caviar to pesto sauce. At lunch
they offer a variety of hot and cold
salads, rice dishes and smoked salmon or
trout. Home-made pastries too. All
take-out.

Dinah's Cupboard
50 Cumberland St. near Yonge
921-8112
Fresh breads every day and a whole
range of pastries, including excellent
Nanaimo bars. Gourmet coffees and
teas, home-made pâtés, cheeses and
much much more.

Fenton's Food Shop
2 Gloucester St. at Yonge
961-8485
One of the city's best gourmet take-
outs. Great picnic baskets. You can buy
the same fine quality meat and fish that
the Fenton chefs prepare in their excellent restaurant next door.

Pastissima
2633 Yonge St. near Briar Hill
482-4175
A wonderful little gourmet shop that
sells spinach, egg, tomato and basil
pastas (to name a few) as well as take-
out sandwiches, gelato fresco and various coffees. They make the pasta right
in front of you, so you know it's fresh.

Paul's French Food Shop
425 Spadina Rd. near Lonsdale
483-9304
A Forest Hill institution. One of the
oldest gourmet take-outs in the city.

Serving Spoon
382 Bloor St. W. near Spadina
967-7666
Excellent selection of coffees, cheeses,
breads, sweets, jams and jellies.

Sperling's Simply Splendid Foods
2558 Yonge St. at Briar Hill
482-8696
Choose from an array of salads, pastries,
home-made pâtés and cheeses. Lunch
and dinner entree specials can be
savoured in their cozy 50-seat restaurant. Also Sunday brunch.

David Wood Food Shop
1110 Yonge St. near Roxborough
968-6967
417 Spadina Rd. near Lonsdale
489-0108
Fabulous. The best of its ilk in Toronto.
All food is prepared fresh on site.
Known for their imaginative dinner specials and wonderful desserts like choco-
late/lemon/raspberry mousse in a
chocolate cup and chocolate paradise
cake. In summer they prepare picnic
baskets on request.

According to the Guinness Book of World Records, *Honest Ed's neon sign is the largest in the world. (Photo by Margaret MacKenzie)*

SPECIALTY STORES

Gold's Luggage Shop
212 Queen St. W. near University
598-3469

They not only sell brand-name luggage at some great prices but they also repair luggage, handbags and golf bags. Major airlines use their repair services.

Honest Ed's
581 Bloor St. W. at Bathurst
537-1574

Not really a specialty store, but a *special* store. Honest Ed's is more than a department store—it's a Toronto landmark. Over 10 million customers a year. The reason? Bargains! Proving that he is a master of marketing, Honest Ed offers unbelievable specials on merchandise of every kind to keep them coming back. Shopping as a form of entertainment.

The Last Wound-Up
91 Cumberland St. near Bay
926-8996

Nowhere else can you find this number and variety of wind-up toys and music boxes.

Lovecraft
63 Yorkville Ave. near Bay
923-7331

Sexy gifts, novelties and erotica.

Perly's Toronto
1050 Eglinton Ave. W.
near Bathurst
785-MAPS

Canada's largest selection of atlases, globes, paper maps, map-measurers and pins.

Touch the Sky
836 Yonge St. near Bloor
964-0434
Queen's Quay Terminal
362-5983

The quintessential kite store.

Gordon V. Thompson
29 Birch Ave. near Yonge
923-6441

Toronto's best supply of sheet music.

Winston and Holmes
138 Cumberland St.
near Avenue Rd.
968-1290
(other locations)

Specialty tobacconists. Domestic and imported cigars including Davidoff.

WITH THE KIDS 13

KIDS AND ANIMALS

Riverdale Farm
Winchester St. at Sumach
392-6794

Situated on a height of land overlooking Riverdale Park, a 19th-century farm has been recreated in the heart of Cabbagetown, one of Toronto's oldest neighbourhoods. As you walk through the barns and past the outdoor pens and ponds, you'll see pigs, cows, sheep, goats, turkeys, hens, ducks and geese. Check with the farm attendants to find out which of the animals can be petted. You can watch the cows and goats being milked by hand each morning at 9:30 and 10 respectively.

Activities during the year include craft classes, candle-making and quilting displays, and demonstrations of spinning, dyeing and weaving the wool that has been shorn from the farm's own sheep. Especially good times to visit are during the farm's Fall and Christmas festivals, and of course in the spring when baby animals are everywhere.

Open daily 9 A.M. to sunset. Dogs and bicycles are not allowed. Best of all, admission is free.

Far Enough Farm
Centre Island (Toronto Islands)
392-8186

Take in this petting zoo as part of a day trip to the Toronto Islands. There are the familiar barnyard animals on hand—piglets, geese, cows, rabbits, ducks, chickens and donkeys. Pony rides are available.

Admission is free, although you will need to pay for the ferry ride to Centre Island. For zoo information call 392-8186. For ferry times and rates call 392-8193.

There's always something for kids to do at Harbourfront. (Harbourfront Corporation)

Metro Toronto Zoo
Hwy. 401 at Meadowvale Rd.
Scarborough
392-5900
See Sightseeing/Attractions.

A must-see for all ages, but the zoo holds special events and exhibits primarily for children. Littlefootland, just north of the main entrance, is the setting for close encounters with some of the zoo's tamer beasts. Here kids can pet farm animals, watch chicks hatch, ride ponies, place their own footprints alongside those left behind by elephants, giraffes and the like at an African watering hole, and compare their athletic abilities with those of animals in the specially designed children's playground. Animal feeding times are posted at the main gate. The polar bears are fed at noon each day and can be watched from above or from an underwater viewing station. Meet the Zookeeper, a popular summertime program, makes zookeepers available to answer questions about the animals in their care.

The Family Centre provides a haven for lost children, a baby-changing area and an on-duty nurse. Strollers can be rented at the entrance area for $1. Pets are not allowed.

Open every day except Christmas Day. Summer: 9 A.M. to 7 P.M. Winter: 9:30 A.M. to 4:30 P.M. For admission rates and special events call 392-5902 (recorded message).

The polar bear exhibit is one of the most popular attractions at the Metro zoo. (Metro Toronto Zoo)

High Park Zoo
Bloor St. W. and Parkside Dr.
392-7545
A smaller, traditional zoo with deer, bison, yaks, llamas, sheep, peacocks and rabbits. Migrating birds use Grenadier Pond in the southwest corner of the park as a stopover. Bird watchers should also check out the small sanctuary by the children's playground. Free admission. Open every day 8 A.M. to dusk.

Fishing

Grenadier Pond in High Park is a great place for kids to throw in a line. Among other species, there are a variety of pan-fish such as black crappie and pumpkinseed. The pond at Hanlan's Point on Centre Island (Toronto Islands) is so well stocked with rainbow trout that success is almost guaranteed. Some of the rivers that course through the city ravines to Lake Ontario offer good fishing, although many of the fish are contaminated and should not be eaten. For information on fishing and guidelines for eating your catch, see Sports/Recreation.

Horseback Riding

See Sports/Recreation

OUT-OF-TOWN

African Lion Safari
Cambridge
See Sightseeing

Marineland
Niagara Falls
See Sightseeing

DAY TRIPS

Toronto's parkland, waterfront shoreline, ravines, and nearby conservation areas are perfect for family outings. In particular, the Toronto Islands, High Park, Scarborough Bluffs, the Beaches, Leslie St. Spit, Wilket Creek Park and the Kortright Centre for Conservation are recommended. See Parks/Gardens.

If you are looking for a place to spend the day that has lots of programmed activity for both children and adults, Ontario Place, Harbourfront, and Canada's Wonderland are sure bets. See Sightseeing.

Chinatown

A day spent in the Dundas W./Spadina area is a cultural experience not soon forgotten. Eat at one of the many authentic Chinese restaurants, shop for fun gifts—paper fans, kites, something made of silk—or just sit and take in the sights, sounds and smells of the colourful streetlife. Driving your car into Chinatown is not a good idea—it's just too busy—so take the TTC and walk. See Restaurants (Chinese) and Shopping.

Fruit Picking

Many farms and orchards within a few hours' drive of Toronto have pick-your-own operations. The Ontario Ministry of Agriculture puts out an annual "Pick Your Own" listing of all participating farms in southern Ontario; phone 1-800-268-3735 or 965-4008 for your free booklet. Harvest times vary with

Children can meet their favourite cartoon characters in Hanna-Barbera Land at Canada's Wonderland.

the weather, so call the farm *before* you set out to make sure the crop is ready.

A family favourite is Chudleigh's Apple Farm near Milton, 30 minutes west of Toronto. Here you can see how apple cider is made, take a horse and wagon ride, and of course pick just-ripened apples. Phone 826-1252 for directions.

Sunshine Beach Water Park
Brampton
794-0468

Sunshine Beach is touted as Canada's largest outdoor water park. Here you will find every conceivable way to get wet and stay wet. The park features an 1850-m² (20,000-sq.ft.) wave pool, two 7-storey-high "screamer" speed slides, body flume slides, whirlpool hot tubs, and a children's water playground with tot slides and a waterfall. A gift shop, eating facilities and 20 ha (50 acres) of picnic grounds encourage you to make a day of it.

On Finch Ave, 2 km (1 mi.) west of Hwy. 427. Open daily in the summer, 10 A.M. to 8 P.M. Admission: adults $12.95, seniors $7.95, children 4–9, $10.95; children 3 and under, free, after 4 P.M. $7.95.

Toronto by Vintage Trolley Car

A 90-minute tour of the city on a restored trolley car. By Toronto Tours. See Sightseeing/Touring Toronto.

MUSEUMS

The world-renowned Royal Ontario Museum and Ontario Science Centre both provide a wealth of opportunity for children to learn about the world. Don't miss them. Other museums of interest are: the Puppet Centre, Hockey Hall of Fame, Canada Sports Hall of Fame, the David Dunlap Observatory, the Marine Museum and the HMCS *Haida* destroyer. For information about these museums and others, see Museums/Art Galleries.

ENTERTAINMENT

Young People's Theatre (YPT)
165 Front St. E. near Sherbourne
864-9732

Dedicated to presenting innovative theatre for young audiences in addition to traditional family classics, YPT is well known for its quality programming.

A performance of Jacob Two-Two Meets the Hooded Fang *by the Young People's Theatre. (Photo by Michael Cooper)*

YOUNG PEOPLE'S THEATRE

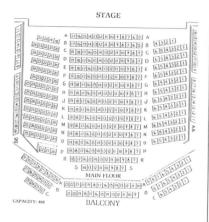

STAGE

MAIN FLOOR

BALCONY

CAPACITY: 468

Where else could you find *Jacob Two-Two Meets the Hooded Fang, The Effect of Gamma Rays on Man-in-the-Moon Marigolds* and *The Prince and the Pauper* produced in one company's season? Phone for an up-to-date schedule and ticket information.

Blue Jays Baseball
The SkyDome
595-0077

This professional baseball organization takes their young fans seriously. Twice each summer, the team is available for pre-game autographs and picture-taking. Call to find out the dates. Kids 14 and under can buy $10, $7 and $4

Waiting to take to the ice at one of Toronto's many outdoor skating rinks. (Photo by Ottmar Bierwagen)

tickets at half-price for all Sat home games and all home games with a 12:35 P.M. starting time. Throughout the season there are lots of sponsored promotions where kids can take home free goodies. Call to find out when Bat Day, Watch Day, Wallet Day, Cap Day (to name a few) are scheduled.

Kidsummer

Toronto Life magazine and radio station CHFI (FM 98) sponsor an annual festival of free summer events for children of all ages accompanied by an adult. Throughout July and Aug, each day offers a different freebie, whether it's a tour of the stables of the Metropolitan Toronto Mounted Police Unit or a chance to dig for artifacts at a local archaeological site. Some of the events require pre-registration, so call the Kidsummer hotline (366-CHFI) for a schedule and information.

Toronto Summer Music Festival

The city's Department of Parks and Recreation, in conjunction with other sponsors, orchestrates a wonderful live music festival, which is held in various city parks all summer long. Well-known jazz groups, chamber music groups, rock bands and dance troupes perform. Call 392-7251 for information about who is appearing where. Free.

Observation Points/High Spots

Many of the highest buildings in the city offer terrific views for free. See the "10 Best Views" list in Sightseeing.

Harbourfront
Queen's Quay W.
973-3000

Most days in the summer and most weekends during the rest of the year

The Wilderness Adventure ride, one of the many exciting attractions at Ontario Place for children and adults alike.

Arts and crafts classes are frequently offered at Harbourfront throughout the summer. (Harbourfront Corporation)

there is something happening for kids at Harbourfront. Plays, concerts, games, crafts, canoeing and dance are regular children's fare. To discover the current program, check Harbourfront's advertisements in the *Globe and Mail* and the Toronto *Star* entertainment sections, as well as *NOW* and *Metropolis* magazines.

Special Annual Events

Special entertainment extravaganzas occur throughout the year. Events such as the Canadian National Exhibition, the Royal Agricultural Winter Fair, the CHIN International Picnic, Caravan and Caribana attract thousands of kids (and adults too). For dates and detailed descriptions of these and other annual festivities, see Sightseeing/Calendar of Events.

Also
Tour of the Universe,
see Sightseeing/Attractions
Ontario Place,
see Sightseeing/Attractions

RESTAURANTS

Chuck E. Cheese's
2452 Sheppard Ave. E.
at Victoria Park
497-8855
2200 Jane St. near Wilson
244-1188
This restaurant has built its reputation on providing more for kids than just a children's menu. There are rides, video games, a ball room, and dressed-up characters (including Chuck E. Cheese himself) to entertain the kids all night long. It's a good idea to make reservations, especially on weekends. L, D daily. Major cards.

Fran's
20 College St. near Yonge
923-9867
2275 Yonge St. near Eglinton
481-1112
21 St. Clair Ave. W. near Yonge
925-6336
A family restaurant open 24 hours a day. The menu provides smaller portions for children and old-fashioned milkshakes and sundaes. B, L, D daily. Major cards.

Ginsberg and Wong
Village by the Grange
70 St. Patrick St. near Queen W.
979-3458
Oversize portions of fun food combinations from this Jewish/Chinese partnership will please most palates. Kids especially love the 32-oz. pop drinks. Wandering musicians every Fri and Sat night. L, D daily. Major cards.

Golden Griddle Pancake House
Many locations including
45 Carlton St. near Yonge
977-5044
11 Jarvis St. near Front E.
865-1263
This reliable chain operation serves up a dependable all-day breakfast. Carlton St. opens at 6 A.M. daily, also L, D daily. Jarvis St. open 24 hours daily. Major cards.

Mr. Greenjeans Emporium
Eaton Centre, mews level
Yonge St. at Dundas
979-1212
The menu offers *big* hamburgers, hot dogs and desserts, including one called Hats Off that comes in a wearable clear plastic top hat filled to the brim with ice cream, cake and candy. The music is up-to-date and fairly loud. A number of larger round tables can accommodate families, friends and birthday parties. L, D daily. Some cards.

The Old Spaghetti Factory
54 The Esplanade near Yonge
864-9761
One of Toronto's best-known family restaurants has a children's menu, but the atmosphere is really what the kids enjoy. Antiques galore, including a decorative 1920 carousel and a full-scale eat-in streetcar. Video games too. Reservations can be made for groups of 15 or more, otherwise it's first-come, first-served. L, D daily. Major cards.

Organ Grinder
58 The Esplanade near Church
364-6517
Every strange-looking musical instrument you can think of is used as decoration here. Remote-controlled strobe lights, glockenspiels, xylophones, Wurlitzer organ and other instruments create a sound and light show that kids love and parents tolerate. Menu includes burgers, chicken wings, pizza and pasta. L, D daily. Major cards.

Victoria Station
190 Queen's Quay E.
at Sherbourne
366-4985
Dine on wholesome food in real railway cars. The kids will love it too! L Mon to Fri, D daily. Major cards.

SHOPPING

TOYS

If you're after something special—unique or educational—try the following:

Kidstuff
738 Bathurst St. near Bloor
535-2212
Here the focus is on quality stuffed toys, wooden toys, dolls, art supplies, European puzzles and games—and highly personal service. Don't expect any war toys.

Merryland Toys
15 Bloor St. W. near Yonge
968-9010
Royal Bank Plaza
Front St. at Bay
368-5975
2 First Canadian Place
King St. at Bay
361-1840
Merryland imports toys from all over the world and is one of Toronto's largest toy stores. They carry heirloom-quality English rocking horses, German wooden toys, Steiff animals and lots of educational toys. On their three floors at the Bloor store you'll find toys ranging from 99¢ to a motorized Ferrari worth $4,000.

Science City Jr.
50 Bloor St. W. near Yonge
968-2627

We love this store and its more adult version across the corridor. They not only carry chemistry and scientific kits and equipment for kids but also puzzles, kaleidoscopes, model kits, kites, books and lots of dinosaurabilia.

The Toy Circus
2036 Queen St. E. near Lee
699-4971

Many of the toys in this cozy little shop in the Beaches have an educational bent—and you won't find much in the way of mechanical toys. The shelves are stocked with stuffed animals, books, games, arts and crafts supplies and lots of dolls.

The Toy Shop
62 Cumberland St.
near Avenue Rd.
961-4870

One of Toronto's oldest toy stores. Two floors of fine-quality imported and Canadian-made toys for children of all ages. They carry a good selection of hand puppets, stuffed animals, dolls and doll houses (including Madame Alexander collector dolls), Lego and Playmobils. Lots of educational toys and costumes too.

CLOTHING AND SHOES

Laura Ashley
18 Hazelton Ave.
near Avenue Rd.
922-7761

In addition to their well-recognized women's clothing and home furnishing fabrics, this international chain sells beautiful girls' clothing. Dresses, skirts, lacy blouses and accessories with an emphasis on small prints and paisleys in traditional feminine styles.

Cansave Children's Shop
1240 Bay St. near Bloor
921-6465

Without a sign out front it's easy to miss—so watch for the street number. All the profits of this operation go to the Canadian Save the Children Fund. Volunteers make and sell children's sweaters, doll clothes, blankets and more at very reasonable prices.

Cotton Basics
162 McCaul St. near Dundas W.
977-1959

Kids' 100% cotton clothing. They manufacture and dye their own label sweatshirts, rompers, pyjamas, flannel-lined pants and more in cheerful primary colours. From newborn sizes up to adult XL. Stylish and reasonably priced.

Cotton Ginny for Kids
153 Cumberland St. near Bay
926-8999
(other locations)

Canadian-made cotton casual wear including fleece-lined sweats, skirts, jumpsuits, sweaters and T-shirts. Good quality, moderate prices.

Little Ones
243 Eglinton Ave. W.
near Avenue Rd.
483-5989
One of the city's most expensive children's clothing stores. They carry lines from the Netherlands, France, Austria and Italy for newborns up to teens. They also sell fashionable shoes to complement the outfits.

Mimosa
1108 Yonge St.
near Summerhill subway
927-7512
This tiny shop specializes in high-quality, mostly imported clothing in newborn up to size 4. Expensive.

Minimi
Hazelton Lanes
55 Avenue Rd. at Yorkville
921-9909
3328 Yonge St. near Fairlawn
489-8313
Exclusive designer wear for kids. Almost all lines are European imports. Infant sizes up to size 14. Some baby accessories such as front carriers, chairs and carry bags are stocked.

Also
Marks and Spencer and **Winners,** see Women's Clothing

SLIGHTLY USED

Play It Again
683 St. Clair Ave. W.
near Christie
651-7711
Used clothing on consignment. You'll often find high-quality brand-name children's garments such as Absorba, Elen Henderson and Ralph Lauren's Polo line. They also carry fashionable second-hand maternity clothes and recycled playpens, strollers, cribs and car seats.

Play 'n' Wear
1722 Avenue Rd. near Fairlawn
782-0211
New and used clothing for infants and children up to size 16. As well, you'll find books, tapes, some toys, and furniture. They also rent out cribs, strollers and car seats for those who have the kids for weekends or holidays. Large stock of costumes for rent too.

CHILDREN'S FURNITURE

The Children's Marketplace
10149 Yonge St.
Richmond Hill
883-4244
Large display of children's furniture as well as toys and clothing. Some used furniture deals.

Storkland
3291 Yonge St. near Lawrence
488-1141
A huge store packed with children's furniture, toys, clothing, strollers and much more. An in-store repair service is offered on items purchased here.

Also
Ikea ,
see Shopping/Home Furnishings

CHILDREN'S BOOKSTORES

The Children's Bookstore
604 Markham St. near Bloor W.
535-7011
A delightful Victorian house in the heart of Mirvish Village is the home of one of North America's largest specialty children's bookstores.

Lindsay's Books for Children
131 Bloor St. W. near Bay
968-2174
Centrally located near the Bay and Bloor intersection, Lindsay's features a balanced selection of popular and classic books.

Mabel's Fables
662 Mt. Pleasant Rd.
near Eglinton
322-0438
A warm and cozy store with a gem-like interior named after its resident cat. A wide range of books, accessibly presented.

Tiddely Pom
47A Colborne St. near Church
366-0290
A cheerful, well-stocked downtown bookstore near St. Lawrence Market.

LIBRARIES FOR CHILDREN

Boys and Girls House
40 St. George St. near College
393-7746

Spaced-Out Library
40 St. George St. near College
393-7748

INDEX

Note that stores, tour companies, rental firms and sports facilities are indexed by type, product or activity, not by individual names.

Index

Index